Wittgenstein and the Social Sciences

ANTHEM STUDIES IN WITTGENSTEIN

Anthem Studies in Wittgenstein publishes new and classic works on Wittgenstein and Wittgensteinian philosophy. This book series aims to bring Wittgenstein's thought into the mainstream by highlighting its relevance to twenty-first-century concerns. Titles include original monographs, themed edited volumes, forgotten classics, biographical works, and books intended to introduce Wittgenstein to the general public. The series is published in association with the British Wittgenstein Society.

Anthem Studies in Wittgenstein sets out to put in place whatever measures may emerge as necessary in order to carry out the editorial selection process purely on merit and to counter bias on the basis of gender, race, ethnicity, religion, sexual orientation, and other characteristics protected by law. These measures include subscribing to the British Philosophical Association/Society for Women in Philosophy (UK) Good Practice Scheme.

Series Editor
Constantine Sandis – *University of Hertfordshire, UK*

Wittgenstein and the Social Sciences

Action, Ideology, and Justice

Robert Vinten

ANTHEM PRESS

Anthem Press
An imprint of Wimbledon Publishing Company
www.anthempress.com

This edition first published in UK and USA 2021
by ANTHEM PRESS
75–76 Blackfriars Road, London SE1 8HA, UK
or PO Box 9779, London SW19 7ZG, UK
and
244 Madison Ave #116, New York, NY 10016, USA

First published in the UK and USA by Anthem Press in 2020

Copyright © Robert Vinten 2021

The author asserts the moral right to be identified as the author of this work.

All rights reserved. Without limiting the rights under copyright reserved above,
no part of this publication may be reproduced, stored or introduced into
a retrieval system, or transmitted, in any form or by any means
(electronic, mechanical, photocopying, recording or otherwise),
without the prior written permission of both the copyright
owner and the above publisher of this book.

British Library Cataloguing-in-Publication Data
A catalogue record for this book is available from the British Library.

Library of Congress Control Number: 2021937603

ISBN-13: 978-1-83998-174-6 (Pbk)
ISBN-10: 1-83998-174-1 (Pbk)

This title is also available as an e-book.

This book is dedicated to the memory of a former supervisor of mine, Bob Arrington, who sadly died in 2015. My discussions with him have had an enormous influence on the way that I think about philosophy.

CONTENTS

Acknowledgements	ix
Introduction	1

Part 1 The Nature of Philosophy and of Social Science

1. Is There Such a Thing as a Social Science?	25
2. Wittgenstein and Relativism	49

Part 2 Does Wittgenstein's Work Have Ideological Implications?

3. Was Wittgenstein a Conservative Philosopher?	69
4. Was Wittgenstein a Liberal Philosopher?	87
5. Leave Everything as It Is	113
6. Eagleton's Wittgenstein	133

Part 3 Applying Wittgenstein's Work to Problems in Social Philosophy

7. Wittgenstein and Freedom of the Will	161
8. Wittgenstein and Justice	177
Bibliography	203
Index	213

ACKNOWLEDGEMENTS

I would like to thank the Fundação para a Ciência e a Tecnologia[1] for their financial support throughout my PhD in Lisbon as well as for my postdoctoral work there. They also funded a visit to Argentina for me to present a paper in La Plata and in Córdoba during August and September of 2017 ('Interpretaciones de Wittgenstein por marxistas ingleses: una crítica'). I would like to thank Andrés Oliva for translating that paper into Spanish. Material from the English version of that paper appears in this book in Chapters 5 and 6. Pedro Karczmarczyk helped to arrange the trip and also arranged my accommodation (with the wonderful and kind Angélica Sangronis and Luis Alberto Pacheco). I am very grateful to him and to Angélica and Luis. It was Guadalupe Reinoso in Córdoba who arranged my talk there. I am grateful to her for arranging that and for showing me around the campus there. She was a fabulous host! The audiences who were present at my talks in La Plata and Córdoba also gave me valuable feedback on my work. I met a Spanish Wittgensteinian, Isabel Gamero, while I was in Argentina and I would like to thank her for stimulating discussion as well as for her help with practical matters in La Plata and Buenos Aires.

In Portugal I would like to thank Nuno Venturinha and Diogo Pires Aurélio, who were my advisors during my doctoral studies. Nuno, in particular, has been very helpful not only with advice about my philosophical work but also with administrative business in the university and outside of it. He helped to arrange for me to travel to Granada, Spain, to give a talk there (a paper about justice which appears, in slightly revised form, as Chapter 8 of this book), and has also invited me to speak at conferences at Universidade Nova de Lisboa.

I would like to thank the MLAG group at the Universidade do Porto for giving me the opportunity to present my paper about Wittgenstein and

---

[1] The Portuguese Foundation for Science and Technology (FCT), the Portuguese national funding agency. My PhD (2014–18) was funded by a PhD grant (SFRH/BD/94166/2013) and my current position as a research fellow is funded by the project Epistemology of Religious Belief: Wittgenstein, Grammar, and the Contemporary World (PTDC/FER-FIL/32203/2017).

Freedom of the Will at their conference (the organisers of the conference were Anna Ciaunica, Sofia Miguens, João Alberto Pinto, José Pedro Correia, Diana Couto, and Luís Veríssimo). That paper has now become Chapter 7 of this book.

In Spain I would particularly like to thank Vicente Sanfélix Vidarte. He arranged for me to visit the Universitat de València to present a paper about Wittgenstein and Liberalism. That paper has since appeared in the Spanish journal *Teorema* (in English) in 2017 and in the Colombian journal *Análisis* (in Spanish) in 2018. I'm grateful to participants in the seminar in Valencia for their comments. Nicolas Sanchez Dura, in particular, was very involved in the discussion both during and after the talk. Carlota Sánchez Garcia translated my paper into Spanish before the talk so that those who wanted to read it in Spanish could read it. It is her translation that appeared in *Análisis*. I am very grateful to her. I am would also like to thank Simon Glendinning for comments on an earlier draft of that chapter as well as to two anonymous referees at the journal *Teorema*. A revised version of that paper appears within this book as Chapter 4.

Various people have commented on my published work during the course of the past six years. I would like to thank participants in the Dimensões da Epistemologia conference, held at Universidade Nova de Lisboa on 6 September 2016, for their comments on an earlier draft of the first chapter of this book. Modesto Gómez-Alonso gave me very helpful comments after the event, which helped me in redrafting my work. I am grateful to Wayne Blackledge, António Caeiro, Philip Cartwright, Pedro Karczmarczyk, Gavin Kitching, Nigel Pleasants, Constantine Sandis, and George Wrisley for their comments on my papers 'Leave Everything as it is' and 'Eagleton's Wittgenstein'. Their comments on those papers prompted me to make changes to the criticisms that I made of Anderson, Callinicos, and Eagleton in Chapters 5 and 6 of this book. I would also like to thank participants at the MLAG conference in Porto for comments on an earlier version of Chapter 7. Javier Cumpa, Manuel de Pinedo, Nils Kurbis, Carla Carmona, and Neftalí Villanueva all gave me very valuable feedback on an earlier draft of Chapter 8 at the University of Granada. At the same conference there was also a discussion of epistemic injustice (featuring Manuel Almagro, Carla Carmona, María José Frápolli, Alba Moreno, Llanos Navarro, Jesús Navarro, Eduardo Pérez, Nuno Venturinha, and Neftalí Villanueva) which was useful in thinking about the issues in Chapter 8.

Constantine Sandis deserves special thanks as the editor of this series and also as someone who has produced great work in philosophy that has influenced my own. Constantine has read a lot of my work over the years and has given me sage advice.

I would like to thank my parents, Janet Szpakowski, Michael Szpakowski, and David Vinten for their support throughout the writing of this book (and for reading various parts of it). My brother and sister, Jack Vinten and Anna Szpakowska, have also been supportive and Jack has produced the cover for this book. I'm grateful to him for that.

Finally, I want to thank Gabriela Ferreira for her support as I have worked on this book. She has been incredible!

INTRODUCTION

This book aims at exploring the implications of Wittgenstein's philosophy for social philosophy and the social sciences. I should make clear at the outset that I will be particularly concerned with Wittgenstein's later philosophical work – his work from the 1930s until his death in 1951. When I talk about 'Wittgenstein's philosophy' I will primarily be talking about the mature philosophy of the *Philosophical Investigations*[1] and *On Certainty*[2] rather than his earlier work in the *Tractatus Logico-Philosophicus*,[3] that he criticized in the later work. However, I will occasionally refer to his earlier work and note certain elements of continuity in Wittgenstein's work.

According to Wittgenstein (throughout his career) philosophy is a discipline that is not based on observation and experiment. It is not an empirical discipline and, more particularly, philosophy is not a science.[4] This book defends the later Wittgenstein's take on philosophy and attempts to show its usefulness for social philosophy and social science. So, this book is not a work of social science and it will not rely on empirical data about our current or past social and political circumstances. I will not be attempting to formulate prescriptions for, say, politicians, social workers, or political activists based on evidence drawn from observations, questionnaires, medical records, interviews, or crime statistics. The aim is not to provide advice about policy or information that might help social scientists to solve particular concrete problems that concern them. Rather, this is a book that is primarily concerned, as Wittgenstein

---

[1] L. Wittgenstein, *Philosophical Investigations*, revised 4th edition by P. M. S. Hacker and Joachim Schulte, trans. G. E. M. Anscombe, P. M. S. Hacker, and Joachim Schulte, Oxford: Wiley-Blackwell, 2009.
[2] L. Wittgenstein, *On Certainty*, Oxford: Blackwell, 1969.
[3] L. Wittgenstein, *Tractatus Logico-Philosophicus*, London: Routledge, 1961.
[4] In the *Tractatus* Wittgenstein says that philosophy 'is not one of the natural sciences' (4.111) and that it 'aims at the logical clarification of thoughts' (4.112). He says of psychology that it 'is no more closely related to philosophy than any other natural science' (4.1121). In the *Philosophical Investigations* Wittgenstein says that 'our considerations must not be scientific ones […] And we may not advance any kind of theory. There must not be anything hypothetical in our considerations. All *explanation* must disappear' (*PI* §109).

was, with conceptual matters. The focus will be on examining conceptual matters in social philosophy and the social sciences with an eye to showing that Wittgenstein's philosophy can be helpful in overcoming confusions.

However, although this work is primarily focused on conceptual matters and is not a work in social science, I take it that it is of relevance to social science and that social scientists have something to learn from Wittgenstein. We cannot make a neat separation between the conceptual cartography engaged in by philosophers and the practices of social scientists. In order to produce good work in social science we must achieve some clarity about the concepts we are using. To say something true about social phenomena we must make sense. The kinds of confusions that Wittgenstein was so skilled in identifying in his philosophical work are confusions that are still rife among social scientists.

Of course, social philosophy is an incredibly broad area and I cannot possibly hope to get rid of all confusion in it within this book. Indeed, it is not clear that it is possible to entirely get rid of all conceptual confusions within social philosophy. New developments in society will undoubtedly lead to new frameworks for understanding society and there is always potential for confusion as new attempts at understanding are made. Furthermore, there are some areas of recent social philosophy that I barely touch upon. For example, I say relatively little about religion within the book, although Section 6.5.6. is dedicated to a critical engagement with Terry Eagleton's discussion of Marx, Wittgenstein, and religion. What I will do in this book is take a look at some of the issues in social philosophy that I take to be central – (i) issues about the nature of social sciences, whether they can be properly called scientific; (ii) the issue of reductionism, whether social sciences can be explained in terms of the (perhaps more fundamental) natural sciences; (iii) the issue of the proper form of explanation in the social sciences (if indeed there is a proper form of explanation in the social sciences); (iv) the issue of relativism, whether social scientists should contemplate some form of relativism about truth, justification, knowledge, existence, or concepts; (v) the issue of ideology – whether Wittgensteinian philosophy favours a particular ideological standpoint; (vi) the issues of freedom of the will and responsibility; and, finally, (vii) the issue of justice.

However, as mentioned above, in dealing with these issues I will not be making arguments based on observational or statistical evidence. This book is a work in philosophy rather than a scientific or empirical work. Its negative aim will be to clear away confusions about the nature of philosophy, the nature of social sciences, and to clear up some confusions that arise in contemplating particular problems within the philosophy of social science such as freedom of the will, control, responsibility, and justice. Its positive aims will be to enrich our understanding of those areas and to show that Wittgenstein's philosophy can be very useful for philosophers of social science, as well as for social scientists.

In order to fulfil those aims I will use methods particularly suited to philosophy as conceived by Wittgenstein. In the first place I will take care in reading the work of philosophers working in social philosophy as well as the work of social scientists and attempt to diagnose cases of conceptual confusion as well as cases of failure in interpretation (e.g. in interpreting Wittgenstein's work). So, this book will to some extent be a work in exegesis and interpretative criticism. In trying to achieve my positive aims of producing clarity and understanding in social philosophy I will attempt to follow Wittgenstein's suggestion that we should construct 'surveyable representations' of regions of grammar. What that means is that I will provide explanations of the meaning of terms that are causing confusion (such as, e.g. 'reasons', 'explanations', 'consciousness', 'control', 'justice') and discuss how those terms are related to other terms (other terms that are etymologically related, other terms that belong to the same family, or terms as they are used in specifically philosophical (as opposed to ordinary) life). If those explanations are successful then the upshot should be enhanced understanding.

Why is it important to do all of this? I think it is important because the kind of scientism[5] that Wittgenstein criticised is still rife in social philosophy and the social sciences. Philosophers and social scientists are still confused about the nature of their subjects. There is still confusion about the nature of explanations in social studies. Social scientists still attempt to bring methodologies and standards from the natural sciences into the social sciences where they are not always appropriate (see Chapter 1). And philosophers and social scientists still think that greater precision can be achieved by trying to redefine psychological expressions in terms from natural science, particularly neurophysiology (see Chapter 6). Producing confused work in social philosophy and the social sciences is time-consuming and that time would be better spent if the questions asked were formulated clearly and answered in terms that we can understand. Of course, the confusion of 'theorists' can also spread to the audiences who read the work. It is also worth getting clear about the

---

[5] I should be clear here that Wittgenstein was not wholly opposed to science. He was deeply interested in engineering, mathematics, and psychology and thought that valuable work was done in all of the various scientific disciplines. The scientism that he was opposed to is the tendency to think that scientific knowledge is a superior kind of knowledge, such that it should be extended into all areas of life (see Hans-Johann Glock's *A Wittgenstein Dictionary*, where he talks about scientism as 'the imperialist tendencies of scientific thinking which result from the idea that science is the measure of all things' (H.-J. Glock, *A Wittgenstein Dictionary*, Oxford: Blackwell, 1996, p. 341)).

nature of Wittgenstein's philosophy so that we can see clearly that it does not support a particular ideological standpoint but that it can be used to clear away confusions in ideological work in political theory.

0.1 Overview of the Contents of the Chapters

In order to answer the question of whether Wittgenstein's philosophy has social and political implications it is best to first get clear about what Wittgenstein's conception of philosophy *is* and to get clear about where Wittgenstein's conception of philosophy stands in relation to other disciplines. This helps us to achieve some clarity about the import that his philosophy *might* have for social science and politics.

To that end, in the first chapter I discuss the issue of reductionism – whether social sciences are reducible to natural sciences – and I conclude that they are not reducible to natural sciences. I also distinguish explanations in terms of reasons (which are particularly prominent in social sciences) from explanations in terms of causes (which are more prominent in natural sciences). Having distinguished reasons from causes I go on to look at the question of methodology. I will argue that there are a great variety of methodologies we might use in our various inquiries, some of which are particularly appropriate to social sciences and others which are particularly appropriate to natural sciences. The question of progress also needs to be addressed. Why is it that enormous progress has been made in the natural sciences and yet philosophers are still discussing many of the same questions as the ancient Greeks and social scientists seem incapable of resolving deep disagreements?

My answer will be that the considerations about reductionism, reasons, and methodology tell us that the different disciplines have different subject matters, different forms of explanation (and description), and so they have very different standards by which we might judge their progress. Disciplines like psychology and philosophy *have* made some progress but the nature of progress in each of these disciplines is very different to the nature of progress in the natural sciences. I will conclude that philosophy, as Wittgenstein conceived it, is quite a different kind of discipline to either social scientific disciplines or the natural sciences but I also want to make clear that philosophy has something to say to other disciplines – that social scientists and natural scientists are susceptible to philosophical confusions that affect their endeavours. Philosophy aims at clearing up grammatical confusions. It enriches our understanding, whereas cognitive disciplines, such as the natural and social sciences, add to our stock of knowledge. But in order to add to our stock of knowledge the cognitive disciplines must achieve clarity about the concepts they are using and must achieve some clarity about how it is that we are to understand their objects (we must try to understand the concepts and practices of those we are studying). We can point to differences between philosophy and the social and natural sciences but those differences are not so great that philosophy is just irrelevant to the cognitive disciplines. Issues of sense and understanding are clearly very important in the social sciences.

In the second chapter I examine various questions about relativism. I ask whether it is a serious objection to Wittgenstein's conception of philosophy that he subscribed to some form of relativism. I use Maria Baghramian's taxonomy of the different forms of relativism to look at various forms of relativism and assess them.[6] I argue that ontological relativism, alethic relativism, and some forms of cognitive relativism are implausible, and also that they cannot be attributed to Wittgenstein. A more plausible form of relativism is conceptual relativism and it is reasonable to describe Wittgenstein as a conceptual relativist. This chapter responds to some of his critics, who claim that Wittgenstein's philosophy implies implausible forms of relativism. My conclusion is that Wittgenstein *is* a kind of relativist but that the fact that he is a kind of relativist does not undermine his philosophical views.

The form of relativism Wittgenstein adopts does not obviously commit him to any particular ideological stance (and I will argue in the following chapters that Wittgenstein was not a conservative, a liberal, or a socialist). However, I will argue in the final chapter that his conceptual relativism would lead him to reject transcendental theories of justice such as Rawls's theory, and Peter Winch has argued convincingly that Wittgenstein's conception of practical rationality (which is connected to his conceptual relativism) would lead him to reject traditional accounts of the relationship between rationality and authority, such as Hobbes's view (and Rawls's too).[7] So, a Wittgensteinian take on philosophy reveals confusions in quite a lot of what has gone by the name of 'political theory' but does not commit Wittgenstein to a full-blown ideology or theory himself. That is not to say that the impact of Wittgensteinian philosophy on political philosophy has to be a wholly negative one – destroying houses of cards. There is a positive aspect to Wittgensteinian philosophy which is that it can aid our understanding of things like practical rationality, authority, and justice. Improved understanding will likely lead to the construction of better political theories.

The chapters on social sciences and relativism form the first part of the book where I am trying to get clear about Wittgenstein's conception of philosophy

---

[6] From Maria Baghramian's recent book about relativism (M. Baghramian, *Relativism*, Abingdon: Routledge, 2004).

[7] P. Winch, 'Certainty and Authority', *Royal Institute of Philosophy Supplement*, vol. 28, 1990, pp. 223–37.

and its relationships to other disciplines. In the second part of the book I look at political ideologies and ask whether Wittgenstein's philosophical remarks imply that he was committed to a particular ideological stance.

Chapter 3 is dedicated to conservatism and I focus particularly on the most prominent conservative interpretation of Wittgenstein which has been presented by J. C. Nyiri. He has argued in a series of papers that Ludwig Wittgenstein is a conservative philosopher. In 'Wittgenstein 1929–31: The Turning Back'[8] Nyiri cites Wittgenstein's admiration for Grillparzer as well as overtly philosophical passages from Wittgenstein's *On Certainty*[9] in support of that thesis. I argue, in opposition to Nyiri, that we should separate Wittgenstein's political remarks from his philosophical remarks and that nothing Wittgenstein says in his philosophical work obviously implies a conservative viewpoint, or any other kind of political viewpoint (which is not to say that no conclusions whatsoever about political theory follow from Wittgenstein's remarks). In his philosophical work Wittgenstein was concerned with untangling conceptual confusions rather than with putting forward a political viewpoint and the two kinds of activities are quite different. There is, however, some evidence of elements of conservatism in the stances that Wittgenstein took on political issues, although there is also some evidence of sympathy for left-wing views, particularly during the 'late' period of Wittgenstein's work after he returned to philosophy at the end of the 1920s. Wittgenstein's philosophical work cannot be claimed by conservatives or socialists as their own but it can be used to untangle philosophical problems in the work of a great variety of political philosophers.

In Chapter 4 I turn to liberalism. The question of whether Wittgenstein was a liberal philosopher has received less attention than the question of whether he was a conservative philosopher but, as Robert Greenleaf Brice has recently argued, there are hints of liberalism in some of his remarks,[10] and some philosophers, like Richard Eldridge, have argued that a kind of liberalism follows from Wittgenstein's later philosophy.[11] Richard Rorty has also drawn liberal conclusions from a philosophical viewpoint which draws on Wittgenstein's work and Alice Crary has suggested that the lessons learned

---

[8] J. C. Nyiri, 'Wittgenstein 1929–31: The Turning Back', in Stuart Shanker (ed.), *Ludwig Wittgenstein: Critical Assessments (Vol. 4)*, London: Routledge, 1986.

[9] Wittgenstein, *On Certainty*.

[10] R. G. Brice, *Exploring Certainty: Wittgenstein and Wide Fields of Thought*, Lanham: Lexington Books, 2014.

[11] See R. Eldridge, *Leading a Human Life: Wittgenstein, Intentionality, and Romanticism*, Chicago: University of Chicago Press, 1997; and R. Eldridge, 'Wittgenstein and the Conversation of Justice', in Cressida Heyes (ed.), *The Grammar of Politics: Wittgenstein and Political Philosophy*, Ithaca, NY: Cornell University Press, 2003, pp. 117–28.

from her own interpretation of Wittgenstein are 'reflected in forms of social life that embody the ideals of liberal democracy'.[12] In the fourth chapter I argue both that Wittgenstein was *not* a liberal and that his philosophy does not imply a liberal viewpoint. The authors discussed in the chapter do not demonstrate that any broad ideological conclusions follow from Wittgenstein's philosophical remarks.

In Chapter 5 I look at the relationship between Wittgensteinian philosophy and Marxist philosophy, focusing on the work of two English Marxists: Perry Anderson and Alex Callinicos. Both of them have produced excellent work in political theory, cultural theory, and philosophy. However, they have both misinterpreted the work of Ludwig Wittgenstein. I argue that Wittgenstein's conception of philosophy is not in tension with Marxist philosophy in the ways that they suggest and that Wittgenstein did not make the errors attributed to him by Anderson and Callinicos. Marxists would benefit from taking Wittgenstein's work more seriously because it would help them to see the nature of epistemological and metaphysical problems more clearly and would complement and enrich their own accounts of philosophical confusion. One political implication of Wittgenstein's philosophical remarks that I identify in the chapter is that we can get rid of philosophical problems by changing society, by making changes to our practical life.

The sixth chapter focuses on the work of another Marxist, the cultural theorist Terry Eagleton. The influence of Wittgenstein's work on Eagleton's oeuvre is clearer than in the case of Anderson and Callinicos. He wrote the script for a film about Wittgenstein's life and work,[13] wrote a novel which included Wittgenstein as a character,[14] and his work in literary theory and cultural theory more generally is clearly indebted to Wittgenstein to at least some extent. His recent book *Materialism* combined insights from Marx and Wittgenstein (as well as the work of other philosophers, such as Nietzsche).[15] In the chapter about Eagleton I look at his article 'Wittgenstein's Friends' and argue that his account of Wittgenstein there is flawed. His criticisms of Wittgenstein do not hit their target. I then go on to look at his more recent book about materialism and suggest that Eagleton also misrepresents Wittgenstein's work there.

---

[12] A. Crary, 'Wittgenstein's Philosophy in Relation to Political Thought', in Alice Crary and Rupert Read (eds), *The New Wittgenstein*, London: Routledge, 2000, p. 141.

[13] K. Butler, T. Eagleton, and D. Jarman, *Wittgenstein: The Terry Eagleton Script, the Derek Jarman Film*, London: BFI, 1993.

[14] T. Eagleton, *Saints and Scholars*, London: Futura, 1987.

[15] T. Eagleton, *Materialism*, New Haven, CT: Yale University Press, 2017.

The final two chapters form the third part of the book and they look at applications of Wittgenstein's philosophical remarks to particular problems that have arisen in the work of political philosophers: the problem of freedom of the will (including problems about self-control and responsibility) and problems concerning justice.

In the seventh chapter I argue that Wittgenstein's grammatical remarks about psychological concepts as well as his remarks about philosophical methodology can help to dissolve conceptual problems that are clearly relevant to political philosophy. My focus in that chapter will be on Patricia Churchland and Christopher Suhler's paper 'Control: Conscious and Otherwise',[16] where they formulate what they think of as a neurobiological account of control. They do so in an attempt to tackle problems about the extent to which we ought to hold people responsible in cases where they are not conscious of the way in which circumstances affect their choices. Some philosophers and cognitive scientists have argued that empirical research shows that circumstances have such a large impact on people's choices that we ought to say that a person's control over what they do in many cases is very limited. Given the lack of control we ought not to hold people responsible for their actions to the extent that we do. This is known as the 'Frail Control' hypothesis and Churchland and Suhler think that their account of control undermines it.

The debate clearly has implications concerning questions of justice in society – implications concerning the way in which we ought to hold people accountable for the things they do. It is also clearly a version of old problems about freedom of the will. Wittgenstein's philosophical remarks can help clarify the terms in which the debate is conducted and to untangle some of the conceptual confusions involved. Churchland and Suhler are right to challenge the Frail Control hypothesis and some of their conclusions are correct. However, the arguments they use to get to their conclusions are confused in various ways. The aim of the seventh chapter is to suggest that Wittgenstein's remarks can help us to dissolve confusions surrounding problems about freedom of the will – help us to achieve clarity. A better understanding of Wittgenstein's philosophy can help us achieve a better understanding of political philosophy.

The eighth and final chapter is focused on the question of justice. In the first half of the chapter I look at ways in which we might get clearer about the concept 'justice' and I use insights gleaned from Hanna Pitkin's *Wittgenstein and Justice*[17] in doing that. In the second half of the chapter I look at whether

---

[16] P. S. Churchland and C. L. Suhler, 'Control: Conscious and Otherwise', *Trends in Cognitive Science*, vol. 13, no. 8, 2009.

[17] H. Pitkin, *Wittgenstein and Justice: On the Significance of Ludwig Wittgenstein for Social and Political Thought*, Berkeley: University of California Press, 1972.

Wittgenstein's philosophical remarks imply that we should adopt a particular conception of justice and I argue that although his remarks do not imply that we should accept a particular conception of justice his remarks do nonetheless imply that we should reject certain conceptions of justice for making unwarranted assumptions or for having confused conceptions of practical rationality.

Within Chapter 8 I also look at some remarks that Wittgenstein made in *On Certainty*[18] and I suggest that Wittgenstein has things to teach us about the form that political disagreements might take. Political disagreements may well not just involve conflicts of opinion; they might also involve disagreements in evidential standards, disagreements about concepts, or perhaps even a difference in worldview. I conclude that although Wittgenstein acknowledges that disagreement, contestation, or rebellion have a role to play throughout our normative practices, this does not imply that his philosophical remarks are suggestive of a particular form that society should take. In particular I do not think that Wittgenstein's remarks provide support for the kind of pluralistic democracy favoured by Chantal Mouffe and José Medina. However, I think that the tools Wittgenstein provided us with can be used to help us to understand oppression and injustice and suggest ways in which that might be done.

0.2 How Is This Book Different to Other Books about Wittgenstein and Social Science?

There are already several book-length discussions of Wittgenstein's relation to social and political theory. In this part of the introduction I would like to make clear where my own work differs from other book-length treatments of these questions. One obvious difference between the work in this book and earlier treatments of the topic, such as Hanna Pitkin's *Wittgenstein and Justice*, John W. Danford's *Wittgenstein and Political Philosophy*, and Susan Easton's *Humanist Marxism and Wittgensteinian Social Philosophy*, is that much of the work discussed here has been written in the past two decades. For example, in the first chapter, about social science, I discuss recent work from Phil Hutchinson, Rupert Read, Wes Sharrock,[19] and John Dupré.[20] In the second chapter I discuss recent work on relativism from Maria Baghramian[21] and Hans-Johann

---

[18] Wittgenstein, *On Certainty*.
[19] P. Hutchinson, R. Read, and W. Sharrock, *There Is No Such Thing as a Social Science*, Aldershot: Ashgate, 2008.
[20] J. Dupré, 'Social Science: City Centre or Leafy Suburb', in *Philosophy of the Social Sciences*, May 2016.
[21] Baghramian, *Relativism*.

Glock.[22] In the third chapter I make use of Corey Robin's recent book *The Reactionary Mind*[23] in defining conservatism. It should also be clear that the topics I focus on in this book differ from those earlier writers.

Other, hugely influential, figures I should mention from the (broadly speaking, Wittgensteinian) philosophy of social sciences and philosophy of action are G. E. M. Ancombe and Peter Winch, who both published highly influential works in the late 1950s, soon after the publication of the *Philosophical Investigations*. I have discussed their work in a few places within this book but I did not want to say more about them since there is already a very large literature discussing both philosopher's work. I hope my indebtedness to their groundbreaking work is clear (as well as my disagreements with contemporary Winchians such as Hutchinson, Read, and Sharrock). I would recommend reading classic works like Ancombe's *Intention*,[24] Winch's 'Understanding a Primitive Society',[25] and his book *The Idea of a Social Science*,[26] as well as more recent discussions of their work such as *Value and Understanding* (a collection of essays about Winch edited by Raimond Gaita),[27] Hutchinson, Read, and Sharrock's *There Is No Such Thing as a Social Science* (which I discuss in the first chapter),[28] and Roger Teichmann's excellent recent book about Anscombe's philosophy[29].

Within this introduction, I will briefly look at three recent book-length discussions of Wittgenstein's relation to social and political theory here and make clear how my own work differs. The three books I will discuss are Peg O'Connor's *Morality and Our Complicated Form of Life*,[30] Christopher Robinson's

---

[22] H. J. Glock, 'Relativism, Commensurability and Translatability', in John Preston (ed.), *Wittgenstein and Reason*, Oxford: Blackwell, 2008.
[23] C. Robin, *The Reactionary Mind: Conservatism from Edmund Burke to Sarah Palin*, Oxford: Oxford University Press, 2011.
[24] G. E. M. Anscombe, *Intention*, 2nd ed., Cambridge: Harvard University Press, 2000 [1957].
[25] P. Winch, 'Understanding a Primitive Society', *American Philosophical Quarterly*, vol. 1, no. 4), pp. 307–24, 1964.
[26] P. Winch, *The Idea of a Social Science and Its Relation to Philosophy*, 2nd ed., London: Routledge, 1990 [1958].
[27] R. Gaita (ed.), *Value & Understanding: Essays for Peter Winch*, London: Routledge, 1990.
[28] P. Hutchinson, R. Read, and W. Sharrock, *There Is No Such Thing as a Social Science*, Abingdon: Ashgate, 2008.
[29] R. Teichmann, *The Philosophy of Elizabeth Anscombe*, Oxford: Oxford University Press, 2008.
[30] P. O'Connor, *Morality and Our Complicated Form of Life: Feminist Wittgensteinian Metaethics*, University Park: Pennsylvania State University Press, 2008.

Wittgenstein and Political Theory,[31] and Michael Temelini's *Wittgenstein and the Study of Politics*.[32]

0.2.1 *Morality and Our Complicated Form of Life*

Peg O'Connor's book *Morality and Our Complicated Form of Life* is primarily concerned with metaethical questions, and so its focus differs from the focus of this book. However, there is some overlap between her work and the questions discussed here. For instance, she discusses methodology in social science as well as the question of relativism and the cases she discusses (Frederick Douglass's speech 'What to the Slave Is the Fourth of July?',[33] Hurricane Katrina[34]) have clear relevance to politics. O'Connor makes several recommendations for conducting feminist inquiry and also cites recommendations made by Virginia Held approvingly. I agree with many of the recommendations she makes for feminist inquiry, including the recommendations that she cites from Virginia Held's *Feminist Morality*.[35] For example, I agree with O'Connor (and Wittgenstein) in being wary of scientism in the humanities and in the social sciences.[36] We should resist claims about social sciences being reducible to natural sciences and should also be careful about importing methods from the natural sciences into the social sciences, given differences in subject matter and also in the kinds of explanations appropriate to the different fields. I also agree with Held and O'Connor in not taking Wittgenstein's remarks about 'our craving for generality'[37] to imply that we should eliminate generalizations from explanations in fields concerned with social phenomena. As I will make clear in the first chapter I think that Wittgenstein's remarks about generalizations in *The Blue Book* concern the proper methodology of philosophy rather than the proper methodology of the humanities more generally or of social science.

---

[31] C. Robinson, *Wittgenstein and Political Theory: The View from Somewhere*, Edinburgh: Edinburgh University Press, 2009.

[32] M. Temelini, *Wittgenstein and the Study of Politics*, Toronto: University of Toronto Press, 2015.

[33] F. Douglass's 'What to the Slave Is the Fourth of July?' is available at https://www.thenation.com/article/what-slave-fourth-july-frederick-douglass/ (accessed 26 May 2018) and is discussed on pp. 132–36 of O'Connor's *Morality and Our Complicated Form of Life*.

[34] O'Connor, *Morality and Our Complicated Form of Life*, pp. 158–68.

[35] V. Held, *Feminist Morality: Transforming Culture, Society, and Politics*, Chicago: University of Chicago Press, 1993.

[36] O'Connor recommends that we 'create a moral epistemology that is consistent with much recent work in feminist epistemologies (resisting its reduction or assimilation to an overly scientistic model' (*Morality and Our Complicated Form of Life*, p. 5).

[37] L. Wittgenstein, *The Blue and Brown Books*, New York: Harper & Row, 1958, p. 18.

In fact, I think that generalizations have a very important role to play in the humanities and social sciences, alongside close analyses of particular cases.[38]

O'Connor looks at moral realism and antirealism in the work of John Mackie, Gilbert Harman (both antirealists), and Nicholas Sturgeon (realist) and she argues that neither of these metaethical positions is satisfactory because both are committed to scientistic assumptions about the role of observation, causation, and objectivity in thinking about morality.[39] In the first chapter of this book I discuss scientism, reductionism, reasons, and causes, and come to broadly the same conclusions as O'Connor.

The dispute over realism and antirealism also has obvious implications for what has traditionally been called 'moral epistemology' (O'Connor prefers to use the expression 'moral understandings' in order to distance herself from the tradition).[40] Realists and antirealists do not only make claims about objects, properties, and causes but also make claims about what their theory implies about the kind of knowledge we can expect to have in the area of morality.[41] If scientism creeps into our conception of our subject matter then that will affect the claims that we will make about knowledge in that area. She concludes, and I agree, that we can make sense of talking about truth and knowledge in morality and she offers her own account of objectivity in the context of her 'felted contextualism'.[42] In the first two chapters of this book I discuss the nature of philosophical inquiry, political enquiry, and scientific enquiry as well as questions about relativism and I come to similar conclusions to O'Connor.[43]

---

[38] Held recommends that we should 'proceed not solely on a case-by-case basis (requires some level of generality)' (cited on p. 5 of Peg O'Connor's *Morality and Our Complicated Forms of Life*).

[39] O'Connor, *Morality and Our Complicated Forms of Life*, pp. 22–23. On p. 59 she says that 'neither realism nor antirealism is tenable as a description of the world and their weaknesses trace back to a shared presupposition'.

[40] O'Connor discusses moral epistemology in chapter 6 of *Morality and Our Complicated Forms of Life* (pp. 113–36) and it is on p. 117 that she says that she favours the expression 'moral understandings'. For another account, see N. Venturinha, 'Moral Epistemology, Interpersonal Indeterminacy and Enactivism', in Jesús Padilla Gálvez (ed.), *Action, Decision-Making and Forms of Life*, Berlin: Walter de Gruyter, 2016, pp. 109–20.

[41] For example, A. J. Ayer claims that sentences expressing moral judgements 'are pure expressions of feeling and as such do not come under the category of truth and falsehood. They are unverifiable for the same reason as a cry of pain or a word of command is unverifiable' (*Language, Truth, and Logic*, New York: Dover, 1952, pp. 108–9), and John Mackie famously claimed that 'value statements cannot be either true or false' (*Ethics: Inventing Right and Wrong*, New York: Penguin, 1977, p. 25).

[42] See chapter 7 of *Morality and Our Complicated Form of Life*, pp. 137–68.

[43] For my own take on J. L. Mackie's antirealism see R. Vinten, 'Mackie's Error Theory: A Wittgensteinian Critique', *Kinesis*, vol. 7, no. 13, 2015, pp. 30–47.

In addition to rejecting the dualism of realism and antirealism O'Connor also rejects the dualisms that she thinks underlie the debate – the language-world dualism and the nature-normativity dualism. A related dualism, the dualism between moral absolutism and moral relativism, is another which she thinks involves confusions. As an alternative to all of these she offers her own 'felted contextualism' which preserves claims to truth and objectivity without resorting to moral absolutist claims and she defends the view that 'we can have better or worse answers or resolutions to these [moral] conflicts'.[44]

In explaining her own view, she looks to Wittgenstein's account of the role of authority, training, and normativity in our lives. Conservative accounts have made much of Wittgenstein's stress on the role of authority and rules in Wittgenstein. This is something that I will discuss in my chapter on conservatism and also in my discussion of Michael Temelini's *Wittgenstein and the Study of Politics* below.

0.2.2 *Wittgenstein and Political Theory*

Christopher Robinson's book, *Wittgenstein and Political Theory*,[45] is largely concerned with the question of theory, as the title suggests. Robinson argues that although Wittgenstein's remarks suggest he opposed theory they are best understood as criticizing 'metatheory'[46] and opening up a space for 'a new way of theorizing political life'.[47] According to Robinson's account, *metatheory* is concerned with questions of justification and explanation (traditional epistemological concerns) whereas Wittgenstein's opposing conception of theory understood theorizing as 'an ongoing description of the components and topography of reality from various positions within'.[48] Robinson calls this *immanent theorizing*[49] and he places special emphasis on perception and on mobility (particularly walking). For example, he says that 'for theorists following Wittgenstein's path to immanent theorizing, what is valued above all else is mobility'[50] and he claims that 'there is a palpable therapeutic effect in seeing that theorizing is cast more accurately as a primitive activity involving seeing and walking'.[51] Immanent theorizing, according to Robinson, involves being mobile and seeing things (reality, practices) close up and describing them[52]

---

[44] O'Connor, *Morality and Our Complicated Form of Life*, p. 146.
[45] Robinson, *Wittgenstein and Political Theory*, 2009.
[46] Ibid., pp. 25, 178.
[47] Ibid., p. 13.
[48] Ibid., p. 26.
[49] Ibid., p. 29.
[50] Ibid., p. 29.
[51] Ibid., p. 39.
[52] Ibid., p. 2.

whereas epic theory (metatheory) involves distancing oneself from things and trying to achieve a 'God's eye view' of them. Robinson says that 'the further we stand from people, the less we care what happens to them' and that 'Wittgenstein expresses this distance as at the heart of "the darkness of our time"'.[53] He claims that Wittgenstein abandons 'the pretense of a God's eye perspective'[54] and that 'both Wittgenstein and, more famously, Beckett, work from a street-level where no God's-eye point of view is possible, though we may find ourselves waiting for it'.[55]

Robinson claims that Wittgenstein's 'therapeutic turn' 'promises an erosion of the boundary separating philosophy from other activities'[56] and 'therapy was conceived as a matter of returning philosophers to the pre-linguistic primordial and then guiding them through mazes of contingent, opaque but permeable and overlapping language-games to give a sense of language's capaciousness and insurpassability [...] akin to the speech therapies a patient rendered aphasic as a result of a stroke might undergo'.[57] The outcome of Wittgensteinian therapy, according to Robinson, is that the patient remembers 'what it is to be human'.[58]

While I agree with Robinson that Wittgenstein would likely have recognized problems with epic or transcendental political theory (this will be discussed in my chapter on justice) I have several disagreements with Robinson's interpretation of Wittgenstein and with Robinson's suggestions about the direction political theory should take. In the first place I think that Robinson misunderstands Wittgenstein's remarks on theory. Looking carefully at Wittgenstein's remarks on theory and philosophy it becomes clear that Wittgenstein was not just criticizing metatheory and nor was he proposing or suggesting a new way of theorizing himself. In §109 of the *Philosophical Investigations* Wittgenstein says that 'we may not advance any kind of theory'. There is no mention of 'metatheory' or 'epic theory' at all anywhere in the *Philosophical Investigations*. However, that does not yet demonstrate that Robinson is mistaken. It could be that what Wittgenstein was objecting to when he objected to theory was what Robinson calls 'metatheory'. That, I think, is Robinson's position. So, in order to see if he is right we should look at what Wittgenstein has to say.

---

[53] Ibid., p. 17
[54] Ibid., p. 37. Similarly, on p. 48 Robinson talks about 'the demise of the pretense of a God's-eye point of view in Wittgenstein's world' and on p. 160 he says that 'Wittgenstein and, more famously, Beckett, work from a street-level where no God's-eye point of view is possible, though we may find ourselves waiting for it'.
[55] Ibid., p. 160.
[56] Ibid., p. 171.
[57] Ibid., pp. 49–50.
[58] Ibid., p. 50.

In §109 of the *Investigations*, when Wittgenstein is discussing the nature of philosophy and rejecting the idea that it is theoretical, it seems that (contra Robinson) he does not have in mind political theories which present themselves as offering a 'view from nowhere' (the 'metatheory' that Robinson opposes). What Wittgenstein does in §109 is to contrast philosophy with empirical theories which involve formulating hypotheses, putting them to the test, making observations, and gathering empirical evidence. He says that 'there must not be anything hypothetical in our considerations' and that philosophical problems 'are, of course, not empirical problems'. Robinson is right that Wittgenstein's conception of what he is doing involves description (and not explanation) but he is mistaken about what Wittgenstein says he is describing. Wittgenstein does not suggest that we should walk and see things and describe them from close-up. As we have just seen, the activity he is engages in is not empirical at all. Wittgenstein is not suggesting that we should describe the things that we see. Philosophy's task is not to describe empirical reality but to describe the uses of words, to describe grammar. Philosophical problems, Wittgenstein says, 'are solved through an insight into the workings of our language'.[59] Whereas Robinson presents the Wittgensteinian position as being one where the philosopher-theorist is engaged in 'an ongoing description of the components and topography of reality from various positions within',[60] Wittgenstein himself distinguishes 'the thing' from 'the mode of representation'.[61] His concern is not with looking at objects and describing their qualities (e.g. the ball in front of me is red and squidgy). Wittgensteinian description is description of the mode of representation rather than of things. The descriptions are of 'the workings of our language',[62] of norms of representation, rather than empirical descriptions of *reality*. I take this difference over the nature of the descriptions involved in Wittgenstein's philosophy to be a significant difference between Robinson's account and my own. Philosophy involves arranging grammatical rules, in order to achieve perspicuity about philosophical problems, not the kind of empirical descriptions we might find in science.

That is not to say that Wittgenstein did not also find metatheory, as Robinson describes it, objectionable. It is just to say that he did not mean to replace it with any kind of theory. Wittgenstein's philosophical remarks in *On Certainty* and elsewhere suggest that he not only objected to the idea that we could have a God's-eye view but he also objected to the idea that philosophy was in any way theoretical.

---

[59] Wittgenstein, *Philosophical Investigations*, §109.
[60] Robinson, *Wittgenstein and Political Theory*, p. 26.
[61] Wittgenstein, *Philosophical Investigations*, §103.
[62] Ibid., §109.

But perhaps something like Robinson's position could still be rescued. Wittgenstein's remarks do suggest that certain ways of going about doing political theory are misguided and perhaps we could say that Wittgenstein's remarks do open up a space for a new way of theorizing political life, as Robinson suggests – as long as we do not suggest that this is the activity that Wittgenstein was engaged in when doing philosophy. In coming to understand political situations we do undoubtedly engage in activities that do not just involve describing grammar. We do gather evidence, we do make observations, and we do present and evaluate opinions. Those are activities unlike what Wittgenstein was doing when he was doing philosophy but they are important activities in understanding our political situation (they also involve more than just walking, seeing things from close-up, and describing them – Robinson's 'immanent theorizing').

Given what I have said about Wittgenstein's conception of philosophy above I think it is clear that I also disagree with Robinson's portrayal of Wittgenstein's 'therapeutic turn'. Robinson's account of Wittgenstein's conception of philosophy was supposed to erode boundaries between philosophizing and other activities. However, Wittgenstein was clear throughout his career that philosophy was a different sort of activity to disciplines which seek knowledge of the world around us. In particular he always clearly distinguished philosophy from science. In the *Tractatus Logico-Philosophicus* he remarks that 'philosophy is not one of the natural sciences'[63] and that it 'aims at the logical clarification of thoughts'.[64] In the *Blue Book* Wittgenstein says that philosophers being tempted to answer questions in the way that science does 'is the real source of metaphysics, and leads the philosopher into complete darkness'[65] and in the *Philosophical Investigations* Wittgenstein says that 'our considerations must not be scientific ones'.[66] Furthermore, in what is now called *Philosophy of Psychology – A Fragment* Wittgenstein says that 'we are not doing natural science; nor yet natural history'.[67] Wittgenstein's work is distinct both from the sciences (including psychology) and from other disciplines in the humanities.[68]

---

[63] Wittgenstein, *Tractatus Logico-Philosophicus*, 4.111. In remark 4.1121 Wittgenstein also says that psychology is no closer to philosophy than any other natural science.
[64] Ibid., 4.112.
[65] Wittgenstein, *Blue and Brown Books*, p. 18.
[66] Wittgenstein, *Philosophical Investigations*, §109.
[67] Ibid., PPF xii.
[68] I should acknowledge here that there is some foundation in Wittgenstein's work for understanding his philosophy as being therapeutic and that Wittgenstein is sometimes interpreted in this light. For example, in *The Big Typescript* Wittgenstein describes his philosophical approach as analogous to psychoanalysis (433e) and in *Philosophical Investigations*, §133, Wittgenstein compares philosophical methods to therapies. However, I think too much can be made of the comparison with psychoanalysis or with therapy.

As mentioned above in my comments on Peg O'Connor's work, our conception of our subject affects what we will say about what we can know, believe, or understand about it. Our conception of our subject has epistemological implications. Given that philosophy is an investigation of grammar and that it involves 'assembling what we have long been familiar with',[69] it is not a discipline aimed at expanding our knowledge but rather it is aimed at increasing our understanding.[70]

0.2.3 *Wittgenstein and the Study of Politics*

Michael Temelini's book *Wittgenstein and the Study of Politics* is divided into two halves. In the first half of the book (the first three of six chapters) Temelini discusses interpretations of Wittgenstein's philosophy that stress the role of authority, training, therapy, and forms of scepticism in Wittgenstein's later work. He presents these various interpretations of Wittgenstein under the heading 'therapeutic scepticism'. In the second half of the book Temelini presents interpretations of Wittgenstein which stress making comparisons, dialogue, and understanding. He gathers these interpretations under the heading of the 'comparative dialogical' reading of Wittgenstein and he defends this kind of interpretation as being preferable to therapeutic-sceptical ones.

In the chapters on the 'therapeutic-sceptical' reading Temelini discusses the work of a great variety of thinkers who have interpreted Wittgenstein's work in a variety of ways and who have been inspired by his philosophical remarks. He discusses the work of people who have interpreted Wittgenstein as a conservative, including J. C. Nyiri and Ernest Gellner. He also examines the work of Stanley Cavell,[71] as well as philosophers whose work has been influenced by Cavell, such as Hanna Pitkin,[72] John Danford,[73] and, more recently, the New

---

Peter Hacker makes this case well in his response to Gordon Baker's late interpretation of Wittgenstein (see 'Gordon Baker's Late Interpretation of Wittgenstein', in Guy Kahane, Edward Kanterian, and Oskari Kuusela (eds), *Wittgenstein and His Interpreters*, Oxford: Blackwell, 2007).

[69] Ibid., §109.

[70] P. M. S. Hacker gives an excellent account of the nature of philosophy and contrasts it with other disciplines in his 'Philosophy: Contribution Not to Human Knowledge but to Human Understanding', which has been published in a collection of his essays – *Wittgenstein: Comparisons & Context*, Oxford: Oxford University Press, 2013.

[71] Such as S. Cavell, *The Claim of Reason: Wittgenstein, Skepticism, Morality, and Tragedy*, Oxford: Clarendon, 1979; and S. Cavell, *Conditions Handsome and Unhandsome: The Constitution of Emersonian Perfectionism*, Chicago: University of Chicago Press, 1990.

[72] I will discuss Pitkin's work in my chapter on justice. Pitkin, *Wittgenstein and Justice*.

[73] J. W. Danford, *Wittgenstein and Political Philosophy: A Reexamination of the Foundations of Social Science*, Chicago: University of Chicago Press, 1978.

Wittgensteinians.[74] Also discussed under the heading of 'therapeutic scepticism' are 'Democratic/Liberal' Wittgensteinians such as Cressida Heyes,[75] Gaile Pohlhaus, and John Wright,[76] as well as feminist Wittgensteinians, such as Peg O'Connor[77] and Alessandra Tanesini.[78] Peter Winch is also considered by Temelini to have interpreted Wittgenstein along 'therapeutic/sceptical' lines.[79] Temelini recognizes that these thinkers vary a great deal in terms of their interpretations of Wittgenstein and in terms of their ideological commitments. However, he thinks that all of these interpretations fail to give dialogue sufficient weight, unlike the 'comparative dialogical' interpretations (from Charles Taylor, Quentin Skinner, and James Tully), which he discusses in the later chapters. Temelini also thinks that the 'therapeutic-sceptical' interpretations lead to conservative, negative, or contingent[80] conclusions, whereas the 'comparative dialogical' interpretations present Wittgenstein's work as having positive, progressive implications. Temelini favours the latter position.

However, Temelini is willing to grant that some of the therapeutic-sceptical interpreters of Wittgenstein do have progressive politics. His problem with these interpreters is either that they see the progressive politics as something that has to be tagged on to Wittgenstein's politically neutral philosophy (O'Connor) or their progressive conclusions are rooted in 'various kinds of scepticism or non-realism that are essentially taken for granted as essential to Wittgenstein's method'[81] (Cerbone, Eldridge, Janik, Zerilli, Pohlhaus, and Wright). The problem in those cases, according to Temelini, is not the progressive conclusions but in the fact that those conclusions are drawn from an interpretation of Wittgenstein as some kind of sceptic or non-realist.

---

[74] Crary and Read, *The New Wittgenstein*.

[75] Temelini also categorizes other contributors to Heyes's volume *The Grammar of Politics* as democratic/liberal Wittgensteinians. Heyes, *The Grammar of Politics*.

[76] See, e.g. G. Pohlhaus and J. Wright, 'Using Wittgenstein Critically: A Political Approach to Philosophy', *Political Theory*, vol. 30, no. 6, 2002, pp. 800–27.

[77] See P. O'Connor, *Oppression and Responsibility: A Wittgensteinian Approach to Social Practices and Moral Theory*, University Park: Pennsylvania State University Press, 2002, as well as her book *Morality and Our Complicated Form of Life*, which is discussed above.

[78] See, e.g. A. Tanesini, *Wittgenstein: A Feminist Interpretation*, Cambridge: Polity, 2004.

[79] Juliette Harkin and Rupert Read argue that it is a mistake to categorize Winch in this way in their review of Temelini's book. See J. Harkin and R. Read, 'Book Review – Michael Temelini: Wittgenstein and the Study of Politics', *Review of Politics*, vol. 78, no. 2, 2016, p. 331.

[80] Temelini says of therapeutic/sceptical readings that 'the politics that necessarily derives from this is conservative, negative, or contingent' (*Wittgenstein and the Study of Politics*, p. 95).

[81] Ibid., p. 33.

There are several problems with Temelini's account. In the first place, although Temelini recognizes that there is some variety among the philosophers he gathers under the heading of 'therapeutic scepticism' he does have a tendency to tar them all with the same brush and misrepresent their views. I strongly suspect that the vast majority of them would have no objection to the idea that dialogue can result in mutual understanding and that it should be valued in both political theory and in the practice of politics. Indeed, Juliette Harkin and Rupert Read, in their review of Temelini's book, make this point with regard to the New Wittgensteinians: their 'approach to philosophical praxis is precisely that which Temelini seeks to elevate in his study [...] [t]he import of listening and the practicing of interpretative charity are the central commitments of the New Wittgensteinian's approach'.[82]

Harkin and Read also complain that Temelini misrepresents Winch as a relativist and Cavell as a dogmatic sceptic,[83] and I agree with them in their criticisms of Temelini. I would add that Temelini also misrepresents Winch as conservative, claiming that Winch's position on forms of life is that 'we must accept authority.'[84] But this is a peculiar interpretation of Winch's discussion of authority. Winch *does* think that people might have ingrained habits of obedience such that they do not question authority but he also claims that these habits can be challenged and are in fact challenged: 'If these habits are to be *challenged*, as of course they sometimes are, a basis will still have to be found for the challenge *in* the life of the community.'[85] At no point does Winch claim that habits of obedience or the authority of the state *should* not be challenged.

What Winch does is give an account of authority which conflicts with traditional accounts in philosophy. Winch looks at remarks from Wittgenstein's *On Certainty* in order to give a rich account of practical rationality in opposition to the accounts of practical rationality found in the works of philosophers such as Thomas Hobbes (and also, later, John Rawls). Hobbes's account makes it difficult to see why someone would consent to be subject to another's authority[86]

---

[82] Harkin and Read, 'Book Review – Michael Temelini', p. 330.
[83] Ibid., p. 331.
[84] Temelini, *Wittgenstein and the Study of Politics*, p. 59.
[85] Winch, 'Certainty and Authority', *Royal Institute of Philosophy Supplement*, p. 228.
[86] See pp. 224–25 of Winch's 'Certainty and Authority' where he explains Hobbes's account of practical rationality and some problems with it. Winch presents us with Hobbes's definitions of 'command' and 'counsel' and points out that 'it is striking that, in the case of command, Hobbes cuts off the "action" from any consideration of reasons by the ostensible "agent", whose own beliefs and projects are to be thought of as irrelevant. The difficulty raised by his definition is how the *will* of another person, the one who commands, can be thought of by the one commanded as *on its own* as reason for acting'.

whereas Wittgenstein's helps us to understand this (to make sense of it). One thing to notice here is that Winch is not saying that anyone *should* be subject to another person's authority. What he did was to describe the conditions under which we can come to understand why somebody consents to another's authority – which he thinks traditional theories had made obscure.

Temelini also misrepresents my own views in his discussion of 'therapeutic scepticism.' In the work of mine that he cites, 'Leave Everything as It Is: A Critique of Marxist Interpretations of Wittgenstein,' I neither emphasize the notion of therapy in Wittgenstein (I do not present a therapeutic reading of Wittgenstein) and nor do I subscribe to a form of philosophical scepticism. My work is mentioned briefly in the second chapter of Temelini's book under the heading of 'strong contextualism' and Temelini argues that the thinkers discussed under that heading either think that we are 'thoroughly determined by conventions' or that we are 'at the mercy of autonomous, radically contingent, and historically variable conventions operating largely out of our control.'[87] I do not in fact believe either of these things and the passage that he quotes from my work in order to justify making his claims does not justify him in making the claim that I am a 'strong contextualist'. What I said in my paper 'Leave Everything as It Is', which Temelini cites, was that Wittgenstein and Marx were both 'sensitive to the importance of (social) context'.[88] However, it does not follow from this that I believe that 'individuals […] are thoroughly determined by conventions' or that individuals are 'at the mercy of autonomous, radically contingent, and historically variable conventions operating largely out of our control', as Temelini suggests. So, one problem with Temelini's work is that he misrepresents the work of several of the philosophers he labels 'therapeutic sceptics', including my own work.

Another criticism that can be made of Temelini's book is that where he does interpret people correctly he does not always put a finger on a problem with their work. For example, Temelini takes it to be a problem with interpretations of Wittgenstein's work that they interpret him as not being a realist. However, if we look at Wittgenstein's later work we see that he regularly objects to realist 'theories' in philosophy, and with good reason. For example, in the *Blue Book*, Wittgenstein tells us that 'the trouble with the realist is always that he does not solve but skip[s] the difficulties which his adversaries see' and he claims that realists fail to see 'troublesome feature[s] in our grammar'.[89] In the *Philosophical Investigations*, Wittgenstein says that '*this* is what disputes between

---

[87] Temelini, *Wittgenstein and the Study of Politics*, p. 56.
[88] See Vinten, R. 'Leave Everything as It Is: A Critique of Marxist Interpretations of Wittgenstein', *Critique*, vol. 41, no. 1, 2013, pp. 21–22.
[89] Wittgenstein, *The Blue and Brown Books*, pp. 48–49.

idealists, solipsists and realists look like. The one party attacks the normal form of expression as if they were attacking an assertion; the others defend it as if they were stating facts recognized by every reasonable human being'[90] and in *On Certainty* Wittgenstein says that the realist's claim that 'there are physical objects' is 'a misfiring attempt to express what cannot be expressed like that. And that is does misfire can be shown.'[91] Feminist Wittgensteinians, such as Peg O'Connor, are on firm ground when they interpret Wittgenstein as presenting realism as confused and she makes a good (Wittgenstein-inspired) case that the moral realism of Nicholas Sturgeon is a confused response to Gilbert Harman's (confused) antirealism.[92]

Perhaps the problem with non-realist views in Temelini's mind is that they either leave us with an 'anything goes' relativism, or they leave us unable to make claims to truth or knowledge. However, Wittgensteinians might very well say that it is the various forms of realism that leave us in a confused position and that realism does not do what it sets out to do, that is, ground our knowledge claims. What we need to do is to return from the metaphysical position of realism to the rough ground of our ordinary lives, where we regularly say that moral claims are true and argue with each other about moral issues on the assumption that there are better or worse stances to take up and standards by which we can make judgements. O'Connor certainly claims that we do have standards,[93] that we can have moral knowledge,[94] and that we can have better or worse answers to conflicts.[95] Temelini does not tackle these arguments and so it seems that he is not in a good position to object to interpretations of Wittgenstein on the basis of them being non-realist.[96]

---

[90] Wittgenstein, *Philosophical Investigations*, §402.
[91] L. Wittgenstein, *On Certainty*, New York: Harper & Row, [1969] 1972, §37.
[92] See O'Connor, *Morality and Our Complicated Form of Life*, pp. 26–33.
[93] Ibid., pp. 63, 94.
[94] Ibid., pp. 113–27.
[95] Ibid., p. 146
[96] I think there are further problems with Temelini's book. I agree with Juliette Harkin and Rupert Read that Temelini misinterprets Wittgenstein's comments about forms of life. I also think that he misinterprets what Wittgenstein says about language games and perspicuous representations. But there is not space here to go into detail on all of this. I think that enough has been said here already to distinguish my position from Temelini's and to make it clear that my take on Wittgenstein and politics is different to his. I do also think that Temelini's book has many virtues as well as vices. I agree with him that conservative interpretations of Wittgenstein's philosophy are mistaken (see Chapter 3 of this book) and I think that there is something to be said for highlighting the role of dialogue in understanding and in resolving political disputes (although I also agree with Harkin and Read that too much can be made of this. They ask some rather

0.3 Wittgenstein, the Radical

Wittgenstein's way of philosophising represented a break with traditional ways of philosophising. Traditional philosophers thought of themselves as constructing metaphysical systems, or as adding to our stock of knowledge, or as doing something continuous with science. Wittgenstein presented us with a radically new way of doing philosophy.

I will argue in this book that Wittgenstein's radical philosophy could also be useful in developing the radical politics and social theory that we need around the world now. It is a mistake to view Wittgenstein's philosophy as conservative and Marxist critics of Wittgenstein are wrong to think that there are deep tensions between Wittgensteinian philosophy and radical left-wing politics. We face enormous threats from climate change, rising authoritarianism, bigotry, and war. Wittgenstein's philosophy is useful in challenging the dominant liberalism of today, which does not seem to be up to the task of rising to those challenges, and in developing a clearer, more radical alternative to it. It can help us to get clearer about the nature of disagreements, about what justice requires, and about the justifications given for various forms of society. Wittgenstein himself may not have been a radical in his politics but his philosophy can help radicals to get clearer in their political thought.

---

pointed questions of Temelini – 'Are the underclass and the superrich in need mainly of respectful mutual dialogue? Is dialogue necessarily the answer for Palestinians being driven out of their land? Should Syrian revolutionaries be invited to "listen" to the voice of their "sovereign government"?' (p. 331 of their review of Temelini's book).

Part 1

THE NATURE OF PHILOSOPHY AND OF SOCIAL SCIENCE

Chapter 1

IS THERE SUCH A THING AS A SOCIAL SCIENCE?

I am not interested in constructing a building, so much as in having a perspicuous view of the foundations of possible buildings. So I am not aiming at the same target as the scientists and my way of thinking is different from theirs.[1]

1.1 Introduction

Action is significant in Wittgenstein's later work and Wittgenstein's work is significant in terms of the development of the philosophy of action. In the very first of the numbered remarks in his *Philosophical Investigations* Wittgenstein highlights the way a shopkeeper *acts* in delivering goods to a customer as a way of contrasting his understanding of language with the 'Augustinian' picture of language. In discussing one sense of the expression 'language game' Wittgenstein describes a language game as consisting of 'language and the activities into which it is woven'.[2] In other remarks Wittgenstein discusses the relationships between action and ostensive definition,[3] the action of a machine (in connection with his discussion of rule following/the relationship between a rule and action in accordance with it),[4] action and reasons,[5] action/behaviour and language,[6] acting and

---

[1] L. Wittgenstein, *Culture and Value*, trans. Peter Winch, Oxford: Blackwell, 1980, p. 7.
[2] L. Wittgenstein, *Philosophical Investigations*, revised 4th edition by P. M. S. Hacker and Joachim Schulte, translated by G. E. M. Anscombe, P. M. S. Hacker, and Joachim Schulte, Oxford: Wiley-Blackwell, 2009, §7.
[3] Ibid., see, e.g. §33, §36.
[4] Ibid., §193.
[5] Ibid., see, e.g. §211.
[6] Wittgenstein's 'private language argument' provides a good example of his thinking about language and action but action and language are discussed throughout the *Philosophical Investigations*. See, e.g. §243, §556.

thinking,[7] acting on orders,[8] and action and the will.[9]

In his book *The Idea of a Social Science* Peter Winch developed Wittgenstein's ideas about action, behaviour, language, and rules into a critique of the idea that the disciplines known as the social sciences are scientific in the manner of the natural sciences. Action appears in *The Idea of a Social Science* as a way of distinguishing natural sciences, which feature causal explanations prominently, from social sciences, which focus upon human actions and feature explanations in terms of reasons and motives more conspicuously. Winch distinguishes actions from habitual behaviour and distinguishes actions in terms of motives from causal explanations. Wittgenstein was notoriously opposed to scientism, that is, the attempt to bring the methods of science to bear in areas where they are not appropriate, especially in philosophy.[10] Winch, following Wittgenstein, detailed ways in which social investigations differ from investigations in the natural sciences.

Phil Hutchinson, Rupert Read, and Wes Sharrock have recently defended Winch's account of differences between natural sciences and social disciplines. In their book *There is No Such Thing as a Social Science* they come to the conclusion that calling social disciplines 'sciences' is likely to lead to confusion.[11] However, not all philosophers who have been influenced by Wittgenstein and Winch agree that there is no such thing as a social science. At the British Wittgenstein Society conference in 2015 (on Wittgenstein and the social sciences) John Dupré defended the idea that social studies can be scientific.[12]

---

[7] Ibid., see, e.g. §330, §490.

[8] Ibid., §459–60, §487, §493, §505, §519.

[9] Ibid., §§611–28. In a recent collection of articles on the philosophy of action edited by Constantine Sandis and Jonathan Dancy the editors place this selection of remarks from Wittgenstein at the front of the book because 'the work of Wittgenstein has been seminal in this change [the move towards having graduate classes devoted entirely to the philosophy of action]' ('preface' to J. Dancy and C. Sandis (eds), *Philosophy of Action: An Anthology*, Oxford: Wiley-Blackwell, 2015, p. x).

[10] For example, in the Blue Book Wittgenstein says that 'philosophers constantly see the method of science before their eyes, and are irresistibly tempted to ask and answer questions in the way science does. This tendency is the real source of metaphysics and leads the philosopher into complete darkness' (L. Wittgenstein, *The Blue and Brown Books*, New York: Harper & Row, 1958, p. 18). See also §81, §89, §109, PPF 365, and PPF 371 in Wittgenstein, *Philosophical Investigations*.

[11] P. Hutchinson, R. Read, and W. Sharrock (eds), *There is No Such Thing as a Social Science: In Defence of Peter Winch*, Aldershot: Ashgate, 2008, p. 51.

[12] A video of the talk John Dupré gave can be found here: http://www.british wittgensteinsociety.org/news/annual-conference/conference-videos. The paper he delivered has since been published as 'Social Science: City Centre or Leafy Suburb' in *Philosophy of the Social Sciences*, May 2016.

In discussing whether the disciplines that are known as social sciences[13] are in fact scientific there are a number of different ways in which the question might be approached. (1) One way of arguing that social sciences are scientific is to claim that social sciences are *reducible* to natural sciences. The positivists of the Vienna Circle and philosophers influenced by them (as well as many scientists) have made the claim that social sciences are reducible to natural sciences, that is, that behaviour at the level of social groups can ultimately be explained in terms of objects at another level – cells, or molecules, atoms, physical things, or even sense data. Reductionists often accompany this claim with the claim that laws at one level can be derived from laws at a lower level (e.g. that the laws of chemistry can be derived from the laws of physics). (2) One might not accept reductionism but nonetheless claim that the kind of explanations used in the social sciences are of the same sort as those used in the natural sciences. The debate about whether explanations in terms of reasons are causal explanations is relevant to this. Donald Davidson in the later part of the twentieth century famously argued that reasons are causes. (3) Another relevant issue in deciding whether the social sciences are scientific is *methodology*. Some have defended the claim that social sciences are scientific on the basis that they employ the same methodology as natural sciences.[14] (4) A problem that arises in comparing natural sciences to social sciences is that there does not seem to be the same kind of *progress* in the social sciences as in the natural ones. In the natural sciences we see widespread agreement over a wide range of issues as well as advances in technology and in the sophistication and usefulness of theories. However, in the social sciences disagreement is the rule and doubts are raised about whether any progress has been made (in philosophy in particular). There is certainly no clear agreement among philosophers about, for example, the relationship between mind and body, and philosophers are still puzzled about the question of whether human beings have free will despite centuries of having discussed the question.[15]

---

[13] Social sciences are usually thought to include economics, sociology, anthropology, human geography, politics, and sociology: disciplines which aim at knowledge of the various relationships between individuals and the societies they belong to. There is more disagreement about whether philosophy and history are to be counted among the social sciences.

[14] E.g., Otto Neurath (of the Vienna Circle) claims that it is not tenable to separate cultural sciences from natural ones by saying that each employ special methods (O. Neurath, 'Physicalism: The Philosophy of the Viennese Circle', in *Philosophical Papers 1913–1946 (Vienna Circle Collection) Vol. 16,* edited and translated by Robert S. Cohen and Marie Neurath, Dordrecht: D. Reidel, p. 50).

[15] There is an excellent recent book on the topic of theorizing in social sciences written from a critical Wittgensteinian perspective that I will not discuss here. Leonidas Tsilipakos's *Clarity and Confusion in Social Theory* (Farnham: Ashgate, 2015) discusses

It is worth noting that John Dupré and Hutchinson, Read, and Sharrock would largely agree in how they would think about the issues of reductionism, the varieties of explanation, methodology, and progress. However, they come to different conclusions about whether social studies should be called scientific. In this chapter I will come down on the side of Dupré and conclude that ultimately the question of whether the social sciences are scientific does not rest on whether they are reducible to natural sciences or whether they employ the same methodologies. I will argue that social sciences are not reducible to natural sciences and that social and natural sciences do not employ the same methodologies across the board (and nor should they) but that, nonetheless, disciplines like psychology, sociology, and economics can make some claim to be scientific.

Before going on to discuss reductionism it is first worthwhile mentioning the related, infamous, dispute in the late 1950s and early 1960s between C. P. Snow and F. R. Leavis about whether there were two cultures, literary and scientific, which were mutually uncomprehending of one another. Snow suggested that there were and that in order to correct the situation there should be greater efforts to educate the young in the natural sciences and to introduce more scientific literacy into politics. He thought that this would lead to improvements in society, especially in poorer parts of the world. Snow was accused of scientism for his efforts to promote the role of science in society.[16] Leavis, on the other hand, argued that there was just one culture[17] (and was accused of 'literarism'[18]). Leavis's concerns about Snow's scientism are not of the same sort as Wittgenstein's worries about scientism mentioned above. Whereas Leavis was primarily concerned with the way in which Snow emphasized science education and technological progress at the expense of literature and social science education, which involved a kind of lacuna in terms of what makes for good, meaningful, happy lives (literature has an important role to play, according to Leavis), Wittgenstein's worries about scientism were primarily about the confusion caused by trying to import scientific methods and concepts into the humanities and the social sciences (particularly philosophy but also psychology and other social/humanistic disciplines) and about attempts to reduce social sciences to natural ones. However, that is not to

---

problems with trying to import theoretical frameworks into social sciences. My review of his book appeared in R. Vinten, 'Review of "Clarity and Confusion in Social Theory" by Leonidas Tsilipakos', *Nordic Wittgenstein Review*, vol. 4, no. 2, 2015.

[16] See F. R. Leavis, 'Luddites? Or, There Is Only One Culture', in *Two Cultures? The Significance of C. P. Snow* (with an introduction by Stefan Collini), Cambridge: Cambridge University Press, 2013, p. 103.

[17] Ibid., pp. 101, 106.

[18] Ibid., p. 103.

IS THERE SUCH THING AS SOCIAL SCIENCE? 29

say that there is no overlap at all. Wittgenstein expressed somewhat similar worries to Leavis about progress[19] and Leavis had relevant things to say about the status of social and humanistic disciplines that I will come back to in the conclusion to this chapter.[20]

1.2 Reductionism

1.2.1 *What Is Reductionism?*

Reductionism has been defined as 'a commitment to the complete explanation of the nature and behaviour of entities of a given type in terms of the nature and behaviour of their constituents'.[21] The *Stanford Encyclopedia of Philosophy* entry on reductionism[22] makes the point that 'saying that x reduces to y typically implies that x is nothing more than y or nothing over and above y' and so the scientist Francis Crick's claim that ' "you" [...] are in fact no more than the behaviour of a vast assembly of nerve cells'[23] is an expression of a reductionist view. Crick goes on to argue that a nerve cell in turn can be expected to be understood in terms of its parts, 'the ions and molecules of which it is composed'.[24] So, one might think that social groups are made up of collections of multicellular organisms, and multicellular organisms are made up of cells, which are made up of molecules made up of atoms composed out of sub-atomic particles, and that we can explain entities at one level in terms of the

---

[19] In one of the remarks published in *Culture and Value* Wittgenstein says,

Our civilization is characterized by the word 'progress'. Progress is its form rather than making progress being one of its features. Typically it constructs. It is occupied with building an ever more complicated structure. And even clarity is only a means to this end and not an end in itself. For me on the contrary clarity, perspicuity are valuable in themselves. I am not interested in constructing a building, so much as in having a perspicuous view of the foundations of possible buildings. So I am not aiming at the same target as the scientists and my way of thinking is different from theirs. (Wittgenstein, *Culture and Value*, p. 7)

[20] Leavis and Wittgenstein were briefly friends (see R. Monk, *Ludwig Wittgenstein*, London: Vintage, 1991, pp. 42, 272, 278–79, 569; and also F. R. Leavis, 'Memories of Wittgenstein', in *Recollections of Wittgenstein*, Oxford: Oxford University Press, 1984, pp. 50–67).

[21] M. R. Bennett and P. M. S. Hacker, *Philosophical Foundations of Neuroscience*, Oxford: Blackwell, 2003, p. 357.

[22] 'Scientific Reduction', http://plato.stanford.edu/entries/scientific-reduction/, accessed 29 August 2016.

[23] F. Crick, *The Astonishing Hypothesis*, London: Touchstone, 1995, p. 3.

[24] Ibid., p. 7.

30   WITTGENSTEIN AND THE SOCIAL SCIENCES

lower levels, with the subatomic particles studied by physics at the lowest level of explanation.[25]

1.2.2 *Why Be a Reductionist?*

The fact that this position is advanced by respected scientists like Crick and others such as Colin Blakemore lends it credibility[26] and it is not just the fact that scientists subscribe to it that lends it credibility but also the esteem in which science itself is held. Science is seen to have been very successful in making advances, in technology, medicine, and so on. The success of science makes it tempting to import scientific methods and attitudes into other areas to see if they might not benefit from the same kind of treatment. This issue, the issue of scientific progress, will be discussed in Section 1.5, later in this chapter. Reductionism is also apparently supported by the fact that dualistic conceptions of past philosophy have been discredited and replaced by one or another form of materialism. If everything is made out of the same kind of stuff – matter – then presumably everything can be explained in terms of it. It seems that we have no need for explanations in terms of immaterial substance, and scientific explanation does not rely on such explanations.[27]

1.2.3 *Problems with Reductionism*

One problem for reductionism is that although the rejection of dualism appears to support a unified materialism, the rejection of dualism does not in fact imply materialism and even when it comes to explanations of material things we often do not explain them or things about them in terms of what they are made of. Materialism, if it is taken to be the view that everything that exists is material, is not well supported. There are many things which we would like to say exist but that are not material objects. As Max Bennett and Peter Hacker note, 'Laws and legal systems, numbers and theorems, games and plays are neither material objects or stuffs.' Bennett and Hacker point out that even when it comes to material objects we often explain their behaviour, perfectly legitimately, in terms other than what they are made of. We

---

[25] This is what is known as 'classical reductionism', and the classic formulation of it is Paul Oppenheim and Hilary Putnam's 'The Unity of Science as a Working Hypothesis', in H. Feigl et al. (eds), *Minnesota Studies in the Philosophy of Science*, vol. 2, Minneapolis: University of Minnesota Press, 1958.

[26] See, e.g. C. Blakemore, *The Mind Machine*, London: BBC Publications, 1988, pp. 270–72.

[27] However, it is worth noting that one can be a materialist without being a reductionist and one can be a reductionist without being a materialist. Berkeley, an idealist, thought that everything reduces to minds and ideas.

explain some things in terms of their function (e.g. human organs), others in terms of their goals, reasons, or motives (the behaviour of animals and human beings).[28] Historical events, such as the Russian revolution, are not explained in terms of what they are made of, 'since they are not made of anything'.[29] So, materialism cannot be used in support of reductionism.[30]

Another problem with attempts to reduce social sciences to natural ones is that social sciences often involve reference to the psychological attributes of human beings but psychological attributes of human beings cannot be reduced to any of the usual candidates that reductionist philosophers refer to – cells, molecules, brain states, or sense data. In the *Philosophical Investigations* one case that Wittgenstein brings our attention to is the case of *knowledge*. He carefully examines the grammar of 'know' and 'understand' and helps us to recognize that knowing cannot be a physical state, a mental state, or a disposition. If it were a physical state then there would be (at least) two different criteria for knowing – (i) the correct application of a relevant rule (e.g. a criterion for someone knowing the alphabet is that they can write or say 'A, B, C, D, E,' etc.) and (ii) the criteria for identifying the corresponding physical state or disposition. But it seems that the second criterion is not the one we would use, since even if the brain were in a particular physical state whenever someone recited the alphabet we would not take the presence of the state to indicate knowledge if someone wrote 'A, D, F, Z, 3' when asked to write the alphabet.[31] Rather than being reducible to a physical state or disposition, knowledge is akin to an ability,[32] and an ability is categorially distinct from the usual candidates that reductionists refer to (cells, molecules, brain states, physical things, or sense data). Following Wittgenstein, Bennett and Hacker note, 'The criteria of identity for mental states, events and processes differ from the criteria of identity for neural states, events and processes.'[33] This should be clear from the fact that psychological attributes are attributable to a person or to animals but neurophysiological attributes are attributable to their brains.[34] So, for example, someone might *believe* that voting to leave the

---

[28] This will be discussed in the following section.
[29] Bennett and Hacker *Philosophical Foundations of Neuroscience*, p. 358.
[30] Bennett and Hacker's discussion of materialism leans on John Dupré's discussion of materialism in *The Disorder of Things*. Dupré discusses and rejects several versions of materialism in his chapter on reduction and materialism (J. Dupré, *The Disorder of Things*, Cambridge, MA: Harvard University Press, 1993, pp. 89–94).
[31] See Wittgenstein, *Philosophical Investigations*, §149.
[32] Ibid., §150.
[33] Bennett and Hacker, *Philosophical Foundations of Neuroscience*, pp. 360–61.
[34] See Wittgenstein, *Philosophical Investigations*, §281: 'Only of a living human being and what resembles (behaves like) a living human being can one say: it has sensations; it sees; is blind; hears; is deaf; is conscious or unconscious.'

European Union (EU) was the right thing to do in the recent referendum in the United Kingdom. I attribute that belief to them (not to their brain) on the basis of their behaviour, particularly their linguistic behaviour. I attribute that belief to them, most likely, because they *say* that they believe that voting to leave the EU was right and I have no reason to doubt that they believe that. However, I do not attribute brain states or processes to them on the basis of their linguistic behaviour and those brain states or processes are states *of that person's brain* and not of the person. The person's beliefs cannot be neural states or events because their neural states and events have a location but their beliefs cannot be said to have a location (at least not in the same way). It makes no sense to ask, 'Where do you believe it was wrong to leave the EU?' Some questions sharing this form *do* make sense but they are not answered in a way that suggests that beliefs are neural states. So, for example, it does make sense to ask 'where do you believe the football game between Sporting Lisbon and Benfica will take place?' but this question is not answered appropriately by saying 'in my head', but by something like 'at the Stadium of Light'.

It is also worth noting that not only are social sciences not reducible to natural sciences but natural sciences themselves cannot all be reduced to physics. John Dupré has argued convincingly that ecology is not reducible to any level below biology,[35] and that there are various problems with reductionist projects in genetics.[36] There have been successful reductionist projects but these successes have been very local. Biological science has not been shown to be reducible to physics and we have good reason to think that it cannot be reduced to physics, namely that categorization in biology and much of the rest of science is driven by changing human interests and there is no single privileged taxonomic scheme in biology in terms of which it could be reduced to physics.

Wittgenstein thought that the temptation to reduce phenomena in one area to phenomena in another was one of the causes of philosophical confusion. In the *Blue Book* Wittgenstein says that his worry about philosophers' preoccupation with the method of science is, at least in part, a worry about 'the method of reducing the explanation of natural phenomena to the smallest possible number of primitive natural laws' and that 'it can never be our [i.e. philosophers'] job to reduce anything to anything'.[37] Philosophy is descriptive, that is, it describes norms of representation with the aim of getting clear about the meaning of problematic terms in order to get rid of the confusion at the root of philosophical problems.[38]

---

[35] Dupré, *The Disorder of Things*, 107–20.
[36] Ibid., pp. 121–45.
[37] Wittgenstein, *Blue and Brown Books*, p. 18.
[38] Ibid.

1.3 Reasons and Causes

As mentioned in the introduction to this chapter, one of the debates that is relevant to the question of whether the social sciences are continuous with the natural sciences is the debate about whether explanations in terms of reasons are causal explanations. One approach is to claim that human *actions* are distinct from behaviour resulting from *habits* (which influence our behaviour causally). A way of bringing out this distinction is to compare human activity with the activities of animals. Peter Winch, a Wittgensteinian philosopher, uses the example of a dog learning to balance sugar on its nose and holding it there until its owner issues a command to eat it. In this case the dog has been trained into a habitual response and cannot be said to be reflectively following a rule. Like rule-following cases the dog might be said to have done something correctly or incorrectly but this is only because we are applying human norms analogically to animals, according to Winch.[39] This is unlike the case of a human being continuing the series of natural numbers beyond 100 upon being ordered to do so because 'the dog has been *conditioned* to respond in a certain way, whereas I *know* the right way to go on *on the basis of* what I have been taught'.[40]

The debates in philosophy about the distinctions that Winch makes between rule-governed human behaviour and habitual animal behaviour, and between reasons, motives, and causes, have moved on since the time of *The Idea of a Social Science*. A seminal anti-Wittgensteinian paper, in opposition to the kind of view that Winch presents, is Donald Davidson's 'Actions, Reasons, and Causes' published in 1963.[41] The arguments between Davidsonians, Wittgensteinians, and others continue to this day.[42]

1.3.1 *Social Studies and Natural Science*

The considerations about differences between causal and rule-governed behaviour suggest that human activity cannot be understood in terms of the causal generalizations favoured by natural scientists. However, Winch thinks that explanations of human behaviour in terms of institutions and rules might

---

[39] P. Winch, *The Idea of a Social Science and Its Relation to Philosophy*, London: Routledge, p. 60.
[40] Ibid., p. 62.
[41] D. Davidson, 'Actions, Reasons, and Causes', *Journal of Philosophy*, vol. 60, no. 23, 1963, pp. 685–700.
[42] See, e.g. G. D'Oro and C. Sandis, *Reasons and Causes: Causalism and Anti-Causalism in the Philosophy of Action*, London: Palgrave Macmillan, 2013; and J. Tanney, *Rules, Reason, and Self-Knowledge*, Cambridge: Harvard University Press, 2013.

still be defended by followers of philosophers like John Stuart Mill as being scientific because:

1. 'an institution is, a kind of uniformity'.
2. 'a uniformity can only be grasped in a generalization'.
   And so
   (Conclusion) 'understanding social institutions is still a matter of grasping empirical generalizations which are logically on a footing with natural science'.

However, this argument is defective according to Winch because where we speak of uniformities we must have some kind of criteria of sameness. To characterize something as going on in a uniform manner is to characterize it as being the same in certain respects throughout time. However, what is characterized as being the same by one criterion might not be characterized as being the same by another. For example, someone looking at two pictures (one picture of an African elephant and one of an Indian elephant) might say that both depict the *same* creature, an elephant; however, we might say that they depict *different* species: one is an African elephant and another is an Indian elephant. Someone who is asked whether the two pictures are *the same* would likely be confused until they are told something further about the criteria they are supposed to apply in deciding. They might respond that they are not the same because the pose of the animal is different in each, or they might refer to the dimensions of the pictures and say the second is larger than the first.

As Wittgenstein says, 'The use of the word "rule" and the use of the word "same" are interwoven.'[43] What this means is that if we are to decide whether two things are the same or whether something counts as 'going on in the same way' (as in cases when we are asked to continue a series of numbers) we must do so by reference to a definition or a criterion – a *rule* of one sort or another. And, as Winch says, 'rules [...] rest on a social context of common activity'[44] and so to decide the nature of a particular field of study we must look at the kind of activities which it involves and also at the rules embedded in those activities which tell us whether the objects of the study are of the *same* kind or not, or whether they continue to be the *same* throughout time.

If we look at the kinds of activities engaged in by natural scientists and by those engaged in fields concerned with human activity (psychology, history,

---

[43] Wittgenstein, *Philosophical Investigations*, §225.
[44] Winch, *Idea of a Social Science*, p. 84.

sociology, literature, etc.) then we find that the things studied differ in each case. The rules which we consider in thinking about natural sciences are, for example, the grammatical rules, which constitute scientific concepts, and the rules governing the procedures of the scientists. However, in the case of those studying human activity we must consider not only the rules of the activities of the sociologists but also the rules governing the behaviour of those that the sociologist studies. It is the second set of rules, according to Winch, that tell us about the nature of sociology. It is those rules 'which specify what is to count as "doing the same kind of thing" in relation to that kind of activity'.[45]

The significance of this in thinking about the relation between social fields and the natural sciences is that the two kinds of activities are quite different. John Stuart Mill had argued that studying human society is like studying a complicated mechanism. However, if Winch is correct then the sociologist's 'understanding of social phenomena is more like the engineer's understanding of his colleague's activities than it is like the engineer's understanding of the mechanical systems which he studies'.[46] Explanation in sociology is often not like the causal explanations of natural science. However, that does not imply that it is not scientific at all.

1.3.2 *Is Winch Correct? – Davidson's Argument That Reasons Are Causes*

Winch distinguished explanations in terms of habituation, which he said were causal, from explanations in terms of rules, which he said were non-causal. Donald Davidson, in his 1963 paper 'Actions, Reasons, and Causes', argued, *pace* Winch, that explanation of human action citing the agent's reason for their action (i.e. the kind of action that Winch said was rule-governed) 'is a species of ordinary causal explanation'.[47] Davidson argues for this first of all by pointing out that the division between explanations in terms of reasons and explanations in terms of causes is not obviously mutually exclusive. It may be that nonteleological causal explanations do not have features that explanations in terms of reasons do, namely that explanations in terms of reasons have a justificatory element; nonetheless, 'it does not follow that the explanation is not also – and necessarily – causal'.[48]

---

[45] Ibid., p. 87.
[46] Ibid., p. 88.
[47] Davidson, 'Actions, Reasons, and Causes', p. 685.
[48] Ibid., p. 691.

Davidson also goes further. He doesn't rest satisfied with the claim that it is not obvious that explanations in terms of reasons are not causal. He gives an argument in favour of thinking that explanations in terms of reasons *are* causal. Davidson's argument for this is that people can have a reason to do something and yet *that* reason was not the reason why they did it. Several different reasons in a particular case could serve to make an action intelligible. For example, somebody might raise their arm and wave it around outside of their car window in order to greet a friend or in order to signal a turn or in order to cool their hand. We might ask why somebody raised their arm and waved it around outside of their car as they drove around a bend and they might respond, 'I saw my friend on the corner and waved at him' or 'my hand was hot having been on the warm steering wheel and so I wanted to cool it down' or 'I wanted to signal that I was turning'. How do we pick out the agent's reason from among the reasons that they had, which might have served to make the action intelligible? – Davidson's answer is that 'central to the relation between a reason and an action it explains is the idea that the agent performed the action *because* he had the reason'. And Davidson thinks that in order to 'account for the force of that "because"' we should think of the relation between reason and action as causal.[49]

Davidson argues that his opponents, the Wittgensteinians (including people like Winch), have not accounted for this relation between reason and action by talking about patterns and contexts because 'the relevant pattern or context contains both reason and action'.[50] Davidson might not have produced a conclusive argument in favour of construing the relation between reason and action in causal terms but it seems as though he has nonetheless provided some reason for thinking that explanation in terms of reasons is a kind of causal explanation. If his opponents are to dispute that, he says that they must identify an alternative pattern of explanation.[51]

Davidson's anti-Wittgensteinian arguments are formidable and have been enormously influential in terms of the way that many philosophers nowadays think about explanations of action in terms of reasons. What this demonstrates is that anyone who wants to defend a position along the lines that Winch wanted to defend must now deal with Davidson's arguments. The debate has moved on since Winch published *The Idea of a Social Science* and non-Wittgensteinian thought now predominates in philosophy departments around the world.

---

[49] Ibid., p. 691.
[50] Ibid., p. 692.
[51] Ibid.

1.3.3 *Is Winch Correct? – Tanney's Response to Davidson*

However, that is not to say that Davidson is correct and that a defence of ideas in the spirit of Winch cannot be given. Over the course of the past two decades, Julia Tanney has built up a powerful case against Davidson's conception of explanations in terms of reasons and she has defended the Wittgensteinian view that Davidson attacked. She has written a series of articles about reasons and rule-following that are collected in the recent volume, *Rules, Reason, and Self-Knowledge.*[52]

In her article 'Why Reasons May Not Be Causes',[53] Tanney examines various cases where somebody had a reason but did not act for that reason. This is the kind of case that Davidson suggested calls for thinking of the relation between reason and action in causal terms – to account for the force of the word 'because' where we say 'the agent performed the action *because* they had the reason'. Tanney denies that we have to bring in the notion of causation in order to account for these cases; instead, 'we just need to introduce judgements, weights, and values into the "anaemic" analysis of reasons'. What needs to be added in such cases is not the notion of causation but 'a more complex justificatory machinery'.[54] We can explain why someone acted for one reason rather than some other reason that they had by saying that the reason they acted on carried more weight for them than the others, or by adding something to the account about the agent's values (or both).

Davidson challenged his opponents to identify a pattern of explanation that accounts for the relationship between reason and action in something other than causal terms and Tanney rises to that challenge in her paper, 'Reasons as Non-Causal Context-Placing Explanations'.[55] If the relationship between (1) *a reason* and (2) *the action that it is the reason for* is not causal then what is it? Tanney explains that 'in many cases attributions of motives, intentions and reasons explain a performance by characterizing it as an action of a certain kind'.[56] Rather than assimilating explanations in terms of reasons to causal explanations Tanney suggests that explanations in terms of reasons are similar to other kinds of explanations that are clearly not causal. An example she gives to illustrate this is of somebody walking out of a chemistry classroom and seeing the letters 'c', 'a', 't' written on the board. They might ask one of

---

[52] Tanney, *Rules, Reason, and Self-Knowledge*.
[53] The article forms chapter 5 of *Rules, Reason, and Self-Knowledge*, pp. 103–32.
[54] Tanney, *Rules, Reason, and Self-Knowledge*, p. 109.
[55] This paper was originally published in C. Sandis (ed.), *New Essays on the Explanation of Action*, London: Palgrave Macmillan, 2009, pp. 94–111, and was reprinted as chapter 7 of *Rules, Reason, and Self-Knowledge*, pp. 149–70.
[56] Tanney, *Rules, Reason, and Self-Knowledge*, p. 154.

their classmates, 'why did the teacher write the word "cat" on the board?' and their classmate could explain what was going on by saying that 'the teacher was starting to write the word "catalyst" and you left the classroom before they finished writing'. This is clearly not a case of the model of causation Davidson subscribes to where there must be two logically independent events entering into the causal relation. In this case there is just one event (writing on the board by the teacher) which has not been understood and so an explanation is called for.[57] Explanations of actions in terms of reasons are similar to this in that what they do is to place an event in context and make sense of it. They are also similar, Tanney suggests, because they do not require two independent occurrences related to each other.

The possibility that at least some explanations of human action in terms of reasons are categorially distinct from explanations in terms of causes gives us some reason to think that social sciences are not like natural sciences. As noted in Section 1.2, the existence of explanations in terms of reasons (and in terms of goals and motives) undermines the kind of materialism that says that we are to explain things simply in terms of what they are made of and this in turn undermines reductionists who think that this kind of materialism lends support to their view. Thus far we have two broad reasons for rejecting the view that social sciences are of a piece with the natural sciences. Social sciences are not reducible to natural sciences (Section 1.2) and they employ different kinds of explanations to the natural sciences, namely, explanations in terms of reasons, rules, motives, and so forth (Section 1.3). In the next section I will examine whether we might claim that social sciences are like natural sciences by claiming that they employ the same methodologies.[58]

1.4 Methodology in the Natural and Social Sciences

Claims that the methodologies of the natural sciences are appropriate for use in the social sciences and that they are the only methods appropriate for use in the social sciences are driven by similar kinds of considerations to those that have motivated people to become reductionists. The enormous *progress* made in the natural sciences suggests that there is something right about the

---

[57] Ibid., pp. 156–57.
[58] As I mentioned in the introduction, Peg O'Connor objects to metaethical theories for their scientism with regard to the role that they give to causation. She notes that within metaethics 'there is a tendency to assimilate reasons to causes ... Reasons and causes, however, have very different aims and play very different roles in our lives'. See her *Morality and Our Complicated Form of Life*, University Park: Pennsylvania State University Press, pp. 115–17.

methodologies used in them and hints at the desirability of those methods in areas other than natural science. The rejection of dualism has led people to think that they should adopt a kind of monism, namely materialism or physicalism, and if social sciences study the same kinds of things as the natural sciences, namely physical things, then they should use the same kinds of methodologies. Another motivation for the claim that we should use the methods of the natural sciences to study social phenomena is verificationism. We might think that we cannot verify claims about, for example, other people's mental states or claims about ethics and so all we can do in these areas is study relevant quantifiable physical attributes such as behaviour (construed in physicalist terms). Some logical positivists argued that ethics as traditionally conceived was unverifiable and should be replaced by science. Otto Neurath heralded a new era in which 'instead of the priest we find the physiological physician and the sociological organizer. Definite conditions are tested for their effect upon happiness (*Glückswirkungen*), just as a machine is tested to measure its lifting effect.'[59]

A method is a way of establishing or accomplishing something. The ways in which the natural sciences establish truths within their domains include using observation and experiment. Observations might give us knowledge or they might lead us to infer that something is the case (perhaps something unobservable) or they might lead us to hypothesize that something is the case (which me might then test using further observations). Scientists have also had success by using explanations of phenomena in terms of their causes and by using mathematical notions to quantify and compare things.

It is certainly true that social scientists make observations, that they can sometimes quantify the things they are observing, and that they can test hypotheses that they formulate on the basis of observations. However, as noted above, there are explanations within the social sciences which are not causal explanations. In the social sciences we explain actions in terms of the reasons that people have and give for doing the things they do, their motives, and their goals. This suggests that there will be significant differences in the methods used by social scientists which reflect the fact that they are investigating the reasons and motives for human action rather than the causes of events involving non-human agents. So, for example, social science research involves questionnaires, surveys, polls, and interviews, in which human beings are asked about the things they do and why they do them. Although social investigations, like the natural sciences, involve observation, the character of the observation is different in each. Coming to understand human action through observation involves knowledge of social practices, norms, and

---

[59] Neurath, 'Physicalism', p. 50.

conventions, and the explanations arrived at by social scientists are not *nomological* explanations as they are in the natural sciences.[60] No *laws* of human behaviour or of human psychology have been discovered and we have no good reason to think that they will be.

Moreover, the methods employed by philosophy, of clarifying concepts by presenting overviews of their grammar, are categorially distinct from the methods employed by those working in the natural sciences. Grammatical claims are not hypotheses or reports of observations. They are not justified or tested by reference to empirical reality at all. As Wittgenstein said, 'There should be no theories, and nothing hypothetical, in philosophy.'[61] Getting clear about the meaning of the expressions one uses is something that one should do *before* one embarks on any scientific investigation.

So, it seems that natural sciences and social sciences, as a matter of fact, employ a variety of different methods. What of the motivations for thinking that perhaps they should employ the same methods – verificationism, materialism, and the progress made by science? Problems with materialism have already been discussed in Section 1.2.3 in discussing problems with reductionism. Verificationism, especially the variety presented by the logical positivists, is now widely rejected by philosophers with good reason. Wittgenstein made sharp criticisms of the view that the 'inner' world is hidden from us and all we can see is bare behaviour (although Wittgenstein's criticisms have still not been heeded by many philosophers today). We do not *infer* that somebody is in pain when we see them stub their toe and cry.[62] In that case we can *see* that they are in pain and we can distinguish that case from one in which we do make an inference, for example, when we see a packet of paracetamol opened next to a half-drunk glass of water on the table. There is a *logical* connection between pain and pain behaviour, namely that pain behaviours are (defeasible) criteria for someone being in pain. So, neither materialism nor verificationism provide us with good reasons for thinking that methodology in the social and natural sciences should be the same. The issue of progress in the social and natural sciences will be discussed in the next section below.

1.5 Progress

As already noted above, the impressive progress made in the natural sciences is one of the motivations to have the social sciences emulate the natural ones

---

[60] See Bennett and Hacker, *Philosophical Foundations of Neuroscience*, pp. 362–66, for more on this.
[61] Wittgenstein, *Philosophical Investigations*, §109.
[62] Ibid., §246, §§250–51, §253.

in one way or another. Academic philosophers and scientists have been unimpressed by the results of psychological theorizing and philosophical argument by contrast with rapid developments in physics, biology, and chemistry as well as by the lack of agreement among social scientists in contrast to natural scientists. For example, Semir Zeki, an academic working in neuroesthetics, has complained about 'the poverty of the results' in philosophy 'in terms of understanding our brains and their mental constitution'[63] and the philosopher Paul Churchland has lamented the lack of progress made by 'folk psychology' (the name he gives to our ordinary framework of psychological concepts, which he takes to be a theory of human behaviour) which he thinks has not progressed in 2,500 years.[64] More recently the physicist Stephen Hawking has declared that 'philosophy is dead' and claimed that it has been superseded by developments in science. Zeki thinks that neurobiology should take over problems about the mind (as well as problems concerning justice and honour) from philosophy, Churchland thinks that 'folk psychology' (our ordinary framework of psychological concepts as well as concepts employed in psychology) should be abandoned in favour of a neuroscientific psychology, and Hawking thinks that philosophers should give up on questions like 'why are we here?' and 'where do we come from?' and leave them to science.[65]

There is surely something to these worries about a lack of progress in philosophy. Philosophers still puzzle over Zeno's paradoxes from 2,500 years ago. There are contemporary Aristotelian ethicists but there aren't any contemporary Ptolemaic scientists. Philosophers are still troubled by sceptical doubts about our senses and by disagreements about what it is that we see and hear. More than two millennia ago Plato made attempts to define knowledge and philosophers today are still making similar attempts. Is it any wonder that people like Hawking think that philosophy might as well just be abandoned?

Ludwig Wittgenstein had an explanation for why it is that philosophical confusions have endured for millennia. It is that these problems are conceptual problems, that is, problems that result from misunderstanding certain concepts, and that the 'traps' set by language – the features of language that cause confusion – have remained in place:

---

[63] S. Zeki, 'Splendours and Miseries of the Brain', *Philosophical Transactions of the Royal Society* B, vol. 354, 1999, pp. 2053–65.
[64] P. M. Churchland, 'Folk Psychology', in S. Guttenplan (ed.), *A Companion to the Philosophy of Mind*, Oxford: Blackwell, 1994, pp. 310–11.
[65] Hawking made these claims at Google's Zeitgeist conference in 2011. See 'Stephen Hawking Tells Google "Philosophy Is Dead"', in *The Telegraph*, 17 May 2011, http://www.telegraph.co.uk/technology/google/8520033/Stephen-Hawking-tells-Google-philosophy-is-dead.html (accessed 24 October 2016).

> One keeps hearing the remark that philosophy really makes no progress, that the same philosophical problems that had occupied the Greeks are still occupying us. But those who say that do not understand the reason it is // must be // so. The reason is that our language has remained the same and seduces us into asking the same questions over and over again. As long as there is a verb 'to be' which seems to function like 'to eat' and 'to drink', as long as there are adjectives like 'identical', 'true', 'false', 'possible', as long as one talks about a flow of time and an expanse of space, etc. etc. humans will continue to bump against the same mysterious difficulties, and stare at something that no explanation seems capable of removing.[66]

It could be claimed that progress, of a sort, has been made in philosophy but that some philosophers and scientists have failed to recognize it as such. In his later work Wittgenstein laid out some of the confusions that have troubled philosophers over the centuries and contrasted their confused formulations with 'surveyable representations' of the problematic expressions. Surveyable representations clarify the meaning of expressions that are causing confusion, showing the way in which the relevant expression is ordinarily used, and perhaps contrasting it with other similar expressions or giving examples of conceptual connections with other expressions – whatever helps to reduce confusion and produce clarity and understanding. One example of this is Wittgenstein's discussion of the concept of 'knowledge' (discussed above, in Section 1.2.3). Elsewhere he dissolves problems from the pre-Socratic philosopher Heraclitus, 'Can one step into the same river twice?';[67] clarifies a centuries-old question from Augustine, 'how is it possible to measure time?';[68] describes the correct use of words like 'know', 'believe', 'certainty', and 'doubt' in dissolving sceptical problems;[69] discusses problems resulting from thinking of sensations as private;[70] as well as many other philosophical problems from over the past centuries.

Whereas progress in science consists in making empirical discoveries and devising ever more powerful theories, progress in philosophy consists in clarification of concepts which are causing puzzlement and does not involve

---

[66] L. Wittgenstein, *Big Typescript*, pp. 423–24 (page 312e of *The Big Typescript: TS 213*, German-English Scholars' edition, edited and translated by C. Grant Luckhardt and Maximilian A. E. Aue, Oxford: Blackwell, 2005).
[67] Ibid., 220, §111.
[68] Wittgenstein, *Blue and Brown Books*, p. 26.
[69] Wittgenstein, *On Certainty*.
[70] See, e.g. Wittgenstein, *Philosophical Investigations*, §246.

constructing theories at all. Philosophy should not be blamed for failing to uncover or discover truths about our brains since that is the task of biology and of neuroscience. What philosophers can do is clarify concepts employed in neuroscientific and psychological research (and in other areas of scientific and social scientific research) and thus help to formulate appropriate questions and to ensure that the results of research are expressed clearly. As Bennett and Hacker say in *Philosophical Foundations of Neuroscience*, philosophy's task 'is to clarify the conceptual scheme in terms of which our knowledge is articulated. Its achievements are its contribution to our reflective understanding of the logical structure of our thought and knowledge about the world. It cannot contribute to knowledge about the brain, and it should not be expected to. Philosophers are not closet scientists.'[71]

People like Semir Zeki, Paul Churchland, and Stephen Hawking are confused if they think that philosophy is to be blamed for failing to solve problems that science might solve, since philosophy is of a different nature to the natural sciences. We hope for increases in our knowledge and improvements in theory from science, discarding falsehoods and accumulating truths along the way. However, we cannot hope for such things from philosophy because philosophy is not a cognitive discipline. It aims at developing our understanding rather than contributing to our knowledge of the universe and the natural world. Its progress can be measured in terms of problems that have been clarified and understanding gained rather than in terms of knowledge.

As for psychology, Churchland is confused if he thinks that it can be replaced by neuroscience.[72] Our ordinary psychological expressions do not constitute a theory, although various theories might be formulated employing those psychological expressions. Churchland's position involves various paradoxes (philosophical or conceptual problems). For one thing, he cannot fault 'folk psychology' for failing to explain memory or the ways in which learning transforms us if he is correct in thinking that psychological expressions should be eliminated, since psychological expressions are employed in formulating the problems.[73] Given that our ordinary concepts are not a theory we cannot expect theoretical progress from them, although we might expect some kind

---

[71] Ibid., p. 404.
[72] In Chapter 7 I will look in more depth at problems with eliminativism – the philosophical approach of Paul Churchland and Patricia Churchland.
[73] See Bennett and Hacker, *Philosophical Foundations of Neuroscience*, pp. 376–77, where they develop this criticism of Churchland and present other similar criticisms. There are detailed objections to both Zeki and Churchland on pp. 366–77 and 396–407 of *Philosophical Foundations of Neuroscience*.

of progress from theories that employ psychological terms – from psychological theory – and it is indeed the case that empirical theories in psychology have advanced.[74]

Psychology cannot be reduced to neuroscience and nor is it similar to sciences like physics in the way that some psychologists have thought. For example, Wolfgang Köhler thought that psychology in the present day was like physics in its infancy. Physics had succeeded in moving from qualitative observations to quantitative measurement and psychology can hope to do the same, he thought.[75] But Wittgenstein objected that 'the confusion and barrenness of psychology is not to be explained by its being a "young science"; its state is not comparable with physics, for instance, in its beginnings [...] For in psychology, there are experimental methods *and conceptual confusion*'.[76] The 'objects' of psychology – mental states, events, and processes – are not hidden to others and only observable in their effects, like electrons. As Wittgenstein observed, we can *see* (at least sometimes) that someone is sad[77] or that they are fearful[78] or in pain.[79] However, none of this implies that psychology is not a science at all. Psychology can be said to have an empirical subject matter, to engage in systematic gathering and accumulation of knowledge, and psychologists might engage in experiments and gather data from those experiments.

Similar things might be said about other social disciplines. Given that they are not reducible to natural sciences, that they employ different kinds of methods and different kinds of explanations, we should not expect exactly the same kind of progress from them. However, political scientists, economists, human geographers, anthropologists, and sociologists *do* add to our stock of knowledge; these disciplines *can* be said to have an empirical subject matter, to aim at truth, to gather data, and to make useful generalizations from that data.

---

[74] See Bennett and Hacker, *Philosophical Foundations of Neuroscience*, p. 373, for a discussion of progress in psychology.

[75] See chapter 2 of W. Köhler, *Gestalt Psychology*, Liveright: New York, 1929.

[76] L. Wittgenstein, 'Philosophy of Psychology – A Fragment', in *Philosophical Investigations*, 4th edition, §371.

[77] L. Wittgenstein, *Last Writings on the Philosophy of Psychology*, vol. 1, edited by G. H. Von Wright and H. Nyman, translated by C. G. Luckhardt and M. A. E. Aue, Blackwell: Oxford, 1982, §767.

[78] L. Wittgenstein, *Remarks on the Philosophy of Psychology*, vol. 1, edited by G. E. M. Anscombe and G. H. Von Wright, translated by G. E. M. Anscombe, Blackwell: Oxford, 1980, §1066–68.

[79] Wittgenstein, *Philosophical Investigations*, §246.

1.6 Conclusion

In the preceding sections of this chapter I have presented arguments in favour of saying that social sciences are not *reducible* to natural sciences, that they involve different kinds of *explanations* to the natural sciences (i.e. explanations of action in terms of reasons, motives, and goals), that the *methodologies* involved in social sciences are at least sometimes different to those employed in the natural sciences, and that the kind of progress that might be expected in social sciences differs from the kind of progress that might be expected in natural sciences (and progress in social sciences amounts to something different than progress in philosophy).

In their book *There is No Such Thing as a Social Science* Phil Hutchinson, Rupert Read, and Wes Sharrock argue that due to these considerations about reductionism and so on there is no such thing as a social science. In the introduction to the book they consider the possibility that the analytical rigour of social studies, the responsiveness to evidence in social studies, and the willingness to learn from other modes of enquiry found among those studying the social realm might be reasons to call social studies social *sciences*. However, they reject this on the grounds that neither of these considerations is sufficient for calling something a science.

In contrast to Hutchinson, Read, and Sharrock, I want to stand by the claim that social sciences are indeed scientific – that there is such a thing as a social science. Although the kinds of considerations alluded to by Hutchison, Read, and Sharrock are not, taken individually, sufficient to call something a science they might nonetheless be jointly sufficient (or it may be that together with other considerations they are jointly sufficient). One reason to claim that social studies are, or at least can be, scientific is that calling something 'scientific' plays a role in legitimizing that discipline. As John Dupré has recently pointed out, the term 'unscientific' is used as a term of criticism[80] and we live in a world where social sciences and humanities come under attack from governments for being unscientific.[81] The mere fact that social sciences are unlike natural sciences in various ways does not imply that they are illegitimate courses of study or that they are any less valuable than the natural

---

[80] J. Dupré, 'Social Science: City Center or Leafy Suburb', *Philosophy of the Social Sciences*, May 2016, pp. 8–9. Dupré asks, 'Is there [...] anything in principle unscientific about the delineation of the rules that exist in a particular society?' and answers, 'I cannot see why. Language is profoundly normative, but this does not make the science of linguistics impossible.'

[81] See, e.g. 'The War against Humanities at Britain's Universities', in *The Guardian*, 29 March 2015, https://www.theguardian.com/education/2015/mar/29/war-against-humanities-at-britains-universities (accessed 26 September 2016).

sciences. Psychologists, economists, anthropologists, sociologists, and human geographers uncover truths and increase our knowledge of human society. Understanding ourselves as human beings and being able to make progress in the way that we relate to each other as economic, political, and social beings are all immensely important.

F. R. Leavis, mentioned in the introduction above, emphasized the importance of social studies. One point that he made was that the objects of study in social studies are in a sense *prior* to studies in the natural sciences:

> There is a prior human achievement of collaborative creation, a more basic work of the mind of man (and more than the mind), one without which the triumphant erection of the scientific edifice would not have been possible: that is the creation of the human world, including language.[82]

Leavis thought that the study of the human world, including language, was immensely important for various reasons. Social disciplines can work in conjunction with natural sciences by helping to decide the ends which (largely instrumental) natural sciences aim at. Thinking carefully about human ends and more generally about what makes human lives significant, meaningful, happy, and rich as well as about how to bring about rich, interesting, happy human lives is the work of social sciences and the scientism of C. P. Snow, that Leavis was responding to, does not recognize the importance of this. Simply aiming at a 'rising standard of living', as Snow did, fails to engage with questions about what makes life worth living. So, social disciplines are to be called 'sciences' partly because they are important and so *worthy* of the title.

Another consideration in favour of calling social disciplines 'sciences' is that practitioners within these disciplines, for the most part, consider what they are doing to be science of sorts. In his recent book *The Puzzle of Modern Economics: Science or Ideology?* Roger Backhouse defends the idea that economics is a science despite recognizing that economics differs from natural sciences in many ways.[83] Similarly, the economist Ha-Joon Chang considers his discipline to be a science despite recognizing that 'economics can never be a science in the sense that physics or chemistry is'.[84] Psychologists also very often talk about

---

[82] F. R. Leavis, 'Two Cultures? The Significance of C. P. Snow (1962)', in *Two Cultures? The Significance of C. P. Snow* with an introduction by Stefan Collini, Cambridge: Cambridge University Press, pp. 73–74.

[83] R. Backhouse, *The Puzzle of Modern Economics: Science or Ideology?*, Cambridge: Cambridge University Press, 2010.

[84] H-J Chang, *Economics: The User's Guide*, London: Pelican Books, 2014, p. 5.

their discipline as a science. Recent introductions to psychology include *Thinking about Psychology: The Science of Mind and Behaviour*[85] and *Understanding Psychology as a Science*.[86] Universities throughout the world have faculties of social science incorporating departments of anthropology, economics, business, politics, psychology, sociology, and human geography (and, less often, departments of history and/or philosophy). It is fair to say that calling social disciplines 'sciences' is the way that we ordinarily talk about them. A divergence from ordinary use requires more than just showing that social disciplines differ from natural sciences in significant ways, since this is recognized by many of those who quite happily talk about social sciences.[87]

So, I conclude that social sciences *deserve* to be called sciences because they are empirical, knowledge-producing disciplines which, done properly, involve analytical rigour and responsiveness to evidence. Here I take social sciences to include economics, sociology, anthropology, human geography, politics, linguistics, and sociology.

However, there are some disciplines which do not fit easily into either the natural or social sciences. Philosophy is one of them. As Wittgenstein pointed out, many of the problems of philosophy are the upshot of confusion about concepts and the way to tackle those problems is not to look at empirical evidence but to get clear about the problematic concepts. Literature and literary studies are also disciplines which are of great value but which do not fit comfortably in either of those categories. There is such a thing as a social science but we should be careful to keep an eye on differences between the various scientific disciplines and not assimilate them in ways that lead to confusion.[88]

In this chapter my intention was to establish that philosophy, as understood by Wittgenstein, is a discipline which undertakes grammatical investigations in order to dissolve philosophical problems and to distinguish it from social and natural sciences. In the next chapter I will discuss another topic which has particularly vexed social and political philosophers, the

---

[85] C. T. Blair-Broeker, R. M. Ernst, and D. G. Myers, *Thinking about Psychology: The Science of Mind and Behavior*, New York: Worth Publishers, 2007.

[86] Z Dienes, *Understanding Psychology as a Science: An Introduction to Scientific and Statistical Inference*, Basingstoke: Palgrave-Macmillan, 2008.

[87] The British Wittgenstein conference at which John Dupré presented the paper I have mentioned was given the title 'Wittgenstein and the Social Sciences' (see http://www.britishwittgensteinsociety.org/news/annual-conference/20–2, accessed 22 October 2016).

[88] Interestingly, even Hutchinson, Read, and Sharrock suggest that it doesn't matter whether social studies get called social sciences 'so long as one keeps a clear view of what is thus named, and what its character is', ibid., p. 51.

problem of relativism. Getting clear about this problem helps to get clearer about Wittgenstein's relation to social and political philosophy and also helps us to see that Wittgenstein's philosophy has some implications for the way that political philosophers should understand their work. I will ask whether Wittgenstein himself was a relativist and also ask whether some form of relativism is credible.

Chapter 2

WITTGENSTEIN AND RELATIVISM

2.1 Introduction

Ludwig Wittgenstein has been accused of being a relativist by various philosophers. In this chapter I will focus particularly on accusations of cognitive relativism levelled at Wittgenstein by Roger Trigg. Accusations of relativism, of various sorts, have been thought to undermine Wittgenstein's philosophical approach.[1] However, there are some philosophers, such as Robert Arrington, Natalie Alana Ashton, Gordon Baker, Hans-Johann Glock, Peter Hacker, and Martin Kusch, who have found relativism in Wittgenstein's work and thought that it is a benign or even a positive feature of his philosophy.[2] Still others argue

---

[1] For example, Trigg suggests that Wittgenstein's relativism amounts to an 'implicit attack on the possibility of unprejudiced reason, the removal of the possibility of truth as a standard – [...] a direct onslaught on the very possibility of rationality' (R. Trigg, 'Wittgenstein and Social Science', in A. Phillips Griffiths (ed.), *Wittgenstein Centenary Essays*, Cambridge: Cambridge University Press, 1991, pp. 209–22: 218). Ernest Gellner has also claimed that Wittgenstein subscribes to a pernicious form of relativism in various places (see, e.g. E. Gellner, *Language and Solitude*, Cambridge: Cambridge University Press, 1998, pp. 5, 72, 75–77, 95, 119, 145, 177, 191).

[2] See, e.g. Hans-Johann Glock's *A Wittgenstein Dictionary*, Oxford: Blackwell, 1996, pp. 22, 32, 48–50, 110, and his 'Relativism, Commensurability and Translatability', in J. Preston (ed.), *Wittgenstein and Reason*, Oxford: Blackwell, 2008, pp. 21–46 (originally published in vol. 20, no. 4 of *Ratio*), as well as Robert Arrington's defence of a form of conceptual relativism, inspired by Wittgenstein in *Rationalism, Realism and Relativism*, Ithaca, NY: Cornell University Press, 1989. Gordon Baker's take on the 'relativism' present in Wittgenstein's work is different to that of Arrington and Glock and is discussed in '*Philosophical Investigations* Section 122: Neglected Aspects', in R. Arrington and H.-J. Glock (eds), *Wittgenstein's Philosophical Investigations: Text and Context*, London: Routledge, 1991, pp. 35–68. Peg O'Connor rejects metaethical relativism and absolutism but holds onto the view that there is a 'framework or context to which judgements are relative' (*Morality and Our Complicated Form of Life: Feminist Wittgensteinian Metaethics*, University Park: Pennsylvania State University Press, 2008, p. 141). More recently, Natalie Alana Ashton has argued that both feminist standpoint theory and perspectival realism are forms of 'non-silly' relativism (silly relativism, which she and just about everybody else reject, is the view that all perspectives are just as good as one another), and her philosophical viewpoint is

that Wittgenstein is not a relativist at all.³ In this chapter I will start by looking at the various forms of relativism and then go on to consider whether Wittgenstein can be placed in one or another of the relativistic camps and throughout the chapter I will look at the credibility of various forms of relativism.

There are, I think, good reasons for thinking that Wittgenstein was a certain kind of relativist, although he certainly did not think that 'anything goes' in the moral, religious, epistemic, or conceptual spheres or that all positions staked out in these spheres were of equal value. What kind of reasons are there for thinking that Wittgenstein was a relativist? For one thing it is clear that Wittgenstein rejected certain kinds of realist positions within philosophy. Realists who set themselves up in opposition to idealism in philosophy are subject to the same kinds of confusions as idealists, according to Wittgenstein. So, for example, in the *Blue Book* Wittgenstein says that 'the trouble with the realist is always that he does not solve but skip the difficulties which his adversaries see, though they too don't succeed in solving them',⁴ and in *On Certainty* Wittgenstein argues that the 'claim' that 'there are physical objects' is nonsense.⁵ Wittgenstein rejected the idea that our concepts are somehow imposed on us by reality and he acknowledges the possibility that our concepts might be very different if the world were different in certain ways.⁶ It seems clear

---

shaped by Wittgenstein (see Ashton's 'Scientific Perspectives, Feminist Standpoints, and Non-Silly Relativism', in Ana-Maria Crețu and Michaela Massimi (eds.), *Knowledge from a Human Point of View* (Synthese Library), Cham: Springer, 2020). Martin Kusch is also open to the idea that there are benign forms of relativism and says that 'sometimes a form of relativism is the right response' to disagreement (in 'Disagreement, Certainties, Relativism', *Topoi*, June 2018, p. 1).

³ See, e.g. John Gunnell's *Social Inquiry after Wittgenstein & Kuhn*, where Gunnell suggests that Wittgenstein can be absolved of accusations of relativism because 'relativism is a philosophical abstraction and invention' (p. 3) and that 'relativism is not really a position at all' (p. 30). Danièle Moyal-Sharrock argues that 'our universally-shared form of life [...] rules out a thoroughgoing relativism' in her 'Fighting Relativism: Wittgenstein and Kuhn' (in C. Kanzian, S. Kletzl, J. Mitterer, and K. Neges (eds), *Realism-Relativism-Constructivism*, Berlin: Walter De Gruyter, 2017, p. 227).

⁴ L. Wittgenstein, *The Blue and Brown Books*, New York: Harper & Row, 1965 [1958], p. 48.

⁵ L. Wittgenstein, *On Certainty*, Oxford: Blackwell, 1969, §§35–37.

⁶ E.g. in *Zettel*, §331, where Wittgenstein says, 'One is tempted to justify rules of grammar by sentences like "But there really are four primary colours". And the saying that the rules of grammar are arbitrary is directed against the possibility of this justification, which is constructed on the model of justifying a sentence by pointing to what verifies it.' And 'Philosophy of Psychology: A Fragment', xii, where Wittgenstein says, 'If anyone believes that certain concepts are absolutely the correct ones, and that having different ones would mean not realising something that we realise – then let him imagine certain very general facts of nature to be different from what we are used to, and the formation of concepts different from the usual ones will become intelligible to him.'

that Wittgenstein rejects the idea that there is a single best way to divide up the world with concepts and the idea that a certain conceptual scheme might be absolutely correct. He also rejected the idea that we can achieve a neutral 'view from nowhere' was opposed to science intruding upon spheres where it did not belong, and argued that people might have different hinge commitments. But where does that leave us? Does someone opposed to realism, scientism, and the idea that we can achieve a view from nowhere necessarily end up being a relativist? If so, what kind of relativist was Wittgenstein? Was he an alethic relativist (a relativist about truth), an ontological relativist (a relativist about what exists), a cognitive relativist (a relativist about rationality or about what we know), or a conceptual relativist?

2.2 Varieties of Relativism

In her masterly critical overview of varieties of relativism Maria Baghramian distinguishes three broad categories of 'cognitive, moral and aesthetic relativism'. Within cognitive relativism she distinguishes between *alethic* relativism (relativism about truth), relativism about *rationality*, and relativism about *knowledge-claims* (epistemic relativism).[7] She then makes further distinctions, between subjective, social/cultural, and conceptual relativism, according to what it is that the cognitive, moral, or aesthetic values are being relativized to (psychological states of individual agents, social and cultural conditions, and conceptual schemes, respectively).[8] So, for example, there might be a form of alethic relativism in which truth is relativized to individuals or one where truth is relativized to a social group. In fact, this is the way in which Alan Sokal and Jean Bricmont have defined relativism – as the claim that 'the truth or falsity of a statement is relative to an individual or social group'.[9]

Baghramian's taxonomy suggests that Sokal and Bricmont's definition is far too narrow in excluding other forms of relativism[10] and, as Hans-Johann

---

[7] M. Baghramian, *Relativism*, Abingdon: Routledge, 2004, p. 6.
[8] Ibid., p. 7.
[9] J. Bricmont and A. Sokal, *Intellectual Impostures*, London: Profile, 1998, pp. 50–51.
[10] Susan Haack's 'Reflections on Relativism: From Momentous Tautology to Seductive Contradiction' (*Philosophical Perspectives*, vol. 10, pp. 297–315) has been influential in recent discussions of relativism. Martin Kusch offers his own taxonomies of relativism in 'Annalisa Coliva on Wittgenstein and Epistemic Relativism', *Philosophia*, vol. 41, 2013, pp. 38–41: 37, and also in his 'Primer on Relativism' in the *Routledge Handbook on Relativism*. There has been a flurry of work on relativism recently coming from a project in which Kusch was the principal investigator (The Emergence of Relativism project at the University of Vienna) and which involved Natalie Alana Ashton, Katherina Kinzel, Robin McKenna, Johannes Steizinger, Katharina, Sodoma, and Niels Wildshut. They have produced a lot of articles and books on various philosophical themes as well as

Glock has suggested, Sokal and Bricmont's definition excludes more credible forms of relativism.[11] Alethic relativism lacks credibility because it leads to ontological relativism, the idea that what is real or what exists is relative. Glock explains why this is so in his 'Relativism, Commensurability and Translatability' where he presents

> two truisms about truth and falsehood:
> (i) That witches exist is true ↔ witches exist
> (ii) That witches exist is false ↔ witches do not exist

Given the truth of these truisms and the (alethic) relativist's claim that what is true is true relative to a society it would have to be that witches exist for one society 'A' (a society that accepts or believes that witches exist) but not for another 'B' (a society that does not accept or believe that witches exist). If that were the case then the two societies must inhabit different worlds but, as Glock comments, this 'is surely absurd. Among other things, it makes it difficult to explain how members of B-type societies could have been so successful at exploiting, oppressing and killing members of A-type societies. Are we to suppose, for example, that the bullets which colonial troops fired [...] managed to traverse an ontological gap before they hit their targets'.[12] But the fact that alethic and ontological relativism lack credibility does not mean that other forms of relativism are not credible, since excluding these options still leaves cognitive and conceptual relativism concerning various kinds of values available.

2.3 Wittgenstein and Relativism

2.3.1 *Wittgenstein and Cognitive Relativism*

Wittgenstein is accused of cognitive relativism by Roger Trigg, who claims that 'the refusal to distinguish between the subject and object of knowledge, the implicit attack on the possibility of unprejudiced reason, the removal of the possibility of truth as a standard – all of this adds up to a direct onslaught on the very possibility of rationality [in Wittgenstein's work]'.[13] The reason for

---

historical material on relativism. There is also a new volume on relativism from Maria Baghramian and Annalisa Coliva which includes a taxonomy of relativisms in the first chapter (*Relativism (New Problems in Philosophy)*, London: Routledge, 2019).

[11] Glock, 'Relativism, Commensurability and Translatability', pp. 22–25.
[12] Ibid., pp. 23–24.
[13] Trigg, 'Wittgenstein and Social Science', pp. 218–19.

which Trigg thinks that Wittgenstein's philosophy removes the possibility of truth as standard is unclear but he claims that in Wittgenstein's work 'reason [...] cannot be wrenched apart from [language games] so as to pass judgment from the standpoint of some contextless and external realm of truth',[14] that 'where language-games and forms of life as such are concerned no room is left for the notions of truth and falsity'[15] and that according to Wittgenstein 'beliefs held within a way of life cannot claim any truth which ought to be accepted by non-participants'.[16]

However, it is at best unclear why we should need to be able to pass judgement from the standpoint of an 'external realm of truth' in order to say things that are true or false or in order to reason. Indeed, it is unclear what an 'external realm of truth' might be. While it is true that Wittgenstein does not think that language games are true or false[17] that does not mean that nothing is. It is the things we say that are true or false not the form of life or the language in which those things are said. This is a grammatical reminder about how we apply the term 'true'. What Wittgenstein says in one of the relevant passages cited by Trigg is this:

> 'So you are saying that human agreement decides what is true and what is false?' – It is what human beings *say* that is true and false; and they agree in the *language* that they use. That is not agreement in opinions but in form of life.[18]

Here Wittgenstein is clear that he does not think that human agreement decides what is true and what is false. What is true is *not* necessarily what the community or individual says is true. Wittgenstein is clearly not claiming that truth is relative to a conceptual scheme, or to a form of life. As Peter Hacker points out, 'It is not truth that is relative to conceptual schemes, but – pleonastically – concepts. Differences between conceptual schemes result not in relative truth but in incommensurable truth.'[19] Different communities might employ

---

[14] Ibid., p. 215.
[15] Ibid., p. 216.
[16] Ibid., p. 217.
[17] What sense can be made of claiming that 'giving orders' (an example of a language game from *Philosophical Investigations*, §23), for example, is true?
[18] L. Wittgenstein, *Philosophical Investigations*, ed. P. M. S. Hacker and Joachim Schulte, trans. G. E. M. Anscombe, P. M. S. Hacker, and Joachim Schulte, 4th edition, Oxford: Wiley-Blackwell, 2009, §241, cited on p. 211; Trigg, 'Wittgenstein and Social Science'.
[19] P. M. S. Hacker, 'On Davidson's Idea of a Conceptual Scheme', *Philosophical Quarterly*, vol. 46, no. 184, July 1996, p. 303.

different concepts and it may be that truths expressible in a language used by one community cannot be translated into the language used by another community but this does not imply that there is any disagreement between the communities over *truth*. An example used by Hacker to illustrate this point is a community whose members are all afflicted by Daltonism (red-green colour blindness). They could have a single colour word that applies to what we call red, green, and grey things. In that case they could truthfully say that 'poppies, grass and clouds are the same colour' but they could not translate our true assertion that 'poppies differ in colour from grass'. Both claims are true, and not true-relative-to-a-community. Disagreement in concepts does not generate *alethic* relativism, that is, relativism about truth.[20]

Indeed, as Hans-Johann Glock points out,[21] Wittgenstein says things about truth, both in his early and late work, which are incompatible with alethic relativism. In the *Tractatus Logico-Philosophicus*, where he says that 'if an elementary proposition is true, the state of affairs exists: if an elementary proposition is false, the state of affairs does not exist'.[22] Wittgenstein presents an obtainment theory of truth. In his later work Wittgenstein presents us with what might be called a form of deflationism,[23] although given that Wittgenstein did not want to advance any kind of theory or explanation and that he wanted to simply describe our language – that is, to remind us of relevant norms of representation – this should not be taken as an attribution of a theory of truth to Wittgenstein. In his later work he simply describes our ordinary use of the term 'true' with the aim of dissolving philosophical problems. In both cases, as Glock says, 'the fact that a proposition is true neither entails nor is entailed by the fact that the proposition is being stated or believed (etc.) to be true by someone, or that it would be useful to believe it, etc.'[24] What this means is that truth is not relative either to the psychological states of individuals or to communities. To say that beliefs can be either true or false is to make a grammatical claim about truth. Somebody believing something does not imply that the thing believed is true and nor does a whole community believing something imply that it is true. As Peter Hacker says, 'What is said, when something

---

[20] Ibid., p. 304.
[21] Glock, 'Relativism, Commensurability and Translatability', p. 24.
[22] L. Wittgenstein, *Tractatus Logico-Philosophicus*, London: Routledge, 1961, 4.25.
[23] See, e.g. *Remarks on the Foundations of Mathematics*, Appendix III, §6 (p. 117), where Wittgenstein asks, 'For what does a proposition's "*being true*" mean? "*p*" *is true = p*. (That is the answer)'; and also *Philosophical Investigations*, §136.
[24] Glock, 'Relativism, Commensurability and Translatability', p. 24.

is said in a language, is true if things are as they are said to be, and there is nothing relative about that.'²⁵

Wittgenstein recognizes that alternative forms of representation are possible in the case of things like measuring and counting. Different practices relating to different needs and interests might result in different concepts. We do not need to look to invented 'language games' in order to come up with examples. One case is the medieval practice of measuring by the ell, which is the length of a person's arm. Cloth was measured in ells until the early nineteenth century and the ell was never standardized in England. Given that people's arms vary in length it is clear that this system of measurement and the associated practices are different from our own practices of measurement in the present day. This might lead one to believe that Wittgenstein's position was that anything goes, that we could adopt different norms of representation in any area, as we like.

However, Wittgenstein does say that adopting different rules can be 'practical' or 'impractical'²⁶ and we should remember that our concepts are interrelated in such a way that we cannot alter one without altering others. Laws of logic are closely linked to notions like 'reasoning', 'thinking', 'proposition', and 'language' and so practices that do not conform to them 'would be unintelligible to us, and would not count as language'.²⁷ This suggests that Trigg is wrong to attribute a radical relativism about rationality or truth to Wittgenstein.²⁸

Peg O'Connor talks about other kinds of limitations on altering frameworks or norms. She says that we cannot move from framework to framework at will: 'We cannot simply just move away from the spatiotemporal framework of the planet Earth or the solar system [...] These frameworks do provide limitations. Similarly, I cannot of my own free will jump from the human form of life to the form of life of a lion.' The language games we use and the frameworks we inhabit are not freely chosen.²⁹

---

²⁵ Hacker, 'On Davidson's Idea of a Conceptual Scheme', p. 303.
²⁶ L. Wittgenstein, *Wittgenstein's Lectures, Cambridge 1932–1935*, from the notes of A. Ambrose and M. Macdonald, ed. A. Ambrose, Oxford: Blackwell, 1979, p. 70.
²⁷ Glock, *A Wittgenstein Dictionary*, pp. 49–50.
²⁸ Although it seems clear that Wittgenstein is not a radical relativist about truth or rationality, the position that Trigg presents is far from the most plausible form of cognitive relativism. There have been more plausible varieties of epistemic relativism presented by philosophers inspired by Wittgenstein. For example, Natalie Alana Ashton makes a good case that both feminist standpoint theory and perspectival realism are (non-silly) forms of epistemic relativism in her 'Scientific Perspectives, Feminist Standpoints, and Non-Silly Relativism'.
²⁹ O'Connor, *Morality and Our Complicated Form of Life*, p. 155.

2.3.2 *Was Wittgenstein a Relativist?*

However, the fact that Wittgenstein was not committed to alethic, ontological, or cognitive relativism in the forms attributed to him by critics does not imply that he was not a relativist at all. As noted above, Peter Hacker suggests that Wittgenstein was committed to the view that *concepts* are relative to conceptual schemes and that conceptual schemes might differ according to the forms of life they are intertwined with. Similarly, Hans-Johann Glock tells us that Wittgenstein was committed to a form of conceptual relativism, namely the view that 'the conceptual framework we use is not simply dictated to us by reality or experience; in adopting or constructing such frameworks there are different options which cannot be assessed as more or less rational from a neutral bird's eye view'[30] and Robert Arrington, in his book *Rationalism, Realism, and Relativism*, describes his own form of moral epistemology (inspired by Wittgenstein) as conceptual relativism[31] and by this he means that 'moral claims are made relative to our concept of morality'.[32] Arrington also makes it clear that he thinks that this kind of conceptual relativism applies to claims beyond the moral sphere as well, to common sense and to scientific beliefs.[33]

There is evidence in the work of Wittgenstein that he did indeed adhere to the claims attributed to him by Hacker, Glock, and Arrington (among others). So, for example, in the *Philosophical Grammar* Wittgenstein says that 'grammar is not accountable to any reality. It is grammatical rules that determine meaning (constitute it) and so they themselves are not answerable to any meaning';[34] in other words, our conceptual scheme is not in some way forced on us by reality and it does not make sense to say that our conceptual scheme is justified by the way things are. Elsewhere, in the collection of remarks published as *Zettel* Wittgenstein says, 'Why, don't I call cookery rules arbitrary, and why am I tempted to call the rules of grammar arbitrary? Because cooking is defined by its end whereas "speaking" is not [...] if you follow grammatical rules other than such-and-such ones that does not mean you say something wrong, no, you are speaking of something else.'[35] What this means is that because the end of

---

[30] Glock, 'Relativism, Commensurability and Translatability', p. 25.
[31] See pp. 248–315 of Arrington, *Rationalism, Realism, and Relativism*.
[32] Ibid., p. 257. Arrington also makes it clear that he does *not* commit himself to the view that 'what is right and wrong is so relative to our standards of morality' (p. 255).
[33] Arrington says that 'all empirical judgements are relative to the concepts governing their constituent terms [...] empirical judgements in common sense and science are as non-objective as moral judgements'. Ibid., p. 262.
[34] L. Wittgenstein, *Philosophical Grammar*, ed. Rush Rhees, trans. Anthony Kenny, Berkeley: University of California Press, 1974, p. 184.
[35] L. Wittgenstein,, *Zettel*, ed. G. E. M. Anscombe and G. H Von Wright, trans. G. E. M. Anscombe, Berkeley: University of California Press, 1967, §320.

cooking is identifiable independently of the rules for cooking (i.e. edible food) it can be used to evaluate the rules used whereas in the case of concepts the rules in question serve to identify their goals. So, for example, we cannot justify colour concepts or the grammatical rules concerning colour by reference to the way the world is. One reason is that it makes no sense to talk of justifying concepts and another is that the grammatical rules for colour expressions tell us what colour *is* and what the colours are and so are presupposed by any claim about colour that might be used in an attempt to justify something.

With regard to forms of life Wittgenstein says that 'the *speaking* of language is part of an activity, or of a form of life' and that 'what has to be accepted, the given, is – one might say – *forms of life*'.[36] These passages serve as reminders that our concepts are grafted onto prelinguistic behaviour, such as wincing and crying, and also that our language is tied up with other forms of activity which are involved in learning and explaining those concepts and so are internally related to what we mean when we say something. The second passage cited above is again a grammatical reminder that our forms of life are not justified, and indeed nothing would count as justifying them. That is not to say that we cannot criticize certain ways of living or that any one form of life is the only one possible, but only that we cannot justify what lies at the bottom of our conceptual framework (i.e. a form of life). Justification goes on within a conceptual framework and so presupposes it.[37]

Hacker, Glock, and Arrington are not the only Wittgenstein scholars to find relativism in Wittgenstein's work and think it a benign or even positive feature of his work. Gordon Baker argues that 'Wittgenstein seems to have been subscribing to a form of relativism which most of his would-be followers reject'.[38] However, the form of relativism that Baker thinks Wittgenstein subscribed to is one that Hacker, Glock, and Arrington object to. According to Baker, Wittgenstein thinks that there are various 'modes of representation' which each reveal aspects of the grammar of our words. These each represent different ways of seeing things (so, e.g. (i) the Augustinian conception of language discussed at the beginning of the *Philosophical Investigations* and (ii)

---

[36] Wittgenstein, *Philosophical Investigations*, §23, PPF 345 (also see §19, §241 (the passage cited by Trigg, mentioned above), as well as 'Philosophy of Psychology: A Fragment (PPF)', 1). For an overview of the different occurrences of 'forms of life' in the Wittgenstein papers, see N. Venturinha, 'Introduction', in António Marques and Nuno Venturinha (eds), *Wittgenstein on Forms of Life and the Nature of Experience*, Bern: Peter Lang, 2010, pp. 13–19.

[37] Wittgenstein's claim that 'what has to be accepted, the given, is – one might say – *forms of life*' (PPF, xi §345) has sometimes been presented as evidence of his conservatism. I will discuss this in Chapter 5 in the section about Terry Eagleton's interpretation of Wittgenstein.

[38] Baker, '*Philosophical Investigations* Section 122: Neglected Aspects', p. 59.

the proposal that the meaning of a word is its use[39] are examples of different modes of representation). Whereas Hacker, Glock, and Arrington think that Wittgenstein was critical of the *positions* of traditional philosophers and that he *argued* against their positions (e.g. referentialism, behaviourism, Cartesian dualism, Platonism), Gordon Baker thinks that these different modes of representation can each be used to clear away the philosophical vexation of different particular philosophers on particular occasions. Whereas Hacker, Glock, and Arrington think of Wittgenstein as disputing the work of other philosophers by pointing out inconsistencies or lack of sense in the things they say, Baker thinks of Wittgenstein's work more as therapeutic. I will return to the dispute between Baker and other Wittgenstein scholars in Section 2.4 below.

Given the evidence of some kind of relativism in Wittgenstein's work and the plausible development of Wittgenstein's claims by various Wittgenstein scholars it seems reasonable to claim that Wittgenstein was a kind of relativist, namely a conceptual relativist, but is conceptual relativism a credible form of relativism?

2.3.3 *Davidson's Challenge to Conceptual Relativism*

The most prominent critic of conceptual relativism in recent times is Donald Davidson. In his article 'On the Very Idea of a Conceptual Scheme'[40] Davidson argues that conceptual relativism is incoherent, that we cannot make sense of the idea of completely untranslatable schemes, and also argues that we cannot even make sense of the idea of partial untranslatability of conceptual schemes.

Davidson defines conceptual relativism in such a way that reality is relative to a scheme and different schemes are possible: 'What counts as real in one system may not in another.'[41] He argues against conceptual relativism by a series of moves. First of all, he objects to the analytic-synthetic distinction as it is found in the work of Kant, the logical positivists, and Peter Strawson. This distinction, he argues, has been undermined by Quine's considerations in his paper 'Two Dogmas of Empiricism'[42] and by Kuhn and Feyerabend's arguments against meaning invariance, which Davidson suggests result in the observation that 'meaning [...] is contaminated by theory, by what is held to be true'.[43] Davidson then argues that once the analytic-synthetic distinction

---

[39] See Wittgenstein, *Philosophical Investigations*, §43.
[40] D. Davidson, 'On the Very Idea of a Conceptual Scheme', *Proceedings and Addresses of the American Philosophical Association*, vol. 47, 1973–74, pp. 5–20.
[41] Ibid., p. 5.
[42] W. V. O. Quine, 'Two Dogmas of Empiricism', *Philosophical Review*, 60, 1951, pp. 20–43.
[43] Davidson, 'On the Very Idea of a Conceptual Scheme', p. 9.

is undermined a form of conceptual relativism becomes tempting. Kuhn and Feyerabend's considerations lead us to the view that changes in science do not just involve rejecting some false statements and accepting some other statements as true. With new theories come new concepts, for example, the concepts of space and time are different in the physics of Newton and Einstein's physics: 'What [...] [speakers of a language] come to accept, in accepting a sentence as true, is not the same thing that they rejected when formerly they held a sentence to be false.'[44] As science advances new conceptual schemes emerge that are incommensurable with the old ones. However, Davidson objects to the kind of conceptual relativism found in the work of Kuhn and Feyerabend on the grounds that 'retention of some or all of the old vocabulary in itself provides no basis for judging the new scheme to be the same as, or different from, the old' since for all Davidson (or anyone else) knows, the new concepts introduced by a theory might play the role of the old ones.[45]

Davidson also considers and rejects forms of conceptual relativism that talk about schemes being related to the world or to experience where the schemes are said to *organize* the *world* or *experience*. He points out that it makes no sense to talk about organizing a single thing (the world/experience) just as it makes no sense to speak about organizing a wardrobe as opposed to organizing the various things within it.[46]

Having considered and rejected these forms of conceptual relativism Davidson considers a form of conceptual relativism where conceptual schemes are said to *fit* or *face* experience. In this case a 'theory' (an expression Davidson uses interchangeably with 'language' and 'scheme') fits experience 'provided it is borne out by the evidence'.[47] But for a theory to fit the evidence is just for it to be *true*, according to Davidson, and the notions of 'fitting' or 'facing' the world/experience do not add anything to the claim that the theory is *true*. Davidson adds to this that he thinks that the best way of thinking about truth is in terms of Tarski's theory of truth, according to which,

> a satisfactory theory of truth for a language L must entail, for every sentence *s* of L, a theorem of the form '*s* is true if and only if p' where '*s*' is replaced by a description of *s* and '*p*' by *s* itself if L is English and by a translation into English if L is not English.[48]

---

[44] Ibid., p. 10.
[45] Ibid., pp. 10–11.
[46] Ibid., p. 14.
[47] Ibid., p. 15.
[48] Ibid., p. 17.

The language here is slightly obscure but the kind of sentences and corresponding 'theorems' Tarski had in mind are cases like the following:

Sentence s 'Snow is white';

corresponding theorem ' "Snow is white" is true if and only if snow is white.'

Davidson thinks about conceptual schemes in terms of intertranslatable languages[49] (because different languages share the same concepts, e.g. 'Il pleut' (French) means the same as 'it is raining' (English)), and given the fact that Tarski's theory of truth makes essential reference to translation and the fact that the model of conceptual schemes under consideration makes essential reference to truth, Davidson thinks that we cannot make sense of the idea of a true theory/conceptual scheme that is untranslatable. As a result, Davidson concludes that the model of conceptual schemes where schemes are said to fit or face reality is not one we can make sense of either.

2.3.4 *Problems with Davidson's Arguments*

However, there are various problems with Davidson's route to his conclusion. In the first place his early moves in the argument are a series of non sequiturs. One can be committed to a version of the analytic-synthetic distinction without having to be committed to meaning invariance or to Kantian, logical positivist, or Strawsonian versions of the distinction. Agreeing with Kuhn and Feyerabend that concepts change and that those changes have ramifications does not obviously imply giving up a distinction between specifications of the meaning of a term and specifications of theoretical truths[50] and, as Hans-Johann Glock argues, one can make a distinction between conceptual scheme and empirical content without committing oneself to the kind of models Davidson considers, that is, those that present the division in terms of scheme and raw material (the world or experience), by recognizing the division as one that is drawn within language, between grammatical claims and empirical ones. Glock points out that drawing the distinction in this way does not involve the kind of objectionable commitments that Davidson and Quine mention, that is, 'mentalistic metaphors, psychologistic doctrines or the empiricist myth of the given'.[51] So, Davidson's conclusion that the analytic-synthetic distinction must be jettisoned

---

[49] Davidson, 'On the Very Idea of a Conceptual Scheme', p. 7.
[50] See Hacker, 'On Davidson's Idea of a Conceptual Scheme', p. 295.
[51] Glock, 'Relativism, Commensurability and Translatability', p. 31.

does not follow from the arguments that he employs. Davidson may well be correct that Kuhn and Feyerabend's conception of conceptual schemes is untenable but he has not demonstrated rejecting their view leaves us with only the model of scheme-fitting/facing-experience as a plausible option.

Both Glock and Hacker also object to the way in which Davidson uses the term 'theory' interchangeably with 'language' and 'conceptual scheme' when he talks about what it is that fits or faces the world/experience. It is true that the boundaries between theoretical discourse and non-theoretical or pre-theoretical discourse are imprecise (and that they shift) and it may well be that expressions used in formulating theories change as the relevant theories change. However, it does not follow from this that there is no clear distinction between language and theory. If we look at the grammar of the expressions 'language' and 'theory' we can see that there are clear differences in their use. It makes sense to talk about a theory being true (or largely true) or about theoretical claims being true but it is nonsensical to say that a language (such as English or Portuguese) is true or largely true. Things we say in English or Portuguese might be true or false but nothing counts as a language being true or false. One attempt to make sense of the idea of a language being true or false might be to think of it as the totality of sentences or things we say but in that case for every true claim made we could also construct its negation in the same language and there are also interrogatives, orders, expressions of wishes, and so on (which cannot be said to be true). If we take the shift from Newtonian physics to Einsteinian physics as a case of changing conceptual schemes then it is clear that there is a difference between scheme and language or theory and language since both of the theories/schemes can be formulated in the same language and yet be different theories/schemes.[52] While it may be true that it is difficult to determine whether some statements are theoretical or not there are clear-cut cases of non-theoretical statements and non-theoretical uses of language, for example, 'let's go and sit in the park', 'did I leave the oven on?', and 'I want my toy!'

One case where the distinction between (empirical) theoretical statements and statements specifying the meaning of the term becomes problematic is a case mentioned in Davidson's essay – that of *truth*. Davidson presents Tarski's work on truth as a *theory* and yet his argument depends on there being an *essential* connection between truth and translation, suggesting that he is thinking of Tarski's comments about truth as being definitional, that is, specifying the meaning of the term 'truth'. However, as Peter Hacker points out, 'Tarski's Convention T, far from providing an accurate description of the way the word

---

[52] See Hacker, 'On Davidson's Idea of a Conceptual Scheme', pp. 297–98; and Glock, 'Relativism, Commensurability and Translatability', p. 31.

"true" is used, is flagrantly at odds with it. "True" is not a metalinguistic predicate. Truth is not a metalinguistic property of sentences since it is not a property of sentences at all.' Hacker assembles various reminders of how we use the expressions 'sentence' and 'true' to show that it is *what is said* that can be true or false rather than what is used to say it, that is, a sentence:[53]

> What is said [...] is that *p*, and it is this, not the sentence that is used in saying it, that is true or false. Hence, since in saying that *p* one may be making something, namely, a statement, assertion or claim, and since what is made is individuated by its content, namely, that *p*, what is made – but not what is used to make it, i.e. a sentence – may likewise be true or false [...] a written sentence, but not the truth it is used to assert, can be erased with an eraser or can be turned upside down. But one cannot erase a truth or, save metaphorically, turn it upside down.

So, Tarski's 'Convention T' does not provide us with a definition of truth. Contra Davidson, Tarski's work does not embody 'our best intuitions as to how the concept of truth is used'.[54] Hans-Johann Glock makes this point clearer when he points out that

> a Tarskian theory does not provide an explanation of 'true' at all. Instead it allows one to derive T-sentences which state the *conditions* under which sentences of *L* are true. But [...] it is one thing to explain what the English term 'true' means. It is another thing to specify under what conditions we would call individual sentences of *L* true.[55]

So, Davidson's final move in his argument is unsuccessful since it hinges on Tarski's Convention T being an accurate account of how we use the term 'true'. The space for conceptual relativism as it is found in the later work of Wittgenstein is still available.

2.4 Is It Correct to Describe Wittgenstein as a Relativist or as Subscribing to a Relativist Theory?

In their book *There Is No Such Thing as a Social Science*, Phil Hutchinson, Rupert Read, and Wes Sharrock argue that it is wrong to attribute theses or theories to Wittgenstein and that it is also wrong to attribute them to Peter Winch, a

---

[53] Ibid., pp. 299–300.
[54] Davidson, 'On the Very Idea of a Conceptual Scheme', p. 17.
[55] Glock, 'Relativism, Commensurability and Translatability', p. 35.

philosopher whose work was inspired by Wittgenstein. They say of Winch that he 'had no theory'[56] and that 'his message is not [...] really [...] any kind of relativism'[57] and they say that a correct understanding of Wittgenstein's remarks in the *Philosophical Investigations*, specifically sections §§240–42, tells us that 'it is absurd to imagine that philosophers can enunciate true statements, "assertions", "theses", which (would) settle the debate of "rationalism against relativism"'.[58] Hutchison, Read, and Sharrock are loath to attribute a theory to Wittgenstein or to (the Wittgensteinian) Winch, whereas people like Robert Arrington, discussed above, are willing to present cognitive relativism as a *theory* in competition with others within moral philosophy (and presumably in other areas of philosophy) and Hans-Johann Glock and Peter Hacker are content to describe Wittgenstein as a conceptual relativist.

As I said above, it is a mistake to suggest that Wittgenstein wanted to advance any kind of theory. Wittgenstein himself said that 'we may not advance any kind of theory [in philosophy]' and that 'if someone were to advance theses in philosophy, it would never be possible to debate them, because everyone would agree to them'.[59] So, it is surely a mistake for Robert Arrington to describe the Wittgensteinian observations about moral rules, judgements, and principles that Arrington calls 'conceptual relativism' as a *theory*. Wittgenstein saw philosophy as a descriptive enterprise rather than as a theoretical or explanatory one. As he says in his remarks about philosophy in the *Philosophical Investigations*, 'All explanation must disappear, and description alone must take its place.'[60] The description in question being of the grammar of the words appearing in philosophical problems; of the use of words such as 'knowledge', 'being', and 'I'.[61] So, it seems that Hutchinson, Read, and Sharrock are correct to be wary of attributing a theory to Wittgenstein.

We could perhaps say similar things about ascribing a relativist *position* to Wittgenstein. Given that Wittgenstein was in the business of presenting us with grammatical reminders and that it was grammatical reminders that Hacker presented in combatting the views of Davidson (i.e. reminders about the use of 'sentence' and 'truth') it is fair to say that the 'position' he was combatting was little more than conceptual confusion – not a position at all – and that the supposedly theoretical remarks contained in Davidson's article (e.g.

---

[56] P. Hutchinson, R. Read, and W. Sharrock, *There Is No Such Thing as a Social Science*, Aldershot: Ashgate, 2008, p. 57.

[57] Ibid., p. 56.

[58] Ibid., p. 55.

[59] Wittgenstein, *Philosophical Investigations*, §109 and §128, respectively.

[60] Ibid., §109.

[61] Ibid., §116.

about Tarski's remarks on truth) were nothing of the sort. Similarly, we could say that the remarks Hacker assembled in combatting Davidson's position were not assertions or theses but grammatical reminders and so not staking out a position in an argument between competing theories. Another way of denying that Wittgenstein took up a position would be to adopt the interpretation of Wittgenstein found in Gordon Baker's work, mentioned above, and to think of Davidson's considerations as presenting one (or more) *aspect* of the use of the relevant terms (i.e. 'truth', 'relativism', etc.) and of Glock and Hacker as simply presenting another aspect of the use of the relevant terms. The set of considerations that we bring our attention to depends on our own philosophical vexations. We should consider those aspects that might help to bring us peace.

However, Hans-Johann Glock argues convincingly that the *'no position'-position* is implausible. One problem with the idea that Wittgensteinian philosophizing just involves 'grammatical aspect seeing' with the aim of bringing (philosophical) peace to some individual (i.e. a 'therapeutic' take on Wittgenstein, like Baker's) is that it does not allow for a distinction between achieving the goal by external means and achieving it by means internally related to the problem. Somebody might come to philosophical peace by receiving a blow to the head (external) or they might achieve philosophical peace through recognizing conceptual errors, or inconsistencies, in the problem as it has been presented to them (internal).[62] In the case of Davidson, discussed above, there is an inconsistency between Davidson's claim that Tarski's account of truth accurately reflects the way 'true' is used and the way that 'true' is in fact used. Davidson's account can be described as a position because he takes a stand about the way certain words are used ('true', 'theory', etc.), which can be opposed with arguments. The case Glock and Hacker make against Davidson, in the manner of Wittgenstein, is an attempt to achieve philosophical peace through recognizing conceptual errors and correcting them and so is an attempt at philosophical peace by internal means. Their arguments suggest that we should reject Davidson's take on the use of relevant expressions and should reject his conclusion about whether complete untranslatability of schemes makes sense.

John Gunnell, in his recent books about Wittgenstein and social theory, has taken up an intermediate view between those outlined above. Whereas Gunnell is reluctant to describe relativism as a genuine position or theory, he does attribute a theoretical position to Wittgenstein. For example, in *Social Inquiry after Wittgenstein and Kuhn* Gunnell says that 'relativism is not actually

---

[62] See H.-J. Glock, '*Philosophical Investigations* Section 128: "Theses in Philosophy" and Undogmatic Procedure", in R. Arrington and H.-J. Glock (eds), *Wittgenstein's Philosophical Investigations: Text and Context*, London: Routledge, 1991, pp. 83–84.

a problem in social practices, ranging from science to everyday forms of life. It is a philosophical abstraction and invention'[63] and yet he claims that 'Wittgenstein's work constitutes a theoretical account of the nature of conventional phenomena'.[64] Given the remarks above about relativism and theory we can say that there is something correct about Gunnell's argument that relativism is not a position but that he is wrong to attribute a theory to Wittgenstein.

2.5 Conclusion

Despite misgivings about calling Wittgenstein a relativist or attributing a theory to him, it is fair to say that the case made by the likes of Glock and Hacker against Davidson, given that it is made fully recognizing that Wittgenstein's work was non-theoretical, is relatively harmless in ascribing conceptual relativism to Wittgenstein, given that they are assembling reminders in order to dissolve confusions presented by Davidson as being problems with conceptual relativism. The methodology employed by Hacker and Glock is certainly in the spirit of Wittgenstein and they recognize that the reminders assembled do not constitute a theory. If Wittgenstein was a relativist at all (and I think it is reasonable to describe him as a conceptual relativist[65]) it is fair to say that his relativism was a positive contribution to mapping out the conceptual terrain surrounding the grammar of terms like 'sentence', 'truth', and 'form of life'.

What is clear is that it is a mistake to accuse Wittgenstein of other forms of relativism. Wittgenstein was certainly not committed to ontological relativism, alethic relativism, or to cognitive relativism as Trigg describes it.[66]

---

[63] J. Gunnell *Social Inquiry after Wittgenstein and Kuhn*, New York: Columbia University Press, 2014, p. 3.

[64] Ibid., p. 7. Note: Gunnell makes this claim 'fully recognising his [Wittgenstein's] claim that he was not presenting a theory', p. 7.

[65] Note: The definitions of 'conceptual relativism' presented by Glock and Arrington were given in Section 2.3.2 of this chapter.

[66] In her article 'Fighting Relativism: Wittgenstein and Kuhn', Danièle Moyal-Sharrock argues against what she calls 'conceptual relativism'. However, the position that she argues against (the idea that 'anything goes – however a particular culture sees fit to describe the world cannot be gainsaid, becomes a benchmark in its own right' (p. 216)) is not the position that I have described here and attributed to Glock and Hacker. In fact she acknowledges the Kuhnian point that 'languages cut up the world in different ways' (p. 215) and agrees with Wittgenstein about the arbitrariness of grammar, although she is keen to point out that if certain 'basic facts' were different then 'so would our concepts be' (p. 221). So although she rejects 'conceptual relativism' she may well be a conceptual relativist in the sense that I have given it in this chapter.

Part 2

DOES WITTGENSTEIN'S WORK HAVE IDEOLOGICAL IMPLICATIONS?

Chapter 3

WAS WITTGENSTEIN A CONSERVATIVE PHILOSOPHER?

3.1 Introduction

The question of whether Wittgenstein was a conservative philosopher has generated a large literature.[1] Given the enormous scope of the literature there will not be space here to consider all of the various arguments in favour of deeming Wittgenstein a conservative. In particular many have focused in on Wittgenstein's claim in §124 of the *Philosophical Investigations* that philosophy 'leaves everything as it is'. That remark alone is deserving of a long discussion (I discuss it in Chapters 5 and 6 of this book) and if controversies surrounding Wittgenstein's remarks about rule-following, rationality, and relativism were taken into consideration a sizable book could be written on the topic of Wittgenstein's relationship to conservatism. I will restrict myself, in this chapter, to the arguments found in J. C. Nyiri's paper 'Wittgenstein 1929–31: The Turning Back'.

The evidence brought by each side of the debate about whether Wittgenstein was conservative can be roughly divided into evidence concerning Wittgenstein's occasional remarks directly concerning political

---

[1] Perhaps most famously, J. C. Nyiri argued in a series of papers that Wittgenstein was a conservative philosopher (see, e.g. 'Wittgenstein 1929–31: The Turning Back', in Stuart Shanker (ed.), *Ludwig Wittgenstein: Critical Assessments (Vol. 4)*, London: Routledge, 1986). Those agreeing with Nyiri in this include Perry Anderson, Alex Callinicos, and H. C. McCauley. Those arguing that Wittgenstein's philosophy was not conservative include Joachim Schulte ('Wittgenstein and Conservatism', in Stuart Shanker (ed.), *Ludwig Wittgenstein: Critical Assessments (Vol. 4)*,, London: Routledge, 1986), Andrew Lugg (in 'Wittgenstein and Politics: Not Right, Left or Center', *International Studies in Philosophy*, vol. 36, no. 1, 2004, and other papers), Toril Moi (in *Revolution of the Ordinary: Literary Studies after Wittgenstein Austin, and Cavell*, Chicago: University of Chicago Press, 2017, chapter 7, pp. 150–71), and see also my 'Leave Everything As It Is: A Critique of Marxist Interpretations of Wittgenstein', *Critique*, vol. 41, no. 1, 2013; and 'Eagleton's Wittgenstein', *Critique*, vol. 43, 2015. This is just a small selection of all that has been written on the subject.

matters and evidence from among Wittgenstein's philosophical remarks. The reason I say 'roughly' divided is that there is some controversy about the extent to which this division can be made. Within Wittgenstein's typescripts each kind of remark would not be clearly separated; a remark about politics might be followed by a remark about philosophy, and philosophers might think that there is no clear division between the two kinds of remark (or that there aren't two kinds of remark at all). In this chapter I will treat the political remarks and philosophical remarks separately and I hope that by the end of the chapter it will become clearer how a separation can be made. I will argue that philosophical remarks that have been construed as having political implications do not in fact have the implications that some commentators have suggested.[2]

If we can separate out the two kinds of remark then there are really two questions to answer. First, we can ask whether Wittgenstein was conservative in his political views and second, we can ask whether Wittgenstein's philosophical remarks have conservative political implications. To the first question my answer will be that Wittgenstein certainly held some political views that can be deemed conservative (although he also held some views that could be characterized as left-wing and as expressing a deep dissatisfaction with the way things were). But my answer to the second question will be that Wittgenstein's philosophical views are perfectly consistent with radical left-wing views and have no conservative implications. Before looking at the evidence that Wittgenstein held conservative political views we must first have some understanding of what conservatism is.

3.2 What Is Conservatism?

One thing worth getting clear about when discussing conservatism is that the members of Conservative parties are not necessarily conservative in their philosophical outlook and even if they are conservative they may well disagree on many questions. Right-wing liberals have allied themselves with conservatives against the common enemy of socialism. As Anthony Quinton notes in his

---

[2] This chapter is based on my paper 'Was Wittgenstein a Conservative Philosopher?' which was published in *Revista Estudos Hum(e)anos*, 2015. Since that paper was published Joseph Agassi has claimed that my position is that 'Wittgenstein was a conservative' and that 'philosophers should ignore this' (J. Agassi, *Ludwig Wittgenstein's Philosophical Investigations: An Attempt at a Critical Rationalist Appraisal*, Synthese Library, vol. 401, Cham: Springer Nature, 2018, p. 170). This is not my position and never has been. I do not think that Wittgenstein was a conservative (although he was a small c conservative in some respects) and I do not think that philosophers should ignore this, although I do not think that Wittgenstein's philosophy is suffused with conservatism (or any other political ideology).

account of conservatism, 'Conservative parties have absorbed so many right-wing liberals [...] that at times the truly conservative element in them has been almost overwhelmed by liberal individualism.'³ This alliance of liberal individualism and conservatism can be seen in one of the most prominent Conservative prime ministers of the past few decades, Margaret Thatcher. She led the Conservative Party in Britain between 1975 and 1990 (she was prime minister from 1979 to 1990) and she was a great admirer of the right-wing liberal individualist Friedrich Hayek. Hayek himself explicitly disassociated himself from conservatism in his book *The Constitution of Liberty*, to which he appended a postscript, entitled 'Why I Am Not a Conservative'.⁴ The stress on liberty, and especially a stress on the importance of free markets, is characteristic of right-wing liberalism rather than conservatism,⁵ although the two are often found in combination nowadays.

In the entry on conservatism in *A Companion to Contemporary Political Philosophy* Quinton identifies three central doctrines of conservatism: traditionalism, scepticism (concerning political knowledge), and the conception of human beings and society as being organically related.⁶ According to conservatives, societies are like biological organisms in that the parts (organs) all play their role in the functioning of the whole and cannot flourish independently of the whole. Each organ has its place and its role and each organ depends on the whole in order to play that role. Similarly, in societies individuals have their proper place and their proper roles to fulfil and they cannot flourish except by being part of a wider whole, their society. This organicism supports sceptical claims about political knowledge. Individuals are imperfect in that they cannot flourish independently of society. No individual can grasp the whole and so theories formulated by individuals will inevitably be imperfect. Radically altering one aspect of society will have ramifying effects throughout all of society and so drastic change is to be avoided because it will have unpredictable results. Society is enormously complex and interrelated. Any changes made should be gradual and should respect the wisdom that has accumulated in long-standing traditional institutions. According to conservatives traditional institutions should be maintained (conserved) and if change is felt to be necessary we should proceed cautiously, remembering that drastic change could have drastic negative effects elsewhere in society.

---

³ A. Quinton, 'Conservatism', in Robert E. Goodin, Philip Pettit, and Thomas W. Pogge (eds), *A Companion to Contemporary Political Philosophy*, 2nd edition, Oxford: Blackwell, 2009, p. 285.
⁴ F. A. Hayek, *The Constitution of Liberty*, Chicago: University of Chicago Press, 1960.
⁵ See Quinton, 'Conservatism', p. 296.
⁶ Ibid., pp. 285–86.

In his article 'Wittgenstein 1929–31: The Turning Back', J. C. Nyiri relies upon a characterization of conservatism that is closely related to the one given above that was presented by Klaus Epstein in his book *The Genesis of German Conservatism*.[7] The organicism, deemed by Quinton to be a central doctrine of conservatism, can be seen in Epstein's claim that conservatives, 'tend to emphasize the importance of variety whereas their opponents stress general norms'. This supports scepticism about political knowledge (Quinton's second central doctrine of conservatism) in that individuals are unlikely to be able to grasp the whole through norms or generalizations because there is such a great variety of people in a great variety of roles. This means that 'the systematic application of reason to political, economic and religious problems usually leads to disastrous results' and supports the third strand of conservatism identified by Quinton, traditionalism. So, all of the strands identified by Quinton are present in the account of conservatism that Nyiri relies upon in his article discussing Wittgenstein's politics.

However, some social theorists have claimed that characterizations of conservatism like those given above are not sufficient. After all, the belief that change should be gradual and a belief in the interrelatedness (and variety) of people is just as compatible with reformist socialism as it is with those more usually associated with conservatism. George Nash, the author of a classic work on conservatism, notes that 'even Fabian Socialists who believed in "the inevitability of gradualness" might be labelled conservatives'[8] and Corey Robin, in his recent book about conservatism, *The Reactionary Mind: Conservatism from Edmund Burke to Sarah Palin*, takes this as a sign that more needs to be said in order to correctly characterize conservatism. Robin suggests that conservatism is 'a meditation on – and theoretical rendition of – the felt experience of having power, seeing it threatened, and trying to win it back'.[9] He argues, plausibly, that conservatives do not actually protect long-standing institutions unless those institutions fit with the interests of those in power. So, conservatives defend the family and the nation but they often do not view trade unions as valuable defenders of the rights of workers, despite the fact that trade unions have evolved and survived for many years. This fits with the fact that prominent conservative writers have often written in response to revolutionary movements or movements of oppressed groups. For example,

---

[7] K. Epstein, *The Genesis of German Conservatism*, Princeton, NJ: Princeton University Press, 1966, cited in Nyiri, 'The Turning Back', p. 37.

[8] G. Nash, *The Conservative Intellectual Movement in America Since 1945*, Wilmington, DE: Intercollegiate Studies Institute, 1976, p. xiv.

[9] C. Robin, *The Reactionary Mind: Conservatism from Edmund Burke to Sarah Palin*, Oxford: Oxford University Press, 2011, p. 4.

Edmund Burke, the paradigmatic conservative philosopher, wrote in response to the French revolution and Salisbury, the Conservative prime minister, wrote that 'hostility to Radicalism, incessant, implacable hostility, is the essential definition of Conservatism. The fear that the Radicals may triumph is the only final cause that the Conservative Party can plead for its own existence.'[10] This leads Robin to claim that conservatism can be partially defined as 'opposition to the liberation of men and women from the fetters of their superiors, particularly in the private sphere'.[11] So, we can see conservatism as a combination of organicism (with regard to the relation between individual and society), scepticism (about knowledge of society and of politics), traditionalism, and the defence of power.

So, we can distinguish members of Conservative parties from those who adhere to conservative ideology. But we might also distinguish those who adhere to conservative ideology from those who hold certain 'conservative' views about certain institutions, wanting to conserve them. The 'conservatism' of the Fabians, mentioned above, would be an example of this, and it was also left-wingers who were among the targets of Tony Blair when he attacked 'the forces of conservatism' in his 1999 conference speech. Left-wingers, Blair thought, were holding him back from 'modernizing' the Labour Party and British society by adhering to traditional Labour values.[12] Moreover, we might distinguish conservative attitudes within politics from culturally conservative attitudes – a preference for traditional cultural artefacts and a resistance to change.[13]

3.3 Wittgenstein's Politics

3.3.1 *Evidence That Wittgenstein Held Conservative Views*

3.3.1.1 *Wittgenstein's Attitudes towards Women*

One area of politics in which it seems quite clear that Wittgenstein held conservative views is the area of women's rights. There is evidence from a number

---

[10] Cited in Ibid., p. 19.
[11] Ibid., p. 16.
[12] Blair's full speech is available on the BBC website here: http://news.bbc.co.uk/2/hi/uk_news/politics/460009.stm (accessed 23 July 2019).
[13] The focus of this paper will be on politics but I think there is evidence that Wittgenstein held culturally conservative attitudes. As Hans-Johann Glock points out, 'Wittgenstein was a cultural conservative [...] he remained attached to eighteenth- and nineteenth century German culture, especially in music' ('Wittgenstein and Reason', in James Klagge (ed.), *Wittgenstein, Biography, and Philosophy*, Cambridge: Cambridge University Press, 2001, p. 204).

of sources over the course of many years which tell us that Wittgenstein held sexist views. For example, David Pinsent, a close friend of Wittgenstein's, records in his diary on 7 February 1913 that

> we talked about Woman suffrage: he [Wittgenstein] is very much against it – for no particular reason except that 'all the women he knows are such idiots'. He said that at Manchester University the girl students spend all their time flirting with the professors. Which disgusts him very much – as he dislikes half measures of all sorts, and disapproves of anything not deadly in earnest.[14]

Evidence from other sources suggests that Wittgenstein continued to hold sexist views. Fania Pascal attended meetings of the Moral Science Club at Cambridge where Wittgenstein spoke (in 1930–31) and then later gave Wittgenstein lessons in Russian (in the mid-1930s) and became a personal friend of his. She claims that Wittgenstein 'disliked intellectual women and in company literally turned his back on them'[15]. This is corroborated by the physicist Freeman Dyson, who lived nearby to Wittgenstein and had some interaction with him. Dyson claims that 'he was, of course, always extremely insulting to women. He couldn't tolerate women coming to his lectures. He would just simply be so rude that they would have to leave. So, a thoroughly

---

[14] D. Pinsent, *A Portrait of Wittgenstein as a Young Man: From the Diary of David Hume Pinsent 1912–1914*, in G. H. Von Wright (ed.), Oxford: Blackwell, 1990, p. 44. Perhaps some would question whether conservatism should be associated with sexism such as this. One reason for doing so is that conservatives revere existing political institutions and oppose radical change. At the time that Wittgenstein was saying this women did not have the vote in Britain and granting them the vote was a radical change. I think it is clear that many conservatives and members of Conservative parties continue to hold deeply sexist attitudes today. Women disproportionately suffered from the Conservative austerity policies in recent years in the United Kingdom. The conservative president Donald Trump has attacked women's right to an abortion in the United States, has made many sexist remarks, and has been accused of many cases of sexual harassment (see https://www.huffpost.com/entry/donald-trump-sexism-mika-brzezinski_n_595589f2e4b05c37bb7d304c?guccounter=1&guce_referrer=aHR0cHM6Ly93d3cuZ29vZ2xlLmNvbS8&guce_referrer_sig=AQAAAHLfZBq1vHsKwUWdx6HwRoS-MGLamiI8LPPfAwk1XNVTRRJSqQWHxGuVODyRvFbjwx4uFbRc2aHbnZqGtVVMLNYidPf6rcYGAN0IOq7Tx5juWyUoCIurixwASa8o68xLB0pHC3aNil2p6A-5Lo_F5oBMlO3Oxgm2Fn7acydvoULU (accessed 23 July 2019)).

[15] F. Pascal, 'A Personal Memoir', in Rush Rhees (ed.), *Recollections of Wittgenstein*, revised edition, Oxford: Oxford University Press, 1984, p.17.

disagreeable character.'[16] Pascal explicitly describes Wittgenstein as conservative in the early 1930s. She claims that 'at a time when intellectual Cambridge was turning Left he was still an old-time conservative of the late Austro-Hungarian Empire'.[17]

There is some suggestion that Wittgenstein was not quite as extreme in his sexism as Dyson suggests. We know that Wittgenstein's lectures were attended by, among others, Margaret Masterman, Alice Ambrose, Elizabeth Anscombe, Iris Murdoch, and Margaret Macdonald. Masterman and Ambrose were members of the select group of students that made the notes which form Wittgenstein's *Blue Book*, and Ray Monk, one of Wittgenstein's biographers, describes them as being among Wittgenstein's favourite students.[18] Wittgenstein's friend Maurice Drury recalls speaking to Wittgenstein about Weininger's sexist views and Wittgenstein made it clear that he disagreed deeply with Weininger's sexism, exclaiming, 'How wrong he was, my God he was wrong.'[19] Elizabeth Anscombe became a close friend of Wittgenstein's, and later translated his *Philosophical Investigations*, but it seems she was one of a few exceptions to Wittgenstein's general dislike of academic women. According to Ray, Monk Anscombe became an 'honorary male', 'addressed affectionately by him as "old man"'. Monk relates a story of Wittgenstein saying to Anscombe, 'thank God we've got rid of the women!' at a lecture when he found that there were no other female students left in attendance.[20]

So, it is fairly clear that Wittgenstein was sexist but what makes this attitude a conservative one? In the first place it is a defence of the status quo, and a defence of the way that things have traditionally been. Women did not have the right to vote in Britain in 1913, when Wittgenstein announced his opposition to women's suffrage. There is also a kind of organicism in the idea that women should play a different role in society to men and Wittgenstein's attitudes accord with Corey Robin's claim that conservatism involves 'opposition to the liberation of men and women from the fetters of their superiors,

---

[16] F. Dyson, interview on 'Web of Stories' website: http://www.webofstories.com/play/freeman.dyson/47;jsessionid=27BB84B2E9D0A7D1F0C0C403063703B9 (accessed 15 December 2014).

[17] Pascal, 'A Personal Memoir', p. 17.

[18] R. Monk, *Ludwig Wittgenstein: The Duty of Genius*, London: Vintage, 1991, p. 336. Of course, none of this demonstrates that Wittgenstein was not sexist.

[19] Vicente Sanfelix Vidarte brought this remark to my attention (from M. O'C. Drury, 'Some Notes on Conversations with Wittgenstein', in Rush Rhees (ed.), *Recollections of Wittgenstein*, Oxford: Oxford University Press, 1984, p. 91).

[20] Monk, *Ludwig Wittgenstein*, p. 498. Another reason to doubt Dyson's claims is that Dyson did not know Wittgenstein well at all and was a physicist rather than a philosopher. Dyson had limited interaction with Wittgenstein.

particularly in the private sphere'. The Conservative Party at the time was vehemently opposed to extending the vote to women (and to all adult men).[21] So, it is safe to conclude that Wittgenstein was conservative in at least one respect – in terms of his attitudes towards women.

3.3.1.2 *Hostility to Marxism*

There is further evidence of Wittgenstein's conservatism, or at least hostility to left-wing views, in what people who knew him recount of what he said about Marxism. Wittgenstein had some acquaintance with the works of Marx and Lenin and his opinion of their works was in some respects quite low. Rush Rhees reports that Wittgenstein 'used to speak with disgust of Marx's phrase "congealed labour time"' and that 'he could imagine that many people would find Marx an infuriating writer to read'[22] and according to M. O'C. Drury Wittgenstein said that 'Lenin's writings about philosophy are of course absurd'.[23] When Rush Rhees said to Wittgenstein that he was thinking of joining the Revolutionary Communist Party Wittgenstein tried to dissuade him from doing so on the basis that as a philosopher you should always be prepared to change direction and being loyal to a party would not allow you the necessary flexibility to change course.

Of course, opposition to organized Marxism is not sufficient to label somebody a conservative but it is true, at least, that adherents of conservative ideology would share Wittgenstein's hostility to organized Marxism. However, there is some unclarity about the extent to which Wittgenstein really did oppose Marxism and that will be discussed later, in Section 3.3.2.

3.3.1.3 *Wittgenstein's Admiration of Conservative Thinkers*

In his article 'The Turning Back'[24] J. C. Nyiri argues that one thing to be said in favour of the thesis that Wittgenstein was conservative is that he admired Grillparzer and Grillparzer was a conservative thinker (as well as being a famous poet). In fact, Wittgenstein's grandmother on his father's side of the family, Fanny Figdor, was personally acquainted with Grillparzer.[25] Nyiri notes

---

[21] See, e.g. Stuart Ball's article, 'The Conservative Party and the Impact of the 1918 Reform Act', *Parliamentary History*, vol. 37, no. 1, 2018, pp. 23–46.
[22] Rhees said this in letters to John Moran which Moran cites in his article 'Wittgenstein and Russia', *New Left Review*, vol. I/73, 1972.
[23] Drury, 'Conversations with Wittgenstein', p. 126.
[24] Nyiri, 'The Turning Back'.
[25] Ibid., p. 40.

that Wittgenstein made reference to Grillparzer in his notebooks on three occasions between 1929 and 1931. In the first note Wittgenstein talks about Grillparzer as a 'good Austrian'. Wittgenstein says that 'the good Austrian (Grillparzer, Lenau, Bruckner, Labor) is especially difficult to understand'.[26] In the second note Wittgenstein quotes Grillparzer as saying, 'How easy it is to move about in broad distant regions, how hard to grasp what is individual & near at hand.'[27] Nyiri suggests that the distinction here, between 'broad distant regions' and 'what is individual & near at hand' corresponds to the distinction between 'concrete use of language and speculative chatter'[28] that conservatives want to make. According to Nyiri, 'The conservative individual, with his preference for the concrete, for that which is given, is in fact always hostile to theory [i.e. 'speculative chatter'].'[29] In the third remark Wittgenstein says that 'in Bruckner's music nothing is left of the long & slender (nordic?) face of Nestroy, Grillparzer, Haydn, etc. but it has in full measure a round full (alpine?) face even purer in type than was Schubert's'. It is difficult to see how this third remark can be construed as suggestive of conservatism in Wittgenstein's thought; indeed it is difficult to make sense of at all. Nyiri suggests that in order to understand the remark we must place it in the context of the other remarks nearby. In particular, immediately after this remark Wittgenstein said that 'the power of language to make everything look the same which appears in its crassest form in the *dictionary* & which makes it possible to personify *time*, something which is no less remarkable than would have been making divinities of the logical constants'. Nyiri claims that the context of the remark suggests that what connects the remark with those surrounding it is 'the idea of *original multiplicity*, of diversity'[30] and emphasis on diversity is characteristic of conservatism. Nyiri cites Klaus Epstein's definition of conservatism in support of his view. Epstein suggests that 'conservatives [...] tend to emphasize the importance of variety, whereas their opponents stress general norms'.[31]

---

[26] From an entry in Wittgenstein's notebooks on 7 November 1929, cited on p. 41 of Nyiri, 'The Turning Back'. This is Nyiri's translation. In *Culture and Value* it is translated as 'I think good Austrian *work* (Grillparzer, Lenau, Bruckner, Labor) is particularly hard to understand' (my italics).
[27] This remark has been published in L. Wittgenstein, *Culture and Value*, Oxford: Blackwell. Nyiri cites the passage on p. 42 of 'The Turning Back'.
[28] Nyiri, 'The Turning Back', p. 42.
[29] Ibid., p. 38.
[30] Nyiri's discussion of the passage in question appears on p. 41 of 'The Turning Back'.
[31] The quote comes from Epstein, *The Genesis of German Conservatism*, cited in Nyiri, 'The Turning Back', p. 37.

Moreover, Nyiri does not just cite instances where Wittgenstein mentions or quotes Grillparzer. He proposes that conservative remarks are present in Wittgenstein's more overtly philosophical work. Examples of such remarks, Nyiri says, include some that have been published in *On Certainty*. According to Nyiri's interpretation, Wittgenstein maintains that we must 'recognise certain authorities in order to be able to make judgements at all'[32] (OC, §493). Nyiri claims, on the basis of §§47, 644, and 94 in *On Certainty*, that the authorities Wittgenstein thinks we must respect include 'one's school, or an inherited picture of the world'.[33] This kind of respect for inherited institutions fits with the traditionalism of conservatism mentioned above and could perhaps also be seen as a defence of those in power.

3.3.2 *Evidence Which Suggests That Wittgenstein Was Not Conservative*

In this section of the chapter I intend to present evidence that Wittgenstein was not wholly conservative in his *political* opinions. The analysis presented by Nyiri is largely *philosophical* in nature and so I will respond to that in Section 3.4 below.

3.3.2.1 *Wittgenstein's Admiration of Left-Wing Thinkers*

It is clear that Wittgenstein saw something in Grillparzer's views and that Grillparzer was a conservative. I will argue in Section 3.4 that what Wittgenstein gleaned from Grillparzer was more philosophical than political in nature and that Wittgenstein's philosophical views do not imply a conservative political philosophy. However, as has been noted many times already,[34] Wittgenstein also admired thinkers on the left. His friends included people like Nikolai

---

[32] Note here that this is Nyiri's rendering of OC, §493. Wittgenstein in fact puts §493 in the form of a question: 'So is this it: I must recognise certain authorities in order to make judgements at all?' (in *On Certainty*, New York: Harper Row, 1972 (originally published by Basil Blackwell, 1969)).

[33] Nyiri, 'The Turning Back', p. 40. The passages from Wittgenstein he mentions are '*This* is how one calculates. Calculating is *this*. What we learn at school, for example. Forget this transcendent certainty, which is connected with your concept of spirit' (OC, §47), 'For otherwise, wouldn't all assertion be discredited in this way?' (OC, §644), and 'But I did not get my picture of the world by satisfying myself of its correctness; nor do I have it because I am satisfied of its correctness. No: it is the inherited background against which I distinguish between true and false' (OC, §94).

[34] See, e.g. Ray Monk's biography of Ludwig Wittgenstein (*Ludwig Wittgenstein*); F. A. Flowers, *Portraits of Wittgenstein*, Thoemmes Continuum, 1999; and Vinten, 'Leave Everything As It Is', pp. 9–22.

Bakhtin, described by Fania Pascal as 'a fiery communist';[35] George Thomson, a Marxist classics lecturer at Birmingham who had a role in shifting Bakhtin's politics to the left; and Pierro Sraffa, an economist who was friends with the Marxist Antonio Gramsci and who Wittgenstein credits as being the stimulus for 'the most fruitful ideas' of the *Philosophical Investigations*.[36] Wittgenstein was also friends with the communist writer and activist, Maurice Dobb, and shared lodgings with him for a while.[37]

But there is not just evidence that Wittgenstein was friends with many people on the left, there is also evidence that Wittgenstein had some sympathy for their views. Although Wittgenstein said that he saw Lenin's philosophical views as absurd, he followed this by saying 'at least he did want to get something done'[38] and although Wittgenstein disliked Marx's way of expressing himself, Rush Rhees says that this did not mean that Wittgenstein objected to Marx's views.[39] It is worth noting that Wittgenstein, on more than one occasion, expressed a desire to visit communist Russia, first in 1922[40] (soon after the Russian Revolution) and then in 1935, when he did in fact go to Russia.[41] Some have argued that his interest in Russia had nothing to do with left-wing sympathies and more to do with his asceticism or even his (alleged) conservatism. For example, Fania Pascal said that 'to my mind, his feeling for Russia would have had at all times more to do with Tolstoy's moral teachings, with Dostoevsky's spiritual insights, than with any political or social matters'.[42]

However, there is evidence that there was more to Wittgenstein's motivations than this. In a letter of introduction that J. M. Keynes wrote to Ivan Maisky, the Russian ambassador in London, on behalf of Wittgenstein Keynes said that Wittgenstein 'has strong sympathies with the way of life which he believes the

---

[35] Pascal, 'A Personal Memoir', p. 14.
[36] L. Wittgenstein, *Philosophical Investigations (Preface)*, in the revised 4th edition by P. M. S. Hacker and Joachim Schulte, Oxford: Wiley-Blackwell, 2009, p. 4. On the relationship between Wittgenstein and Sraffa, see N. Venturinha, 'Sraffa's Notes on Wittgenstein's "Blue Book"', *Nordic Wittgenstein Review*, vol. 1, 2012, pp. 181–91.
[37] See Monk, *Ludwig Wittgenstein*, pp. 272, 343, 347.
[38] Drury, 'Conversations with Wittgenstein', p. 126.
[39] In a letter to John Moran 'Rhees twice emphasized that Wittgenstein regarded not Marx's views, but "the way he wrote" [...] as infuriating'. See Moran, 'Wittgenstein and Russia'.
[40] In a letter to Paul Engelmann. See P. Engelmann, *Letters From Ludwig Wittgenstein. With a Memoir*, trans. L. Fürtmüller, ed. Brian McGuinness, Oxford: Blackwell, 1967, pp. 52–53.
[41] Pascal, 'A Personal Memoir', p. 29.
[42] Ibid., pp. 44–45. J. C. Nyiri associates Wittgenstein's interest in Russia with conservatism in 'The Turning Back', pp. 45–46.

new regime in Russia stands for'.[43] What did Wittgenstein believe the regime in Russia stood for? According to Rush Rhees, 'Wittgenstein would say [towards the end of the Second World War] "the important thing is that the people have *work*" [...] He thought the new regime in Russia did provide work for the mass of the people [...] He also thought it would be terrible if the society were ridden by "class distinctions".' In a footnote Rhees adds, 'When I said that the "rule by bureaucracy" in Russia was bringing in class distinctions there, he told me "if anything could destroy my sympathy with the Russian regime, it would be the growth of class distinctions."'[44] Furthermore, Ray Monk cites Wittgenstein's friend, George Thomson, as saying that Wittgenstein's attitude towards Marxism was that 'he was opposed to it in theory but supported it in practice' and Monk notes that 'this chimes with a remark Wittgenstein made to Rowland Hutt [...]: "I am a communist, *at heart*." ' Monk concludes that 'there is no doubt that during the political upheavals of the mid-1930s Wittgenstein's sympathies were with the working class and the unemployed, and that his allegiance, broadly speaking, was with the Left'.[45]

So, it seems that Wittgenstein's interest in Russia did have something to do with political and social matters. Wittgenstein admired the Russian regime for providing full employment and for eradicating class distinctions (as he saw it). Wittgenstein, despite having some serious reservations, had some respect for Marxist theory, and this can be seen in the fact that he used the formulation 'the transition "from quantity to quality"'[46] in §284 of the *Philosophical Investigations* which is drawn ultimately from Hegel but which later appeared as Engels's 'first law' of dialectics. And there is new evidence from Rush Rhees's notes of conversations with Wittgenstein, published in *Mind* recently, that Wittgenstein was thinking of Marxist ideas in this passage. According to Rhees, 'Marx got the phrase from Hegel but I think Wittgenstein had Marxist ideas in mind here.'[47] This is not to suggest that Wittgenstein was a full-blown communist but it does at least indicate that Wittgenstein was not conservative in all of his political views. Wittgenstein was deeply conservative in his attitudes towards women but this did not form part of a wider conservative outlook when Wittgenstein was working on his later philosophy.

---

[43] See Monk, *Ludwig Wittgenstein*, p. 349.
[44] R. Rhees, 'Postscript', in Rush Rhees (ed.), *Recollections of Wittgenstein*, Oxford: Oxford University Press, 1984, p. 205.
[45] Monk, *Ludwig Wittgenstein*, p. 343.
[46] Wittgenstein, *Philosophical Investigations*, §284.
[47] G. Citron, R. Rhees, and L. Wittgenstein, 'Wittgenstein's Philosophical Conversations with Rush Rhees (1939–50): From the Notes of Rush Rhees', *Mind*, vol. 124, no. 493, January 2015, pp. 1–71.

3.4 Wittgenstein's Philosophy – Nyiri on Wittgenstein and Grillparzer

In this section I will pick up on the second of the questions I raised in the introduction to this chapter: Do Wittgenstein's philosophical remarks have conservative implications? I will start by looking at Nyiri's arguments concerning Wittgenstein and the conservative poet Franz Grillparzer and then move on to look at the remarks in *On Certainty* mentioned by Nyiri.

Nyiri proposed that Wittgenstein's admiration for Grillparzer and his own family's connections with Grillparzer were good evidence that Wittgenstein was conservative. It should be clear, first of all, that a family connection and a remark from Wittgenstein about the good Austrian work of Grillparzer (among others) do not constitute solid evidence that Wittgenstein was conservative. Your grandmother's acquaintances do not all necessarily hold the same politics as you do and it is possible to have admiration for a poet's work without agreeing with their politics. The second remark from Wittgenstein about Grillparzer was a quote from Grillparzer and we should ask whether it is a case of Wittgenstein highlighting something that he saw as good in Grillparzer's conservatism. However, it is far from clear that this was Wittgenstein's intention. The passage in question was, 'How easy it is to move about in broad distant regions, how hard it is to grasp what is individual and near at hand.' Nyiri defended this as an expression of conservative politics by arguing that Wittgenstein was here contrasting concrete uses of language and speculative chatter. Conservatives, according to Nyiri, favour concrete uses of language ('individual and near') over speculative chatter ('broad distant regions') because they doubt that theorizing about society is worthwhile, or even whether it is possible. But there are clear suggestions elsewhere in Wittgenstein's work that the contrast between concrete uses and speculative chatter is not what he had in mind. In the *Philosophical Investigations*, Wittgenstein looks to the correct use of ordinary terms in contrast to the misuse of terms by earlier philosophers. The contrast that Wittgenstein has in mind in the *Investigations* is the contrast between sense and nonsense. So, for example, at §39 Wittgenstein picks apart referentialist 'theories' of meaning by arguing that

> it is clear that the sentence 'Nothung has a sharp blade' has a *sense* whether Nothung is still whole or has already been shattered. But if 'Nothung' is the name of an object, this object no longer exists when Nothung is shattered into pieces; and as no object would then correspond to the name, it would have no meaning. But then the sentence 'Nothung has a sharp blade' would contain a word that has no meaning, and hence the sentence would be nonsense. But it does have a sense.

Wittgenstein makes a similar point when he argues that 'when Mr N. N. dies, one says that the bearer of the name dies, not that the meaning dies. And it would be nonsensical to say this, for if the name ceased to have meaning, it would make no sense to say "Mr N. N. is dead"' (*PI* §40). Later on in the *Investigations* Wittgenstein clearly connects the tasks of philosophy with this distinction between sense and nonsense when he says that 'the results of philosophy are the discovery of some piece of plain nonsense and the bumps that the understanding has got by running up against the limits of language' (*PI* §119). Seen in this light it seems plausible that Wittgenstein was not contrasting 'concrete' uses of language with speculative chatter about how to organize society, as Nyiri argues; rather, he was contrasting broad attempts to grasp the essence of language or some other phenomenon (which lead us into speaking nonsense) and particular, correct, ordinary uses of language (which make sense). His discussion of the nature of philosophy in the *Philosophical Investigations* suggests that Wittgenstein wanted to look closely at particular uses of language in order to dissolve philosophical problems that arise 'when language goes on holiday', that is, when people do not use words correctly and end up speaking nonsense. So, it is far from obvious that the passage from Grillparzer supports the view that Wittgenstein was a conservative. When Wittgenstein talks about that which is 'individual and near' it seems plausible that he is talking about looking at particular, correct, ordinary uses of language in contrast to the 'broad distant regions' of metaphysical nonsense.

The final passage in Wittgenstein's notebooks where he mentions Grillparzer is the one where he contrasts the 'nordic' face of Grillparzer with the 'alpine' face of Bruckner and Schubert. Nyiri tries to suggest that this passage is indicative of conservatism because it represents a kind of emphasis on diversity that conservatives favour. However, even if Wittgenstein's intention is to highlight diversity, it is unclear that an emphasis on diversity of any and every sort is characteristic of conservatism. For example, the conservative chancellor of Germany, Angela Merkel, has made a point of saying that having diverse cultures within a country does not work. At a meeting in Potsdam in 2010 she said that 'this [multicultural] approach has failed, utterly failed'.[48] David Cameron, the conservative prime minister of Great Britain, made the same point in 2011 at a conference in Munich soon after.[49] This may not be the

---

[48] Quote taken from 'Angela Merkel: German Multiculturalism Has "Utterly Failed"', in the *Guardian* newspaper, 17 October 2010, http://www.theguardian.com/world/2010/oct/17/angela-merkel-german-multiculturalism-failed (accessed 19 December 2014).

[49] See 'PM's Speech at Munich Security Conference', https://www.gov.uk/government/speeches/pms-speech-at-munich-security-conference, 5 February 2011 (accessed 19 December 2014).

kind of diversity (cultural diversity) that Nyiri had in mind but if he does not have this kind of emphasis on diversity in mind it seems a little implausible that we are to look for the diversity favoured by conservatives in the particular instances mentioned by Wittgenstein (i.e. 'faces', musical styles, kinds of poetry).[50] And even if we were to accept that the passage about Bruckner was suggestive of conservatism in Wittgenstein's political views it would not demonstrate that Wittgenstein's philosophy is conservative.

Nyiri argues that the third passage in Wittgenstein's notebooks about Grillparzer (about his 'nordic' face) is to be understood in the light of the comment Wittgenstein makes afterwards. This is where Wittgenstein talks about 'the power of language to make everything look the same […] which makes it possible to personify *time*, something which is no less remarkable than would have been making divinities of the logical constants'. Rather than interpreting this, as Nyiri does, as representing a conservative stress on diversity, it would perhaps be more natural to interpret it again in the light of Wittgenstein's remarks about the nature of philosophy, sense, and nonsense. Given that Wittgenstein makes mention of the 'divinity' of the logical constants here it would make sense to interpret this as a remark which has his predecessors in the philosophy of logic in mind. When Wittgenstein was writing his later philosophy he often attacked the referentialism and philosophy of logic associated with Gottlob Frege and Bertrand Russell. The natural way to interpret the comment would be as an attack on their philosophy which, as Wittgenstein saw it, obscured the understanding of language by assimilating expressions to one another[51] and which made the mistake of thinking that the logical constants must refer to entities (a view which he attacked in both his early and his later work). The point is that it is more natural to understand Wittgenstein as making a philosophical point here (i.e. as one to do with language, logic, sense, and nonsense) rather than as making a political point about the superiority of conservatism over its left-wing or liberal rivals. Indeed, in *The Blue*

---

[50] A similar point can be made about Nyiri's suggestion that conservatives place particular emphasis on particularity – on concrete circumstances. From the opposite end of the political spectrum Vladimir Lenin argued that 'the Marxist dialectic demands a concrete analysis of each specific historical situation' (in *The Junius Pamphlet* (1916) in *CW* 22:316 – where he stressed the importance of knowledge of detail rather than a priori reasoning). This suggests that an emphasis on the concrete is not distinctive of conservatism.

[51] So, e.g. in §10 of the *Investigations* Wittgenstein says 'making the description of the uses of these words [number words, object words, and so on] similar in this way [saying that they all signify something] cannot make the uses themselves any more like one another!' and in §11 he suggests that it would be better to think of words by analogy with tools, with various uses/functions.

Book Wittgenstein says something similar to the passage quoted by Nyiri in the context of discussing conceptual confusions surrounding the notion of 'time'. There he says that 'if we look into the grammar of that word, we shall feel that it is no less astounding that man should have conceived a deity of time than it would be to conceive of a deity of negation or disjunction'.[52]

Similarly, it is more natural to understand Wittgenstein as making philosophical points (which are consistent with any political ideology) in the remarks that Nyiri cites from *On Certainty* than it is to understand them as in some way expressing sympathy for conservative political views. For example, Nyiri cites §47 from *On Certainty* in support of his argument because it mentions school as an authority. What Wittgenstein actually says is, '*this* is how one calculates. Calculating is *this*. What we learn at school, for example. Forget this transcendent certainty which is connected with your concept of spirit.' The context for this remark is a discussion of the concepts of 'knowledge', 'doubt', 'certainty', and 'belief'. Wittgenstein has moved on from discussing Moore's claims to *know* things like 'here is a hand' and is discussing knowledge and certainty in the area of mathematics. An earlier passage sheds some light on what is going on in §47:

> Knowledge in mathematics: Here one has to keep on reminding oneself of the unimportance of the 'inner process' or 'state' and ask 'Why should it be important? What does it matter to me?' What is interesting is how we use mathematical propositions. (*OC* §38)

So, the context is one in which Wittgenstein is arguing that we should move away from thinking about knowledge as an inner state (this is conceptually confused, as Wittgenstein argues elsewhere[53]) towards looking at how we actually use mathematical propositions. In §47 he is recommending that we move away from the conception of certainty that is associated with confused views of the mind (e.g. the view that knowledge is a mental state) and look at how mathematical propositions are learnt and used in practice. Wittgenstein is talking about how the concepts of 'calculating' and 'certainty' are employed. He makes no comment in §47 about whether the ability to calculate must be acquired in a school – school is not seen as a necessary institution but as an instructive example – and nor does he make any comment on whether schools should be preserved as an institution or on whether, say, schoolchildren

---

[52] L. Wittgenstein, *The Blue and Brown Books*, New York: Harper and Row, 1958, p. 6. Wittgenstein also comments on conceptual confusions about time in the *Philosophical Investigations*; see, e.g. §90, §196.

[53] See §§148–55 of *Philosophical Investigations*.

should respect school authorities. No conservative political point is made. The passage is part of an extended discussion which is intended to make our use of various related concepts ('calculate', 'knowledge', 'certainty', 'doubt', 'belief', etc.) more perspicuous with the aim of dissolving epistemological problems (e.g. scepticism is compared to the 'hypothesis of our having miscalculated in all our calculations'[54] – with the purpose of showing that neither is a possible hypothesis). Wittgenstein does, in a way, suggest that we should respect an authority. Before we can challenge mathematical rules we must first be trained in mathematics and what we should respect is the correct uses of these terms. We should respect the correct uses of these terms if we do not want to be led astray into talking nonsense and get caught up in philosophical confusion. This is quite different to the conservative emphasis on respecting authorities such as the church, political authorities, and schoolteachers, which Wittgenstein makes no comment on.

3.5 Conclusion

So, I conclude that none of the philosophical remarks in Wittgenstein's work discussed by Nyiri in his article endorse or imply a conservative viewpoint. Wittgenstein's philosophy concerns confusions about concepts rather than grappling with ideological problems directly. There is some evidence that Wittgenstein was conservative, at least in some respects, in his politics and in his cultural attitudes, but his philosophical work does not have any obvious political implications. I suggest elsewhere in this book that his philosophy *does* have some not so obvious political implications (although not to the extent that it implies endorsing a particular ideology). My principal concern in this chapter has been to demonstrate that some of the arguments offered in favour of Wittgenstein being conservative, by the likes of Nyiri, miss their mark.

---

[54] Wittgenstein, *On Certainty*, §55.

Chapter 4

WAS WITTGENSTEIN A LIBERAL PHILOSOPHER?

4.1 Introduction

There is a substantial literature on the question of whether Wittgenstein was a conservative philosopher[1] but much less has been written on the question of whether Wittgenstein was a *liberal* philosopher despite the fact that, as Robert Greenleaf Brice has recently argued[2], there are hints of liberalism in Wittgenstein's writings.[3] Brice ultimately argues that the case for Wittgenstein

---

[1] See, e.g. J. C. Nyíri, 'Wittgenstein's Later Work in Relation to Conservatism' (in Anthony Kenny and Brian McGuinness (eds), *Wittgenstein and His Times*, Chicago: University of Chicago Press, 1982), 'Wittgenstein 1929–31: The Turning Back' (in Stuart Shanker (ed.), *Ludwig Wittgenstein: Critical Assessments (Vol. 4)*, London: Routledge, 1986), and 'Wittgenstein's New Traditionalism', *Acta Philosofica Fennica*, vol. 27, 1976, pp. 503–9; H. C. McCauley, 'Wittgenstein: Philosophy and Political Thought', *The Maynooth Review*, vol. 2, no. 2, 1976; D. Bloor, *Wittgenstein: A Social Theory of Knowledge*, London: Macmillan, 1983; P. Anderson, 'Components of the National Culture', in R. Blackburn and A. Cockburn (eds), *Student Power: Problems, Diagnosis, Action*, London: Penguin Books, 1969; E. Gellner, *Words and Things: An Examination of, and an Attack on, Linguistic Philosophy*, London: Victor Gollancz, 1959; A. Callinicos, *Marxism and Philosophy*, Oxford: Oxford University Press, 1985; A. Janik, 'Nyíri on the Conservatism of Wittgenstein's Later Philosophy', and 'Wittgenstein, Marx and Sociology', in Allan Janik's *Essays on Wittgenstein and Weininger*, Amsterdam: Rodopi, 1985; G. Pohlhaus and J. R. Wright, 'Using Wittgenstein Critically: A Political Approach to Philosophy', *Political Theory*, vol. 30, no. 6, December 2002; A. Lugg, 'Wittgenstein and Politics: Not Right, Left or Center', *International Studies in Philosophy*, vol. 36, no. 1, 2004; T. Moi, *Revolution of the Ordinary: Literary Studies after Wittgenstein, Austin, and Cavell*, Chicago: University of Chicago Press, 2017 (chapter 7, pp. 150–74); S. Laugier, 'This Is Us: Wittgenstein and the Social', *Philosophical Investigations*, vol. 41, no. 2, April 2018 (pp. 207–9).
[2] R. G. Brice, *Exploring Certainty: Wittgenstein and Wide Fields of Thought*, Lanham: Lexington Books, 2014, pp. 86–94.
[3] It could be argued, of course, that works which try to settle the question of whether Wittgenstein was a conservative philosopher indirectly answer the question of whether he was a liberal. However, I hope to make clear in this chapter that there are specific arguments in favour of Wittgenstein being a liberal that should be addressed in order to answer the question.

being a liberal is no stronger than the case for him being a conservative. In both cases the evidence is a long way from conclusive. However, other philosophers have been less circumspect. In his essay 'Wittgenstein and the Conversation of Justice', Richard Eldridge argues that 'a kind of substantive or weak perfectionist liberalism' follows from 'the condition of the human person that is enacted in *Philosophical Investigations*'.[4] Richard Rorty puts a pragmatist spin on Wittgenstein's work and suggests that liberalism is a mode of thought with greater utility than others – one which allows us to cope better. And Alice Crary, while critical of Rorty, suggests that the lessons learned from her own interpretation of Wittgenstein are 'reflected in forms of social life that embody the ideals of liberal democracy'.[5]

In this chapter I will agree with Brice that there is neither a particularly strong case in favour of Wittgenstein being a liberal and nor is there a particularly strong case to be made in favour of liberalism using Wittgenstein's philosophical writings. In the course of coming to those conclusions I will first examine the variety of positions going by the name of liberalism. I will then go on to look at the case that Brice pieces together in support of the claim that Wittgenstein was a liberal in *Exploring Certainty*. Following that, I will go on to argue that Eldridge, Rorty, and Crary fail to demonstrate that there are liberal

---

[4] R. Eldridge, 'Wittgenstein and the Conversation of Justice', in Cressida Heyes (ed.), *The Grammar of Politics*, Ithaca, NY: Cornell University Press, 2003, pp. 127–28. Like Eldridge, Sandra Laugier as well as Gaile Pohlhaus and John R. Wright argue for a form of political philosophy inspired by Wittgenstein and Cavell but I have chosen Eldridge's work as the focus for criticism in this chapter because he argues that a fairly particular form of liberalism follows from Wittgenstein's work whereas Pohlhaus and Wright are clear that Wittgenstein avoids 'any positive theoretical edifice' ('Using Wittgenstein Critically', p. 802) and say that there is no 'singular "Wittgensteinian" position' or 'specific [Wittgensteinian] program of political thought' ('Using Wittgenstein Critically', p. 804). However, Pohlhaus and Wright do think that Wittgenstein's work is useful in helping us to 'understand our cognitive responsibilities in the difficult process of maintaining a liberal society' (p. 805). Similarly, Sandra Laugier makes no attempt to associate Wittgenstein with a particular political theory or political ideology, although she does think that Wittgenstein's work is relevant to understanding political issues. I agree with Rupert Read in rejecting the kind of liberalism found in Cavell's work and in work inspired by Cavell (see R. Read, 'Wittgenstein vs. Rawls', *Publications of the Austrian Ludwig Wittgenstein Society – New Series*, vol. 14, 2010) but there is not space here to get into that discussion.

[5] A. Crary, 'Wittgenstein's Philosophy in Relation to Political Thought', in Alice Crary and Rupert Read (eds), *The New Wittgenstein*, London: Routledge, p.141. Bernard Williams, in his 'Pluralism, Community and Left Wittgensteinianism', suggests that 'the tendency of Wittgenstein's influence has been distinctly conservative' (p. 34) but thinks that a 'Left Wittgensteinianism' can be gleaned from his work (p. 37). I think Williams's arguments for these claims relies on a flawed understanding of Wittgenstein's use of the expression 'form of life'.

tendencies in Wittgensteinian philosophy. While agreeing with much of what Crary says in her arguments against Rorty I will argue that no broad ideological conclusions follow from Wittgenstein's philosophical remarks.[6]

4.2 Liberalism

The most obvious thing to say about liberalism is that liberals seek after *liberty* or *freedom*. However, there are different accounts of what liberty and freedom amount to and of what it is that should be free. Some philosophers stress negative freedom, that is, freedom from coercion by others,[7] while other philosophers stress positive freedom, arguing that someone is free only if they are autonomous or self-directed[8] or that someone is free only if they have effective power to act.[9] Some liberals emphasize the freedom of people to do what they like as long as their exercise of their freedom does not interfere with other people's whereas others emphasize free markets.[10]

Liberals nowadays often tie their support for freedom to support for democracy but there is no necessary connection between liberalism and support for democracy.[11] In their entry on liberalism in the *Stanford Encyclopedia of Philosophy*

---

[6] Vicente Sanfélix Vidarte has also entered into the discussion about whether Wittgenstein was a liberal. Like me, he does not think that Wittgenstein was a liberal, or that his philosophy has liberal implications, but he focuses on Wittgenstein's earlier philosophy whereas this chapter focuses on Wittgenstein's later philosophy (see 'Was Wittgenstein a Liberal?' in K. Wojchiechowski and J. Joerden (eds), *Ethical Liberalism in Contemporary Societies*, Frankfurt am Main: Peter Lang, 2009).

[7] See, e.g. I. Berlin, 'Two Concepts of Liberty', in *Four Essays on Liberty*, Oxford: Oxford University Press, 1969, p. 122.

[8] See, e.g. T. H. Green, *Lectures on the Principles of Political Obligation and Other Essays*, ed. Paul Harris and John Morrow, Cambridge: Cambridge University Press, 1986 [1895], p. 229.

[9] See, e.g. R. H. Tawney, *Equality*, New York: Harcourt. Brace, 1931, p. 221.

[10] According to Perry Anderson, the term 'liberalism' originated in Spain in the early nineteenth century: '"Liberalism" was an invention of the Spanish rising against French occupation in the epoch of Napoleon, an exotic expression from Cádiz at home only much later in the drawing-rooms of Paris or London' (P. Anderson, *The Origins of Postmodernity*, London: Verso, 1998, p. 3). Michael Broer makes the same claim in *Europe after Napoleon*, Manchester: Manchester University Press, 1996, p. 36. Daniel B. Klein and Will Fleming suggest that 'liberal' was first used in a political sense around 1769, by the Scottish historian William Robertson (and then soon after by Adam Smith in *The Wealth of Nations*) (see 'The Origin of "liberalism"', *The Atlantic*, 13 February 2014, https://www.theatlantic.com/politics/archive/2014/02/the-origin-of-liberalism/283780/ (accessed 29 August 2019)).

[11] In 'Was Wittgenstein a Liberal Philosopher?' Vicente Sanfélix Vidarte notes both that the term 'liberal' is 'far from precise' and that 'though there has been […] no lack of liberals who are democrats, there have been many others who were not', pp. 119 and 120, respectively.

Gerald Gaus, Shane D. Courtland, and David Schmidtz suggest that Thomas Hobbes could be considered a liberal because he adheres to the 'fundamental liberal principle', namely the claim that 'restrictions on liberty must be justified',[12] despite the fact that Hobbes does then go on to argue that severe restrictions on liberty *can* be justified. Hobbes was not a supporter of democracy and it is also questionable whether one of the founding fathers of liberalism, John Locke, was. Locke is rightly credited with inspiring moves towards greater democracy and toleration but he was not in favour of women having the right to vote or of a universal male franchise.[13] Locke argued in favour of religious toleration but did not think that such toleration should extend to atheists or to Catholics.[14] And it is not just liberals from centuries ago that have been ambivalent about democracy; Friedrich Hayek, in an interview with the Chilean newspaper *El Mercurio*, said that he preferred 'a liberal dictator to democratic government lacking liberalism'. The key ingredient of a liberal society, according to Hayek, was free markets. Dictatorship was not his professed ideal but was preferable, in his view, to a democratically elected government that placed severe impediments ('impurities') in the way of free markets, such as democratic trade unions and government-controlled industry. His ideal was a democracy 'clean of impurities'. In his ideal world it seems that he would have liked to avoid having an electorate able to vote for government control of industry or able to organize themselves into unions. In the interview with *El Mercurio* mentioned above Hayek defended the military dictatorship of General Pinochet in Chile,[15] which had overthrown a democratically elected

---

[12] D. Courtland, G. Gaus, and D. Schmidtz, 'Liberalism', in *Stanford Encyclopedia of Philosophy*, http://plato.stanford.edu/entries/liberalism/, (entry first published in 1996, substantially revised 2014, accessed 15 January 2016). Note: Alan Ryan, in his entry on Liberalism in *A Companion to Contemporary Political Philosophy* says that 'it would be absurd to call Hobbes a liberal even while one might want to acknowledge that he supplied many of the ingredients for a liberal theory of politics' (A. Ryan, 'Liberalism', in *A Companion to Contemporary Political Philosophy*, Oxford: Blackwell, 1993, p. 298).

[13] D. L. Thomas, *Routledge Philosophy Guidebook to Locke on Government*, London: Routledge, 1995, p. 41.

[14] Béla Szabados and Eldon Soifer explain why Locke took these stances in their book *Hypocrisy: Ethical Investigations*: 'Locke believed that Catholics, through their acceptance of the authority of the Pope, had in effect declared allegiance to another sovereign and thus could not be tolerated within civil society. Similarly, he believed that the oaths and pledges of atheists could not be relied upon, since they had no divine sanction to back them up' (Toronto: Broadview Press, 2004, p. 214).

[15] All of the references above to the *El Mercurio* article refer to 'Extracts from an Interview with Friedrich von Hayek', *El Mercurio*, Santiago de Chile, 12 April 1981, pp. D8–D9. The text of the interviews with Hayek can be found in B. Caldwell and L. Montes, 'Friedrich Hayek and His Visits to Chile', *Review of Austrian Economics*, vol. 28, no. 3, pp. 261–309.

socialist government and had rounded up thousands of opponents and had them killed. Classical liberals such as Hayek and 'neoliberals' like Margaret Thatcher and Ronald Reagan were of the opinion that Pinochet's dictatorship was better than democratically elected socialists.[16]

However, not all liberals are in the classical mould of Locke and Hayek. Modern liberals in the tradition of J. S. Mill, L. T. Hobhouse, and John Rawls tend to emphasize the ability of individuals to develop themselves in 'manifold diversity'[17] and this also means that they tend towards supporting toleration of other people and their (diverse) opinions. The liberal positions that are most relevant here are those described by Brice, Eldridge, Rorty, and Crary, and in each of these cases it would be fair to say that they are modern liberals or that the liberalism they focus their attention on is of the modern variety.

4.2.1 *Brice on Liberalism*

According to Brice, important elements of liberalism include 'a respect for […] a *reasonable pluralism*'[18] of beliefs and opinions, and with that a recognition of the capacity of human beings for *tolerance* and *acceptance* of others who disagree with oneself. Brice lists further features that he deems essential to liberalism including 'a concern for, and a respect of the working class; a concern for and a respect of the environment; an abhorrence of war, and a willingness to share what one has with others'.[19] On Brice's account John Stuart Mill is a paradigmatic liberal and Rawls is cited in listing the key elements of liberalism. Brice also, rather eccentrically, describes Marx as a liberal thinker,[20] although Marx would more usually be thought of as an opponent of the liberal thought that grew up with capitalism. This suggests that Brice has left-wing ideology more generally in mind rather than just left-wing varieties of liberalism.

The description of liberalism given by Brice stands in stark contrast to the kind of views held by classical liberals like Hayek, which suggests that, as Alan Ryan says, 'we should be seeking to understand liberalisms rather than liberalism'.[21]

---

[16] Interestingly, even Tony Blair and Jack Straw, of Britain's Labour Party, helped Pinochet to avoid being brought to justice (see 'Secret UK Deal Freed Pinochet', *Guardian*, 7 January 2001, http://www.theguardian.com/world/2001/jan/07/chile.pinochet (accessed 19 January 2016)).

[17] J. S. Mill, *On Liberty*, London: Longman, Roberts, & Green, 1869, III. 2.

[18] Brice cites Rawls here, with regard to the use of the expression 'reasonable pluralism' (J. Rawls, *Political Liberalism*, New York: Columbia University Press, 2005, p. 4).

[19] Brice, *Exploring Certainty*, p. 90.

[20] Ibid., p. 90.

[21] Ryan, 'Liberalism', p. 292.

4.2.2 Eldridge on Liberalism

Like many liberals, Richard Eldridge places emphasis on the notion of *freedom*. In particular, Eldridge repeatedly emphasizes the notion of 'expressive freedom' and suggests that achieving expressive freedom is Wittgenstein's primary aim. So, for example, he says that the *Philosophical Investigations* is 'a drama of a continuing struggle to achieve expressive freedom'[22] and that 'there is in *Philosophical Investigations* a continuing tragic not-reaching of a goal, and nonetheless a continuing aspiration to achieve expressive freedom'.[23] Eldridge hints at what he means by this by presenting examples of 'sureness in self presentation' including 'the power and restraint of Gil Shaham's performances of the Prokofiev violin concertos'.[24] So, the *Philosophical Investigations*, according to Eldridge, 'presents a protagonist seeking to articulate the terms for full human self-command and self-expression'.[25]

Eldridge spells out what the liberalism that he finds in Wittgenstein would involve in his 'Wittgenstein and the Conversation of Justice'.[26] There he says that since there are various, reasonably competing, ways of life we should be tolerant of others and mutually respectful. The framework of this variety of liberalism would also involve a commitment to personal autonomy as a substantive good. This, presumably, chimes with the goal of 'full human self-command and self-expression' mentioned above.

4.2.3 Rorty's Utopian Liberalism

Richard Rorty's liberalism is a curious mixture of the kind of politics associated with the left and the politics of the right.[27] On the one hand he stresses the notion of *solidarity* (which he opposes to that of 'objectivity'), supports trade unions in their demands for better wages and conditions,[28] applauds the

---

[22] R. Eldridge, *Leading a Human Life: Wittgenstein, Intentionality, and Romanticism*, Chicago: University of Chicago Press, 1997, p. 92.

[23] Ibid., p. 94.

[24] Ibid., pp. 6–7.

[25] Ibid., p. 7.

[26] Eldridge, 'Wittgenstein and the Conversation of Justice', pp. 117–28.

[27] Pohlhaus and Wright describe Rorty as a 'political liberal' but also as a 'philosophical conservative'. Their take on Rorty is different to mine. For their reasons for associating Rorty with conservatism see 'Using Wittgenstein Critically', pp. 802–3, 818–20.

[28] In his article 'Failed Prophecies, Glorious Hopes' Rorty says that 'the rise of the trade unions is, morally speaking, the most encouraging development of modern times' (in *Philosophy and Social Hope*, London: Penguin Books, 1999, p. 207 (the article first appeared as 'Endlich sieht man Freudenthal', in *Frankfurter Allgemeine Zeitung*, 20 February 1998)).

development of substantial welfare states,[29] and opposes the growth of economic inequality[30] as well as inequality of opportunity;[31] on the other hand he sees a lack of patriotism as a problem with the left,[32] opposes multiculturalism,[33] and sees free markets as indispensable.[34] However, despite the fact that his politics contains right-wing elements Rorty's liberalism is closer to the modern liberalism described by Brice – influenced by Mill and Rawls – than it is to the classical liberalism of Locke and Hayek. Rorty himself recognizes something of a split in his politics and that is reflected in the fact that he calls himself a 'liberal ironist'.

Rorty's discussion of liberalism tends to be an *abstract* one – presenting an ideal rather than describing the way that liberals actually behave. He tends to talk about what 'liberal democracies' do or don't do but not about what, for example, the U.S. government does. So, he says that 'a liberal democracy [...] will use force against the individual conscience just in so far as conscience leads individuals to act so as to threaten democratic institutions'[35] but modern liberal democracies, such as the United States, use force in so many instances that conflict with this that it is highly doubtful whether they even aim at acting on that principle much of the time. Rorty acknowledges that his liberalism is utopian (and his indebtedness to Mill) when he says that the institutions in the society he envisages

> would be regulated by John Stuart Mill's dictum that everybody gets to do what they like as long as it doesn't interfere with other people's doing the same.
>
> As far as I can see, nothing theoretical that we have learned since Mill's time [...] give[s] us reason to *revise* as opposed to supplement our previous descriptions of utopia.[36]

---

[29] See, e.g. 'Trotsky and the Wild Orchids' where Rorty says that 'welfare state capitalism is the best we can hope for' (*Philosophy and Social Hope*, p. 17) and 'Looking Backwards from the Year 2096' where Rorty suggests that 'fully fledged welfare states' will promote economic development and defend against civil unrest (*Philosophy and Social Hope*, pp. 247–50).

[30] Rorty, *Philosophy and Social Hope*, p. 243.

[31] Ibid., p. 231.

[32] Ibid., p. 252.

[33] Ibid., pp. 252–53.

[34] Ibid., p. 204. Also see 'Looking Backwards from the Year 2096' where he says that 'a viable economy requires free markets', in *Philosophy and Social Hope*, p. 244.

[35] R. Rorty, 'Priority of Democracy to Philosophy', in Douglas Tallack (ed.), *Critical Theory: A Reader*, London: Routledge, 1995, p. 374.

[36] Rorty, *Philosophy and Social Hope*, p. 235.

A final aspect of Rorty's liberalism worth noting here is that he sees himself as following in the footsteps of American pragmatists and as being influenced by pragmatist elements in Wittgenstein's thought, as he sees it. This means that he thinks about philosophical and political views in terms of their utility or their inutility,[37] their usefulness, or their point. When thinking about language he wants to focus on words as *tools* for coping with our environment rather than thinking about language as being representational.[38] He contrasts his own view, with its stress on *solidarity*, with the realist view which stresses *objectivity* and emphasizes notions like *truth* and *representation*. One way of advancing towards the liberal utopia that he envisages is to develop a new *vocabulary* that draws people into recognizing the relative utility of liberalism compared to other ways of thinking.[39] On Rorty's view there is no clear distinction to be made between philosophy and other disciplines: 'Both scientists and philosophers help us learn to get around the world better. They do not employ distinct methods.'[40]

Wittgenstein's influence can be seen in Rorty's talk of words as tools. At the beginning of the *Philosophical Investigations* Wittgenstein contrasts the 'Augustinian view', according to which words name objects and sentences combine names (§1), with the view of words as tools. He suggests that we 'think of the tools in a toolbox: there is a hammer, pliers, a saw, a screwdriver, a rule, a glue pot, glue, nails, and screws. The functions of words are as diverse as the functions of these objects.'[41] Rorty also suggests that the Wittgensteinian maxim 'Don't look for the meaning, look for the use' suggests a pragmatic reading of his work. It suggests to Rorty that 'any utterance can be given significance by being batted around long enough in more or less predictable ways',[42] and so leads to Rorty's view that we can formulate more fruitful ways

---

[37] So, e.g. in 'Hilary Putnam and the Relativist Menace' he says that ' "criticism of other philosophers" distinctions and problematics should charge relative inutility rather than "meaninglessness" or "illusion" or "incoherence" ', in *Truth and Progress: Philosophical Papers*, vol. 3, p. 45.

[38] In 'A World without Substances or Essences' Rorty says that we should see language 'as providing tools for coping with objects rather than representations of objects, and as providing tools for different purposes', in *Philosophy and Social Hope*, p. 65.

[39] E.g. he talks approvingly of Dewey hoping that 'we would stop using the juridical vocabulary which Kant made fashionable among philosophers, and start using metaphors drawn from town meetings rather than tribunals' (R. Rorty, 'Pragmatism and Law: A Response to David Luban', in *Philosophy and Social Hope*, p. 111).

[40] R. Rorty, 'Wittgenstein and the Linguistic Turn', in *Philosophy as Cultural Politics: Vol. 4 Philosophical Papers*, Cambridge: Cambridge University Press, 2007, p. 166.

[41] L. Wittgenstein, *Philosophical Investigations*, trans. G. E. M. Anscombe, Oxford: Basil Blackwell, 1953, §11. Wittgenstein continues to use the comparison with tools throughout the *Philosophical Investigations* – see, e.g. §14, §15, §17, §23, §53, §360.

[42] Rorty, 'Wittgenstein and the Linguistic Turn', p. 172.

of talking, such as using a 'vocabulary' employing the term 'solidarity' rather than that of 'objectivity'. We can talk in ways that allow us to cope better and a kind of liberal ironist vocabulary would allow us to do that, according to Rorty.[43] One other way in which Wittgenstein has influenced Rorty is in his talk of 'language games'. Rorty seems to see his talk of *vocabularies* as being similar to Wittgenstein's talk of language games and forms of life.[44]

4.2.4 *Crary and Liberalism*

Alice Crary, in her article 'Wittgenstein's Philosophy in Relation to Political Thought', suggests that the lesson we learn from Wittgenstein about 'investigating established modes of thought and speech' is 'one [she suspects] we would find reflected in forms of social life that embody the ideals of liberal democracy'.[45] What is meant by 'liberal democracy' is not perfectly clear but this term is typically used to distinguish modern, capitalist, representative democracies with elections, human rights, and civil liberties, from both other kinds of democracies (e.g. direct democracies such as in the Paris Commune) and from undemocratic states with limited freedoms (e.g. Saudi Arabia). According to this rough outline countries as different as the United States, Japan, and Sweden would all count as liberal democracies. A state might count as a liberal democracy whether it has a social democratic government or a conservative one and so to say that the lesson we learn from Wittgenstein is reflected in forms of social life embodying the ideals of liberal democracy is not to say that Wittgenstein was a liberal or that his philosophy has liberal implications, and so her claim is weaker than the one made by Eldridge. In 'Wittgenstein's Pragmatic Strain' Crary suggests that lessons from Wittgenstein might help to

---

[43] It is worth briefly noting here that Wittgenstein never actually employed the slogan used by Rorty. It was first offered up by John Wisdom as epitomizing Wittgenstein's view (J. Wisdom, *Philosophy and Psycho-Analysis*, Oxford: Basil Blackwell, 1953, p. 117).

[44] So, e.g. he quotes Sabina Lovibond approvingly when she says that

'an adherent of Wittgenstein's view of language should equate that goal with the establishment of a language game in which we could participate ingenuously, while retaining our awareness of it as a specific historical formation. A community in which such a language game was played would be one [...] whose members understood their own form of life and yet were not embarrassed by it' (quoted in R. Rorty, *Objectivity, Relativism and Truth: Philosophical Papers: Volume 1*, Cambridge, Cambridge University Press, 1991, p. 32, fn. 15 (the passage is originally from S. Lovibond, *Realism and Imagination in Ethics*, Minneapolis: University of Minnesota Press, 1983, p. 158)) and presumably he thinks that Lovibond's talk of establishing a language game parallels his own talk of shifting vocabularies.

[45] Crary, 'Wittgenstein's Philosophy in Relation to Political Thought', p. 141.

resolve disputes between liberals and communitarians and so the suggestion is that her own position combines elements of the two approaches.[46]

Crary acknowledges that she does not build a conclusive case for this conclusion but that is not her intention in the article. Her intention is to demonstrate that widely accepted interpretations of Wittgenstein's philosophy, from both left and right, misunderstand Wittgenstein's account of meaning and so their conclusions about the political implications of Wittgenstein's philosophy are shaky. So, Crary makes something of a negative case for her position by undermining the arguments of people like Ernest Gellner and J. C. Nyiri, who argue that Wittgenstein's philosophy has conservative implications because it does not allow for rational criticism of other forms of life.

4.2.5 *Summary*

The philosophers under consideration in this chapter have a conception of liberalism that is a modern one.[47] What this means is that they emphasize the kind of freedom, democracy, toleration, and mutual respect between people with differing moral and political outlooks that is found in modern capitalist representative democracies and that they seek to broaden the scope of those values within a liberal-democratic framework. However, there are other kinds of liberals: classical liberals and neoliberals, whose emphases are different. In the next section I will consider whether Wittgenstein might be considered a liberal of some sort, whether liberal democracies are particularly conducive to carrying out the kind of philosophical work that Wittgenstein engaged in, and whether Wittgenstein's philosophy might be of help in promoting liberal values.

---

[46] A. Crary, 'Wittgenstein's Pragmatic Strain', *Social Research*, vol. 70, no. 2, Summer 2003, pp. 369–90.

[47] Given that the authors discussed in this chapter are modern liberals, it is primarily focused on modern liberalism rather than classical liberalism. I think that the combination of elements of conservatism in Wittgenstein's thought, his support for social democratic parties (voting for the British Labour Party), and things like his distaste for class division in his (romanticized) view of post-revolutionary Russia already make it fairly clear that Wittgenstein was not a classical liberal. Further support for the claim that Wittgenstein was not a classical liberal can be found in Hayek's recollections of Wittgenstein (Hayek was Wittgenstein's second cousin and Hayek met Wittgenstein on a few occasions). Hayek (a classical liberal) said that when he met Wittgenstein in the early 1940s he avoided talking about politics with him because 'we knew we disagreed politically'. Although it is unclear exactly how Hayek and Wittgenstein disagreed it is at least clear that they did – and to the extent that they would avoid talking about politics (see F. A. Hayek, 'Remembering My Cousin, Ludwig Wittgenstein', *Encounter*, August 1977, p. 22).

4.3 Wittgenstein and Liberalism

4.3.1 *Brice's Case for Wittgenstein Being a Liberal*

In *Exploring Certainty* Robert Greenleaf Brice tries to demonstrate that something of a case can be made in favour of Wittgenstein being a liberal just as some kind of case can be made in favour of saying that Wittgenstein was conservative. However, he is clear that he does not wish to endorse the view that Wittgenstein was a liberal. His point is to argue that 'it is wrong to try to draw any definitive conclusions from the "evidence"',[48] given that both kinds of cases can be made with some force.

Brice starts by examining evidence of Wittgenstein's political views. He cites a passage from Ray Monk's biography of Wittgenstein in which Monk says that 'there is no doubt that during the political upheavals of the mid-1930s Wittgenstein's sympathies were with the working class and the unemployed, and that his allegiance, broadly speaking, was with the Left'.[49] As we saw in Chapter 3, Monk himself cites evidence from friends of Wittgenstein in support of his claim, including George Thomson's claims that Wittgenstein 'supported [Marxism] in practice' and that Wittgenstein, in the 1930s, was 'alive to the evils of unemployment and fascism and the growing danger of war'.[50] As noted in Section 4.2.1 above, Brice thinks that 'a concern for, and a respect of the working class' is essential to liberalism, and so Wittgenstein's sympathy for the working class counts as evidence in favour of him being a liberal, according to Brice.

However, it is debatable whether sympathy for the working class is essential to liberalism. There are liberals, like Hayek, who are content to see trade union rights removed, since these are a barrier to the free markets that he particularly treasures, and it seems that somebody with a particular sympathy for the working class would not be so blasé about removing a worker's right to organize in trade unions. Ideologies particularly associated with sympathy for the working class are socialist and communist ideologies and so the passages Monk relies on would perhaps be better used in support of claiming that Wittgenstein was a socialist or communist rather than to support the claim that he was a liberal. Brice's definition of liberalism is extremely broad – too broad, in that it encompasses Marxist views – but this does not undermine his central claim, that 'it is wrong to try to draw any definitive conclusions from the "evidence"' about Wittgenstein's political views. The fact that there is

---

[48] Brice, *Exploring Certainty*, p. 86.
[49] R. Monk, *Ludwig Wittgenstein: The Duty of Genius*, London: Vintage, 1991, p. 343.
[50] G. Thomson, 'Wittgenstein: Some Personal Recollections', *Revolutionary World*, vol. XXXVII, no. 9, 1979, pp. 86–88.

some evidence of Wittgenstein holding left-wing views undermines the claims made by Nyiri and Bloor about Wittgenstein's supposed conservatism and this supports Brice's conclusion.

Brice also cites passages which suggest that Wittgenstein was opposed to bourgeois thinking,[51] that he was a pacifist (or at least abhorred war),[52] and that he supported the Labour Party in the 1945 elections. However, just as in the case of sympathy for the working class, these stances are not associated particularly with liberalism. The Labour Party in Britain is a social democratic, reformist socialist party, not a liberal one, and the people voting for it are in any case not necessarily entirely in agreement with its views. Opposition to bourgeois thinking is more often associated with Marxism, socialism, and anarchism than with liberalism. In fact, liberalism, as an ideology which defends capitalism, could well be seen as a form of bourgeois ideology itself. Pacifism, again, is not particularly associated with liberals. There are anarchists who are pacifists, socialists who are pacifists, as well as liberals who are pacifists. Moreover, it is clear that Wittgenstein was not a lifelong pacifist, despite sometimes saying things which indicated that he inclined in that direction. For one thing, he was eager to fight in the First World War, and did so as a volunteer, from the beginning of the war in 1914 and after the Second World War Wittgenstein wrote,

> The hysterical fear over the atom bomb now being experienced, or at any rate expressed, by the public almost suggests that at last something really salutary has been invented. The fright at least gives the

---

[51] L. Wittgenstein, L. *Culture and Value (Revised Edition)*, ed. G. H. von Wright and H. Nyman, revised by Alois Pichler, trans. Peter Winch, Oxford: Blackwell, 1998, p. 24e – where Wittgenstein says,

Ramsey was a bourgeois thinker. i.e. he thought with the aim of clearing up the affairs of some particular community. He did not reflect on the essence of the state – or at least he did not like doing so – but on how *this* state might reasonably be organized. The idea that this state might not be the only possible one partly disquieted him and partly bored him. He wanted to get down as quickly as possible to reflecting on the foundations – of *this* state.

[52] In a letter to Norman Malcolm, written shortly after the end of the Second World War, Wittgenstein said,

Perhaps I ought to feel elated because the war is over. But I'm not. I can't help feeling certain that this peace is only a truce. And the pretence that the complete stamping out of the 'aggressors' of this war will make this world a better place to live in, as a future war could, of course, only be started by them, stinks to high heaven &, in fact, promises a horrid future. (in N. Malcolm, *Ludwig Wittgenstein: A Memoir*, 2nd edition, Oxford: Clarendon Press, 2001, p. 97)

impression of a really effective medicine. I can't help thinking: if this didn't have something good about it the philistines wouldn't be making an outcry [...] the bomb offers a prospect of the end, the destruction, of an evil, – our disgusting soapy water science. And certainly that's not an unpleasant thought.[53]

So, the passages that Brice cites do not lend credibility to the conclusion that Wittgenstein was a liberal.

Brice also suggests that support for the thesis that Wittgenstein was a liberal can be found in Wittgenstein's more philosophical writings. He cites Wittgenstein's 'Remarks on Frazer's *Golden Bough*' in attributing to Wittgenstein the traditional liberal value of tolerance. However, the passage that Brice cites from Wittgenstein makes no mention of tolerance of other's beliefs or of acceptance of people with different beliefs. The point that Wittgenstein makes is better described as being about methodology in anthropology and about the correct categories for describing the beliefs of others. In the passage that Brice cites Wittgenstein says,

> Frazer's account of the magical and religious views of mankind is unsatisfactory; it makes these views look like *errors* [...] The very idea of wanting to explain a practice seems wrong to me. All that Fraser does is make them plausible to people who thinks as he does. It is very remarkable that in the final analysis all these practices are presented as, so to speak, pieces of stupidity. But it will never be plausible to say that mankind does all that out of sheer stupidity.[54]

Wittgenstein is suggesting that Frazer is limited in his explanatory framework given that he thinks of magic as a kind of proto-science. We do not have to conceive of magic in this way, Wittgenstein points out. Symbolic and ritualistic behaviour need not involve false beliefs about its instrumental efficacy. Belief in such things as killing a priest in his prime in order to keep his soul fresh (the kind of beliefs that Frazer sought to explain) is not empirical belief. As Peter Hacker points out, 'They are not based on observations of constant conjunctions in nature, and cannot be shown to be mistaken by an *experimentum*

---

[53] Wittgenstein, *Culture and Value (Revised Edition)*, pp. 55e–56e. Note: Although Wittgenstein sneers at 'philistines' being opposed to the bomb in this passage it does not indicate that he was in favour of the bomb himself. What he says is good about the atom bomb is the effect that it has on people's take on science.

[54] L. Wittgenstein, 'Remarks on Frazer's Golden Bough', in *Philosophical Occasions*, Cambridge: Hackett, 1993, p. 119.

crucis or more careful inductive procedures.'[55] In the kinds of cases under consideration by Frazer, Wittgenstein wants to say that 'there is *no* question of an error'.[56] Similar considerations apply to the other passages from Wittgenstein cited by Brice,[57] that is, no mention is made of toleration or acceptance of the beliefs discussed by Frazer; rather, points are made about methodology, explanation, and understanding in anthropology.

Brice also suggests that liberal conclusions about acceptance flow from Wittgenstein's remarks in *On Certainty* about forms of life shifting or changing[58] and he cites Wittgenstein's *Remarks on the Philosophy of Psychology (Vol. II)*[59] in connection with the theme of acceptance: 'Given the same evidence, one person can be completely convinced and another not be. We don't on account of this exclude either one from society, as being unaccountable and incapable of judgement' (§685). However, in none of these instances does Wittgenstein himself draw any conclusions about tolerance or acceptance and nor do such conclusions follow from what he says. It is interesting, for one thing, that in the remark immediately following the one cited by Brice (from *RPP*, vol. II, above) Wittgenstein says, 'But mightn't a society do precisely this?' (§686) with no comment on whether excluding people in such a way would be desirable or not, suggesting that the point he is making is not about tolerance of others but rather one about how we think about judgement.

So, although Brice succeeds in demonstrating, *pace* Nyiri and Bloor, that Wittgenstein was far from a thoroughgoing conservative, he does not produce a convincing case in favour of Wittgenstein being a liberal.[60]

---

[55] P. M. S. Hacker, 'Wittgenstein on Frazer's Golden Bough', in P. M. S. Hacker, *Wittgenstein: Connections and Controversies*, Oxford: Oxford University Press, p. 82.

[56] Wittgenstein, 'Remarks on Frazer's "Golden Bough"', cited in P. M. S. Hacker, 'Wittgenstein on Frazer's Golden Bough', p. 82.

[57] Wittgenstein, *Philosophical Occasions*, pp. 125, 131.

[58] Brice, *Exploring Certainty*, p. 92. Brice cites *OC* §256 ('the language game does change with time'), §559 ('You must bear in mind that the language game is so to say something unpredictable. I mean: it is not based on grounds. It is not reasonable (or unreasonable). It is there—like our life'), and §97 ('The mythology may change back into a state of flux, the river-bed of thoughts may shift. But I distinguish between the movement of the waters on the river-bed and the shift of the bed itself; though there is not a sharp division of one from the other').

[59] L. Wittgenstein, *Remarks on the Philosophy of Psychology, Volume II*, ed. G. H. von Wright and Heikki Nyman, trans. C. G. Luckhardt and M. A. E. Aue, Oxford: Basil Blackwell, 1980.

[60] And, as mentioned earlier, this was not Brice's intention. He says that

> it was not my purpose to argue that *one* social/political interpretation of Wittgenstein is right, or better than another. Indeed, drawing conclusions about Wittgenstein's political temperament by pointing to passages that seem to confirm a particular position, while

4.3.2 *Eldridge, Liberalism, and Wittgenstein*

Recall that Eldridge places particular emphasis on the notion of 'expressive freedom' in his account of Wittgenstein's *Philosophical Investigations*. The path carved out by the discussion between the various voices of the *Philosophical Investigations* is a 'drama of a continuing struggle to achieve expressive freedom'.[61] Elsewhere Eldridge describes the *Investigations* as 'the ongoing reenactment of a condition [the condition of the human subject] – rather than [...] the conclusive establishment via argument (deductive or quasi-deductive) argumentation of theses about the nature of meaning or understanding'[62] and Eldridge goes on to argue that 'what follows [...] from the condition of the human person that is enacted in *Philosophical Investigations* is [...] a kind of substantive or weak perfectionist liberalism'.[63] It is a form of perfectionist liberalism, on Eldridge's view, in part because it aims to 'articulate the terms of full human self-command and self-expression'.[64] The upshot of all of this is a liberalism involving tolerance, mutual respect, and a commitment to autonomy.

The first thing that might make us slightly wary of Eldridge's account is that the elements Eldridge takes to be central do not appear in the *Philosophical Investigations* at all – at least not in the form that Eldridge discusses them. Not only does Wittgenstein not use the term 'expressive freedom' but the central liberal notion of *freedom* or *liberty* is not mentioned in the *Philosophical Investigations* at all. There is also no mention of autonomy, tolerance, or mutual respect. The expression 'self-command' is not used, although early on in the *Investigations* Wittgenstein does talk of commanding 'a clear view of the aim and functioning of the words [in a language game]'[65] and later, again, tells us that commanding 'a clear view of the use of our words'[66] is one of his principal aims.

---

  simultaneously overlooking other passages that may contradict that position, is most certainly wrong [...] Rather, my purpose was to show the distractive power [...] such 'arguments' have on us. (*Exploring Certainty*, p. 93)

[61] Eldridge, *Leading a Human Life*, p. 92.
[62] Eldridge, 'Wittgenstein and the Conversation of Justice', p. 235, fn. 10.
[63] Ibid., p. 127.
[64] Eldridge, *Leading a Human Life*, p. 7. Ray Monk picks up on hints of perfectionism in Wittgenstein's work in the subtitle to his biography of Wittgenstein – 'The Duty of Genius' (thanks to an anonymous referee commenting on my paper 'Was Wittgenstein a Liberal Philosopher?' (*Teorema*, vol. 36, no. 1, 2017) for this point). The current chapter is a revised version of that paper.
[65] Wittgenstein, *Philosophical Investigations*, §5.
[66] Ibid., §122.

So, is there any truth in Eldridge's account? Certainly, it is true that Wittgenstein does not aim at debating or putting forward *theses*.[67] In discussing the nature of philosophy, as he practices it, Wittgenstein says that 'if someone were to advance *theses* in philosophy, it would never be possible to debate them because everyone would agree to them'.[68] It is also true that Wittgenstein does sometimes speak of an element of self-control being involved in philosophizing. Eldridge cites a passage from the 'Big Typescript' in support of his case, where Wittgenstein says,

> DIFFICULTY OF PHILOSOPHY NOT THE INTELLECTUAL DIFFICULTY OF THE SCIENCES, BUT THE DIFFICULTY OF A CHANGE OF ATTITUDE. RESISTANCE OF THE WILL MUST BE OVERCOME. [...] Work on philosophy is [...] actually more of // a kind of // work on oneself. On one's own conception. On the way one sees things [...] THE METHOD OF PHILOSOPHY: THE PERSPICUOUS REPRESENTATION OF GRAMMATICAL // LINGUISTIC // FACTS. THE GOAL: THE TRANSPARENCY OF ARGUMENTS.[69]

Eldridge also cites a remark from the collection that is known as *Culture and Value*, where Wittgenstein says that 'the edifice of your pride has to be dismantled. And that is terribly hard work'.[70] Another respect in which Eldridge's account is at least partially correct is that he claims that Wittgenstein wants to avoid being dogmatic or doctrinaire. So, Eldridge says of Wittgenstein that he wants to 'avoid all at once dogmatism, nihilist skepticism, and simple indifferentism'[71] and that 'onwardness and self-revision, not doctrine and self-completion are pervasive'.[72] There is support for this in Wittgenstein's later work, for example in the *Philosophical Investigations*, where Wittgenstein raises worries about 'the dogmatism into which we fall so easily in doing philosophy'.[73] Wittgenstein

---

[67] See Hans-Johann Glock's '*Philosophical Investigations* Section 128: "Theses in Philosophy" and "Undogmatic Procedure"' for an excellent discussion of what Wittgenstein means by 'theses' in this context.
[68] Wittgenstein, *Philosophical Investigations*, §128.
[69] L. Wittgenstein, 'Philosophy: Sections 86–93 of the So-Called "Big Typescript" (Catalogue Number 213)', in James Klagge and Alfred Nordmann (eds), *Philosophical Occasions 1912–1951*, Indianapolis: Hackett, 1993, pp. 161–63, 171. Cited on p. 109 of Eldridge, *Leading a Human Life*.
[70] Wittgenstein, *Culture and Value (Revised Edition)*, p. 30e. Cited on p. 109 of Eldridge, *Leading a Human Life*.
[71] Eldridge, *Leading a Human Life*, p. 7.
[72] Ibid., p. 89.
[73] Wittgenstein, *Philosophical Investigations*, §131.

makes it clear that he is far from seeking to impose a set of beliefs or opinions (i.e. being doctrinaire), in his lectures (1939) where he said that he was not advancing opinions at all[74] and said that if anyone were to dispute anything he said he would let that point drop and move on to something else.[75]

Nonetheless, there are problems with Eldridge's account of Wittgenstein. Whereas Eldridge contrasts Wittgenstein's opposition to advancing theses in philosophy with 'the ongoing reenactment of a condition', Wittgenstein himself, in the passages on philosophy in the *Philosophical Investigations*, contrasts advancing theses with presenting descriptions of the grammar of our language with the goal of dissolving philosophical problems. So, in the *Investigations* Wittgenstein says that

> we may not advance any kind of theory. There must not be anything hypothetical in our considerations. All *explanation* must disappear, and description alone must take its place. And this description gets its light – that is to say, its purpose – from the philosophical problems. These are, of course, not empirical problems; but are solved through an insight into the workings of our language [...] The problems are solved [...] by assembling what we have long been familiar with.[76]

The purpose of philosophy, as Wittgenstein does it, is not self-command (although an element of self-command is involved in fulfilling this purpose) but to dissolve philosophical problems by assembling relevant grammatical rules that we are already familiar with – by 'assembling reminders' of the correct use of words ('the work of a philosopher consists in marshalling recollections').[77] The element of self-command that is involved – the overcoming of the resistance of the will, or the dismantling of pride – is required because we are 'bewitched' by sentences that appear to make sense but which do not: 'Philosophy is a struggle against the bewitchment of our understanding by the resources of our language.'[78] Similarly, it is not 'onwardness and

---

[74] L. Wittgenstein, *Wittgenstein's Lectures on the Foundations of Mathematics, Cambridge, 1939*, ed. Cora Diamond, Chicago: University of Chicago Press, 1976, p. 103.
[75] Ibid., p. 22.
[76] Wittgenstein, *Philosophical Investigations*, §109.
[77] Ibid., §127.
[78] Ibid., §109. There is a very interesting examination of the gender imagery used by Wittgenstein (and other philosophers) in Phyllis Rooney's 'Philosophy, Language, and Wizardry', in Naomi Scheman and Peg O'Connor (eds), *Feminist Interpretations of Ludwig Wittgenstein*, University Park: Pennsylvania State University Press, 2002. Rooney claims that 'it is useful to examine [...] what Wittgenstein's "bewitchment" image does that wouldn't get done without it [...] Like the earlier gender metaphors that suggest a clear

self-revision', as Eldridge says, that Wittgenstein opposes to dogmatism and doctrine, rather it is the careful examination of the grammar of our language. So, for example, when we are faced with a philosophical problem in mathematics what we should do is to 'render surveyable the state of mathematics that troubles us'.[79] In order to achieve understanding in philosophy we should produce surveyable representations of the relevant region of grammar[80] (i.e. remind ourselves of how the relevant words are ordinarily used).

When Wittgenstein talks about dogmatism in philosophy he does not have in mind the kind of objectionable blinkered or inflexible stances taken in politics that might be contrasted with more open-minded or perhaps liberal stances; rather, he is talking about a kind of philosophy in which an archetype or a model is held onto in such a way that it amounts to a 'preconception to which reality *must* correspond'.[81] His targets were Spengler, who he accused of 'dogmatically attribut[ing] to the object what should be ascribed only to the archetype'[82] and his own earlier philosophy. As Peter Hacker puts it, 'It is characteristic of misguided [dogmatic] philosophy to insist that things *must* be thus-and-so, because this is how one has resolved to represent them.'[83] Wittgenstein's point is that grammatical rules do not describe *de re* necessities; rather, they are rules for the use of words (i.e. not descriptions at all). Wittgenstein's philosophy is not doctrinaire or opinionated because it does not involve presenting opinions at all. The activity that Wittgenstein is engaged in is the description of norms of representation, the description of grammar, with the purpose of getting rid of philosophical (i.e. conceptual) confusion and this is quite different to presenting opinions (i.e. not grammatical claims) on matters in politics, morality, or metaphysics. *Describing* grammar is also a quite different kind of activity to theorizing, which aims at *explaining* some phenomenon.

Eldridge himself acknowledges the appeal of this account of Wittgenstein's philosophy, attributing the view to Gordon Baker and Peter Hacker. He says that it is 'a considerable and powerful view. Put into practice, it yields trenchant criticisms of a great deal of work in linguistics, cognitive psychology, and the

---

division, *bewitchment* also implies a clear demarcation: it has an all-or-nothing sense to it – one is or one is not cast under the spell' (p. 41).

[79] Ibid., §125.
[80] Ibid., §122.
[81] Wittgenstein, *Philosophical Investigations*, §131.
[82] L. Wittgenstein, L. *The Big Typescript: TS 213*, German-English Scholars Edition, ed. and trans. C. G. Luckhardt and Maximilian A. E. Aue, Oxford: Blackwell, 2005, p. 204e.
[83] P. M. S Hacker, 'Wittgenstein on Grammar, Theses, and Dogmatism', in *Wittgenstein: Comparisons & Context*, Oxford: Oxford University Press, 2013, p. 167.

theory of perception.'[84] However, Eldridge thinks that this account is open to serious objections. On the one hand it acknowledges Wittgenstein's remark about philosophy not advancing theses or any kind of theory but on the other it attributes a thesis to Wittgenstein, namely that grammar is autonomous.

However, it is not clear that Eldridge's objection finds its target. For one thing, Baker and Hacker themselves do not refer to 'grammar is autonomous' as a thesis. So, there is no explicit commitment from them to the clash that Eldridge identifies. Moreover, it is not clear that 'grammar is autonomous' *is* a thesis. If it were a thesis then it is, at best, unclear what evidence could be adduced in support of it. An alternative way of viewing the remark that 'grammar is autonomous' is to view it as itself a kind of grammatical remark (and so not the kind of thing such that we might produce evidence for). The remark basically amounts to saying that 'there is no such thing as justifying grammar as correct by reference to reality',[85] and so it rules out philosophical attempts to do that, such as that in Wittgenstein's own earlier work. 'Grammar is autonomous' could be taken to be like 'inner states stand in need of outward criteria', in playing the role of a synoptic description 'drawing together and interrelating a multitude of grammatical propositions that are truisms'.[86]

The other problem facing Eldridge's objection is that it seems as though if he objects to Baker and Hacker on those grounds he would also have to bring the objection against Wittgenstein himself, since Wittgenstein makes remarks in several places that amount to saying that grammar is autonomous. For example, in *Philosophical Grammar* Wittgenstein says that 'grammar is not accountable to any reality. It is grammatical rules that determine meaning (constitute it) and so they themselves are not answerable to any meaning'[87] and in *Zettel* we find Wittgenstein saying that 'one is tempted to justify rules of grammar by statements like "But there really are four primary colours". And the remark that the rules of grammar are arbitrary is directed against the possibility of this justification.'[88] It seems unlikely that Wittgenstein himself would have held both that 'grammar is autonomous' is a thesis and that he would remark that there are no theses in philosophy. This lends support to the view that 'grammar is autonomous' is not a thesis at all.

---

[84] Eldridge, *Leading a Human Life*, p. 103.
[85] G. P. Baker and P. M. S. Hacker, *Wittgenstein: Rules, Grammar and Necessity* (second edition, extensively revised by P. M. S. Hacker), Oxford: Wiley-Blackwell, 2009, p. 336.
[86] Ibid., p. 20.
[87] L. Wittgenstein, *Philosophical Grammar*, ed. Rush Rhees, trans. A. J. P. Kenny, Oxford: Blackwell, 1974, p. 184.
[88] L. Wittgenstein, *Zettel*, ed. G. E. M. Anscombe and G. H. von Wright, trans. G. E. M. Anscombe, Oxford: Blackwell, 1967, §331.

Given the problems with Eldridge's account (i.e. the inconsistencies of his account with Wittgenstein's own professed aims) and the plausibility of Baker and Hacker's account, I suggest that the latter is preferable, and so the case that Eldridge makes for there being a variety of perfectionist liberalism in Wittgenstein's work is seriously undermined.[89] Neither Brice nor Eldridge has made a convincing argument in favour of Wittgenstein being a liberal. In the next section I will turn to Rorty's pragmatic case for liberalism and argue that it does not suggest that there is any kind of liberalism in Wittgenstein's philosophical work.

4.3.3 *Rorty, Wittgenstein, and Liberalism*

In the section above (4.2.3) it was suggested that there were some commonalities between Wittgenstein's and Rorty's philosophies. However, with regard to the topic in question, namely Rorty's pragmatic case for liberal ironism, it is the differences between the two that are more striking. (i) One way in which Rorty and Wittgenstein differ is in *how they conceive their relationship to traditional philosophy*. Rorty's pragmatist line is that 'criticisms of other philosophers' distinctions and problematics should charge relative inutility rather than "meaninglessness" or "illusion" or "incoherence"',[90] whereas, as Alice Crary notes, 'it is a signature gesture of Wittgenstein's philosophy [...] to appeal to nonsense as a term of philosophical criticism'[91] and Crary's take on Wittgenstein is supported by remarks that Wittgenstein himself made, such as his remark that 'the results of philosophy are the discovery of some piece of plain nonsense'.[92] (ii) Wittgenstein does not think of his work in philosophy as consisting in *creating new vocabularies* as Rorty does. Rorty thinks that we should give up on

---

[89] Eldridge is among those interpreters of Wittgenstein who take the *Philosophical Investigations* to be a literary text and so puts pressure on the philosophy/literature distinction. Eldridge wants to suggest that the 'voices' in the text are in a discussion that never comes to resolution, in contrast to, for example, Peter Hacker, who want to suggest that Wittgenstein presents conclusive arguments against certain philosophical positions (including Wittgenstein's own earlier views). See, e.g. 'Gordon Baker's Late Interpretation of Wittgenstein', in G. Kahane, E. Kanterian, and O. Kuusela (eds), *Interpretations of Wittgenstein*, Oxford: Blackwell, 2007.

[90] R. Rorty, 'Hilary Putnam and the Relativist Menace', in *Truth and Progress: Philosophical Papers Volume 3*, Cambridge: Cambridge University Press, 1998, p. 45.

[91] Crary, 'Wittgenstein's Philosophy in Relation to Political Thought', p. 128.

[92] Wittgenstein, *Philosophical Investigations*, §119. Elsewhere Wittgenstein says, 'To say that this proposition ["This is how things are"] agrees (or does not agree) with reality would be obvious nonsense' (§134) and 'only I can know whether I am really in pain: another person can only surmise it. – In one way this is wrong, and in another nonsense' (§246) (see also PI §252, §282, §464, §524).

certain distinctions and ways of speaking associated with past philosophy and promote new, more useful, ways of speaking (such as the liberal ironist vocabulary that he wants to promote). So, for example, he suggests that we set aside 'the subject-object, scheme-content, and reality-appearance distinctions and [think] [...] of our relation to the rest of the universe in purely causal, as opposed to representationalist, terms',[93] that 'we cannot employ the Kantian distinction between morality and prudence',[94] and that we should 'stop using the distinctions between finding and making, discovery and invention, objective and subjective'.[95] Moreover, in line with point (i) above, Rorty suggests that Wittgenstein should have abandoned the distinction between sense and nonsense in the *Philosophical Investigations* and Rorty sees the continued use of the distinction in Wittgenstein's later philosophy as a mistaken remnant of the *Tractarian* philosophy.[96] Wittgenstein, like Rorty, has problems with distinctions made by traditional philosophers but he does not suggest jettisoning the old dichotomies. Instead he says that 'what we do is to bring words back from their metaphysical to their everyday use'.[97] What that means is that we should 'marshal recollections' or 'assemble reminders'[98] of the ordinary use of the words in question so that we can recognize that the way that past philosophers have used the words in question is nonsensical – 'to pass from unobvious nonsense to obvious nonsense'.[99] (iii) The difference in philosophical approaches is summed up by one of James Conant's objections to Rorty. Wittgenstein famously said that his aim in philosophy was 'to show the fly the way out of the fly-bottle'[100] and I take it that this aim was synonymous with the aim mentioned above, of passing from unobvious to obvious nonsense – to make clear where past philosophers were confused and to remind people of how the relevant words are used ordinarily. However, James Conant notes that 'Rorty's recommendation appears to be that one should leave the fly in the fly-bottle and get

---

[93] Rorty, 'Hilary Putnam and the Relativist Menace', p. 49.
[94] Rorty, *Philosophy and Social Hope*, p. xvi.
[95] Ibid., p. xviii.
[96] See R. Rorty, 'Keeping Philosophy Pure: An Essay on Wittgenstein' (in *The Consequences of Pragmatism*, Minneapolis: University of Minnesota Press, 1982) – page 22 – where Rorty talks about 'a set of distinctions ("linguistic facts" versus other facts, convention versus nature, conditional versus unconditional necessity, philosophy versus science, sense versus nonsense, "factual knowledge" versus other realms of discourse) which themselves are left over from the *Tractatus* and which cannot be used without perpetuating the notion of philosophy as a distinct *Fach*'.
[97] Wittgenstein, *Philosophical Investigations*, §116.
[98] Ibid., §127.
[99] Ibid., §464.
[100] Ibid., §309.

on with something more interesting'[101] and Rorty himself, in commenting on this assessment, says that 'Conant here gets me exactly right'.[102] (iv) It follows from Wittgenstein's account of philosophy as involving uncovering or discovering nonsense that he would not want to affirm the negation of the traditional philosophical 'theories' that he examines, because the negation of nonsense is itself nonsense. However, as Alice Crary[103] and Hilary Putnam have observed, Rorty seems to want to do something like affirming the negation of traditional philosophical positions. Rorty objects to realism but responds to it by saying that we can't describe reality in itself.[104] Whether or not Rorty's position is coherent it clearly is not Wittgenstein's one.[105] (v) Rorty and Wittgenstein also differ in their approach to the issue of how philosophy relates to science. Throughout his career Wittgenstein made a clear distinction between philosophy and science. In the *Tractatus Logico-Philosophicus* Wittgenstein said unequivocally that 'philosophy is not one of the natural sciences'[106] and in the *Philosophical Investigations* he says that 'our considerations [in philosophy] must not be scientific ones'.[107] Philosophy, unlike science, describes linguistic norms[108] with the aim of dissolving (conceptual) confusion, according to Wittgenstein. However, Rorty, says that 'both scientists and philosophers help us to learn to get around the world better. They do not employ distinct methods.'[109] (vi) A final difference between Rorty and Wittgenstein that is

---

[101] J. Conant, 'Introduction' to H. Putnam, *Realism with a Human Face*, Cambridge: Harvard University Press, 1990, p. lii. John McDowell makes a similar point in his assessment of Rorty's work in *Mind and World*. McDowell says that Rorty's refusal to address traditional philosophical problems amounts to 'a deliberate plugging of the ears' (J. McDowell, *Mind and World*, Cambridge: Harvard University Press, 1994, p. 151). Gaile Pohlhaus and John R. Wright discuss their take on Rorty's approach to philosophy and his ironist liberalism on pp. 801–3 and pp. 818–20 of their 'Using Wittgenstein Critically', 2002. Pohlhaus and Wright suggest that we cannot succeed in engaging a sceptic in 'the circulation of question and reason-giving answer', in 'resituating these questions [the questions of the philosophical sceptic] in the contexts where they might legitimately arise and make sense' through 'simply rejecting and abandoning the questions (as Rorty suggests), which would mean rejecting the skeptic herself' (p. 803).
[102] Rorty, 'Hilary Putnam and the Relativist Menace', p. 47, fn. 17.
[103] Crary, 'Wittgenstein's Philosophy in Relation to Political Thought', pp. 127–28.
[104] Putnam, *Pragmatism*, p. 39. See also, pp. 27–56 of Putnam's *Pragmatism* for a full discussion of why Putnam thinks that it is mistaken to describe Wittgenstein as a pragmatist.
[105] See, e.g. Wittgenstein's *Blue Book*, where he examines the grammar of the relevant terms involved in disputes between idealists, solipsists, and realists (L. Wittgenstein, *The Blue and Brown Books*, New York: Harper & Row, 1958, pp. 48–49).
[106] L. Wittgenstein, *Tractatus Logico-Philosophicus*, London: Routledge, 1961, 4.111.
[107] Wittgenstein, *Philosophical Investigations*, §109.
[108] Ibid., §124.
[109] Rorty, 'Wittgenstein and the Linguistic Turn', p. 166.

particularly worth commenting on here is their difference over the issue of meaning and use. Rorty presents us with the outline of a '"social practice" theory of language'[110] which he describes as a pragmatic theory 'epitomized in the Wittgensteinian maxim "Don't look for the meaning, look for the use"'.[111] However, according to Wittgenstein's conception of philosophy there could be no *theses* in philosophy and although Wittgenstein is credited with the 'maxim' he never himself said such a thing. Wittgenstein did not recommend replacing talk of meaning with talk of use and he did not think that meaning could be explicated in terms of use in every instance. What Wittgenstein actually said in the *Philosophical Investigations* was that 'for a *large* class of cases of the employment of the word "meaning" – though not for *all* – this word can be explained in this way: the meaning of a word is its use in the language'.[112] Rorty thinks Wittgenstein's thought here suggests that 'any utterance can be given significance by being batted around in more or less predictable ways'[113] but although Wittgenstein would have agreed that any utterance could be *given* a meaning he would have been wary of the thought expressed by Rorty here. As we have already seen Wittgenstein did not think that certain words used in traditional philosophical 'theories' were given a clear sense despite being used in 'more or less predictable ways'. As Daniel Whiting notes in his introduction to a collection of essays about Wittgenstein and language, 'there is a normative dimension to use [...] from the fact that, for example "bachelor" means *eligible, unmarried, adult male*, it appears trivially to follow that it would be wrong or incorrect to apply it to a married woman or to form the sentence, "My sister is a bachelor"'.[114] If someone were to repeatedly say "my sister is a bachelor" at ten o'clock every morning (i.e. bat the phrase about in "more or less predictable ways") the phrase would not become any more meaningful. As in the case of traditional philosophers, if you use a word in a way that flouts the ordinary rules for its use then you need to at least explain what you mean by what you say in order to be understood.[115]

---

[110] Ibid., pp. 172–73.
[111] Ibid., p. 172.
[112] Wittgenstein, *Philosophical Investigations*, §43.
[113] Rorty, 'Wittgenstein and the Linguistic Turn', p. 172.
[114] D. Whiting, 'Introduction', in Daniel Whiting (ed.), *The Later Wittgenstein on Language*, Basingstoke: Palgrave Macmillan, p. 4.
[115] Pohlhaus and Wright suggest that Rorty's misinterpretation of Wittgenstein, attributing a 'use theory of meaning' to him, leads to a kind of 'philosophical conservatism':

> Those who find in Wittgenstein's thought a 'use theory of language' [...] indirectly affirm Wittgenstein's connection to conservatism by claiming to see in Wittgenstein a theory of meaning grounded on conventionally governed practices [...] these views may still yield philosophical support for a political danger, namely that of

These sharp differences between Wittgenstein's philosophy and Rorty's pragmatist philosophy tell us that whatever the virtues of Rorty's pragmatist case for liberalism it is not a case that is strongly rooted in Wittgenstein's philosophy. It might be said to be inspired by Wittgenstein's philosophy but this inspiration consists in taking words and phrases from Wittgenstein's work and twisting them beyond recognition and so Rorty's case does very little to demonstrate that there is any kind of liberalism to be found in Wittgenstein's work. In fact, given that Wittgenstein is primarily concerned with matters of grammar, sense, and nonsense, it seems clear at the very least that his concerns are not political or ideological (although his work may well be of help in dissolving conceptual confusions in the work of political philosophers, which might, indirectly, lead to changes in people's ideology, perhaps by undermining the credibility of the philosopher in question).

4.3.4 *Crary on Rorty and Liberal Democracy*

Alice Crary, in her 'Wittgenstein's Philosophy in Relation to Political Thought', objects to Rorty's arguments in several places. She objects to the way in which he throws out the baby with the bathwater when he suggests that we should drop realist jargon (e.g. objectivity) because realism is incoherent. In this respect she is closer to Wittgenstein than Rorty, in that Wittgenstein only wanted to bring back words from their metaphysical to their ordinary use rather than drop them, as Rorty suggests. As already noted, she also objects to the way in which Rorty moves from rejecting realism to asserting something like its negative and makes a similar objection to the one that Conant has made concerning the way that Rorty just wants to discard traditional philosophy and move onto something more interesting rather than engage with the way in which philosophical problems beguile us,[116] and finally, she objects to views which attribute theses about meaning to Wittgenstein.

Rorty presents us with something like a false dichotomy, between realist philosophy and 'pure language game' philosophy. Crary notes that Wittgenstein 'rejects as the product of metaphysical confusion the idea that we must choose between, on the one hand, having the world and forfeiting responsibility and, on the other, having responsibility and losing

---

repudiating radical challenges to the established order [...] This danger is an inherent part of what we will call 'philosophical conservatism'. ('Using Wittgenstein Critically', p. 801)

They claim that 'to see Wittgenstein as offering a use theory of meaning combined with philosophical quietism is to trivialise him' ('Using Wittgenstein Critically', p. 802).

[116] Crary, 'Wittgenstein's Philosophy in Relation to Political Thought', pp. 127–29.

the world',[117] that is, the kind of division that Rorty has in mind. In place of Rorty's confused 'theorizing' Crary suggests that we adopt a view of Wittgenstein such that he is calling upon us to develop sensitivities acquired when mastering our language. We should, on this view, 'put [...] to use – and perhaps stretch – our *imagination*'.[118] This seems reasonable enough. Wittgenstein's philosophy does involve us having to think about how we ordinarily use the terms that are under consideration and then to assemble to appropriate resources to tackle philosophical problems. However, it is difficult to see how Crary gets from this to the conclusion that the lessons from her interpretation of Wittgenstein's philosophy would be found 'reflected in forms of social life that embody the ideals of liberal democracy'.[119] Crary herself says that this is only a suspicion that she has and she does not specify the ideals that she has in mind. It is also difficult to know quite what she is opposing the ideals of liberal democracy to: is she thinking about private property (liberal) versus public property (socialist), free markets (liberal) versus government control of industry, or perhaps maximal individual liberty versus responsibility to a collective? Without further specification it is difficult to evaluate her conclusion and how she has arrived at it, and so I would suggest that, at best, a weak case has been made for saying that Wittgenstein's thought is reflected in the forms of social life she mentions. We might say that Wittgensteinian philosophizing is particularly encouraged by societies that allow people time to reflect, to develop their imaginative capacities, and which educate them well, but neither of these elements is tied particularly to liberal democracy. In fact, one might argue that the capitalism that has grown up with liberal democracy denies much of the world opportunities to develop in these ways. Tendencies towards specialization, and pressures to publish original material in philosophy journals in liberal democracies, might also be thought to be trends that undermine philosophizing as Wittgenstein suggested.

---

[117] Ibid., p. 141.
[118] Ibid., p. 140. Gaile Pohlhaus and John R. Wright, in their paper 'Using Wittgenstein Critically', also place emphasis on the imagination, taking inspiration from Sabina Lovibond and Stanley Cavell. They argue that 'the development of the imagination is [...] an essential element of getting a clear view of who "we" are, without which we are at the mercy of the unimaginable and inhumane through the denial of a significant aspect of who we are' (p. 823). (See also, S. Lovibond, *Realism and Imagination in Ethics*, Minneapolis: University of Minnesota Press, 1983; and S. Cavell, 'Availability of Wittgenstein's Later Philosophy', in *Must We Mean What We Say?*, New York: Charles Scribner's, 1969).
[119] Ibid., p. 141.

4.4 Conclusion

So, neither Brice, Eldridge, Rorty nor Crary has made a convincing case for there being some kind of liberal or liberal-democratic tendencies in Wittgenstein's thought. As noted in the previous chapter, in his political pronouncements Wittgenstein himself combined elements of conservative influence with sympathy for elements of bolshevism, as well as a 'Tolstoyan ideal of a life of manual work',[120] so if there are hints of liberalism in Wittgenstein's philosophical thought it would seem that Wittgenstein himself was not particularly well attuned to them.[121] Wittgenstein's political thought was not liberal and his philosophy does not obviously have any ideological implications; rather, it was focused on dissolving the conceptual confusions found in the work of past philosophers. I will go on to argue in later chapters that Wittgenstein's philosophical remarks do have some political implications but the implications that they have do not suggest that Wittgenstein was a liberal.[122]

---

[120] H.-J. Glock, *What Is Analytic Philosophy?*, Cambridge: Cambridge University Press, 2008, p. 192.

[121] For a good overview of Wittgenstein's various political opinions see Ray Monk's autobiography of Wittgenstein – Monk *Ludwig Wittgenstein*.

[122] Gaile Pohlhaus and John R. Wright do not claim that Wittgenstein was a liberal but do claim that a Wittgensteinian approach can 'shed light on essential difficulties involved in the formation and maintenance of political bonds in the liberal society' ('Using Wittgenstein Critically', p. 815). This is undoubtedly true and I also agree with much of what Pohlhaus and Wright have to say in objecting to Richard Rorty's philosophical work. I agree with them in objecting to Rorty's refusal to engage with traditional philosophy (insofar as he actually does refuse to engage) and also in objecting to Rorty's dismissal of challenges to liberalism. However, unlike Pohlhaus and Wright I do not think that Wittgenstein's work should be used in service of the aim of 'the difficult process of maintaining a liberal society' ('Using Wittgenstein Critically', p. 805). The inability of liberal societies to deal with problems like climate change, war, and bigotry as well as the kinds of problems Pohlhaus and Wright themselves point out (i.e. radical alienation (p. 816)) suggest to me that we should be looking for more democratic, more equal, peaceful, and sustainable alternatives to liberalism.

Chapter 5

LEAVE EVERYTHING AS IT IS

The philosophers have only to dissolve their language into the ordinary language, from which it is abstracted, in order to recognize it as the distorted language of the actual world and to realize that neither thoughts nor language in themselves form a realm of their own, that they are only *manifestations* of actual life.

Karl Marx, *The German Ideology*

5.1 Introduction

Wittgenstein's philosophy is, more often than not, simply ignored by Marxist philosophers. However, on the rare occasions that Marxist philosophers have tried to give an account of Wittgenstein's philosophy they have often, mistakenly, supposed that Wittgenstein's philosophy stands in opposition to Marxist philosophy.[1] Marx tried to give a scientific account of human society and culture, whereas Wittgenstein was notoriously opposed to theorizing in philosophy. Marx famously said that 'the philosophers have only interpreted the world, in various ways; the point is to change it',[2] while Wittgenstein was concerned with conceptual considerations and had very little to say about workers' struggles. Early, critical, responses to Wittgenstein from figures on the left proved to be influential, including Ernest Gellner's *Words and*

---

[1] Several recent books have examined the differences between continental philosophy and analytic philosophy. One of the aims of these books has been to bridge the gap of mutual incomprehension between the two camps. The aim in this chapter is similar, although it will be restricted to the gap between Marxist philosophers and Wittgensteinians (see, e.g. Simon Critchley, *Continental Philosophy*, Oxford: Oxford University Press, 2001; and Hans-Johann Glock, *What Is Analytic Philosophy?*, Cambridge: Cambridge University Press, 2008).

[2] K. Marx, 'Theses on Feuerbach', Thesis 11, 1845, in K. Marx, *The German Ideology*, 2nd edition, edited and introduced by C. J. Arthur, London: Lawrence and Wishart, 1974.

Things[3] and Herbert Marcuse's *One-Dimensional Man*.[4] However, more recent accounts of Wittgenstein's thought from Marxists in both the continental and analytic traditions have been more sympathetic and have overcome the weaknesses of some of the earlier analyses.[5]

My argument in this chapter will be that the apparent differences between Marxist and Wittgensteinian thought dissolve once one understands the different ways in which Marx and Wittgenstein thought about the nature of philosophy. I will start by looking at some of the mistakes made by Perry Anderson in his attempts to get to grips with Wittgenstein. I will then go on to see how those mistakes have been compounded by Alex Callinicos before finally saying something about what Marxists stand to gain from a better understanding of Wittgenstein's philosophy.[6]

The reasons for focusing on the work of Anderson and Callinicos are, first, that in both cases they have audiences that go beyond academia:[7] Anderson

---

[3] E. Gellner, *Words and Things: An Examination of, and an Attack on, Linguistic Philosophy*, 2nd edition, London: Routledge, 2005 [1959]. T. P. Uschanov's essay 'Ernest Gellner's criticisms of Wittgenstein and ordinary language philosophy' gives a good account of the reception of Gellner's account of Wittgenstein and also makes sharp criticisms of Gellner's work (Uschanov's essay appears in G. Kitching and N. Pleasants (eds), *Marx and Wittgenstein: Knowledge, Morality and Politics*, London: Routledge, 2002). Perry Anderson, whose essay 'Components of the National Culture' will be examined here, describes Gellner's book as a 'classic' and he clearly thinks that Gellner has dealt decisively with 'linguistic philosophy', including Wittgenstein ('Components of the National Culture', in R. Blackburn and A. Cockburn (eds), *Student Power: Problems, Diagnosis, Action*, Harmondsworth: Penguin, 1969, fn. 28, p. 280).

[4] H. Marcuse, *One-Dimensional Man: Studies in the Ideology of Advanced Industrial Society*, 2nd edition, New York: Routledge & Kegal Paul, 1991 [1964].

[5] See, e.g. Kitching and Pleasants, *Marx and Wittgenstein*; A. Badiou, *Wittgenstein's Antiphilosophy*, London: Verso, 2011; and P. Karczmarczyk, 'Althusser and Wittgenstein: Ideology and Therapeutical Analysis of Language', *Rethinking Marxism*, vol. 25, no. 4, 2013, pp. 534–48.

[6] There is not a huge literature on the relationship between Marxist philosophy and Wittgensteinian philosophy but in addition to the books mentioned in the last footnote we could add Susan Easton's *Humanist Marxism and Wittgensteinian Social Philosophy*, Manchester: Manchester University Press, 1983; and David Rubinstein's *Marx and Wittgenstein*, London: Routledge, 1981, and there has recently been a bit of a revival of interest in the relationship(s) between the two philosophers. For example, Dimitris Gakis has published several articles about the relationships between Marxist and Wittgensteinian philosophy (including 'Wittgenstein, Marx, and Marxism: Some Historical Connections', *Humanities*, vol. 4, 2015, pp. 924–37; and 'The Political Import of Wittgenstein's *Philosophical Investigations*', *Philosophy and Social Criticism*, vol. 44, no. 3, 2018, pp. 229–52). Terry Eagleton, whose work will be discussed in the next chapter, has recently published a book about materialism (*Materialism*, New Haven, CT: Yale University Press, 2017) in which he discusses the relationship between Marxism and Wittgensteinian philosophy.

[7] Both are academics. Anderson is Professor of Sociology and History at UCLA and Callinicos is Professor of European Studies at King's College, London.

was, for a long time, editor of the *New Left Review* and regularly writes for other publications, including the *London Review of Books*. Alex Callinicos is an active socialist, editor of the *International Socialism Journal*, and he regularly writes for *Socialist Worker*. Second, the essay of Anderson's that I will focus on, 'Components of the National Culture', has been reprinted numerous times[8] and neither he nor Callinicos has since published anything which indicates a serious switch in attitude towards Wittgenstein.[9] I take it that Anderson and Callinicos are representative of Marxist philosophers more generally in either ignoring or misrepresenting the work of Wittgenstein.[10] Finally, although Marxists like Anderson and Callinicos have ignored or misrepresented Wittgenstein's work they have not ignored philosophy altogether. Marxists have often discussed issues such as the relationship between philosophy and other disciplines as well as epistemological issues and questions about theory.

---

[8] E.g. it has reappeared in P. Anderson, *English Questions*, London: Verso, 1992; A. Milner (ed.), *Postwar British Critical Thought*, vol. 2, London: Sage, 2004.

[9] Wittgenstein is mentioned a few times in Anderson's *The Origins of Postmodernity*, first as an influence upon Lyotard and second in connection with Habermas's critique of postmodernism. Anderson claims that Wittgenstein's notion of 'incommensurable language games' is incoherent and that this incoherence has often been noted (p. 26). Lyotard compounds Wittgenstein's errors, according to Anderson. However, it is worth noting that when Wittgenstein discusses different language games he never makes the claim that they are incommensurable (although they are clearly quite different kinds of uses of language that cannot obviously be 'translated' into one another). It is hard to see how his notion might be thought to be problematic. Wittgenstein uses it to emphasize the fact that spoken language and activities are interwoven and gives 'giving orders, and obeying them, describing the appearance of an object, constructing an object from a drawing, reporting an event, speculating about an event' as examples of language games (§23, *Philosophical Investigations*). Does Anderson want to argue that 'giving orders, and obeying them' is commensurable with 'speculating about an event'? It is, of course, true that there have been debates about issues concerning commensurability in connection with Wittgenstein's work, concerning the commensurability of languages or of theories, but Anderson cannot just brush those issues away as if they are already settled in favour of Wittgenstein's opponents. In connection with Habermas, Anderson argues that Habermas was wrong to castigate Wittgenstein's progeny as postmodernists since many of them are fierce critics of postmodernism – and it is undoubtedly true that Wittgensteinians have been critical of postmodernism (see, e.g. Glock, *What Is Analytic Philosophy?*, pp. 201, 231–61).

[10] A quick search through the archives of *New Left Review* and *International Socialism Journal* revealed that neither journal had acknowledged Wittgenstein's contribution to philosophy. The only article besides Anderson's one on British culture in the *New Left Review* was one that discussed Wittgenstein's attitudes towards Russia and not his specifically philosophical work (J. Moran, 'Wittgenstein and Russia', *New Left Review*, vol. I/73, May–June 1972, pp. 85–96).

It may be tempting to say that the reason Marxists have ignored Wittgenstein is that he has little to say about advancing the class struggle. While that is true I think that Marxists stand to gain a better understanding of philosophy[11] through looking at the work of Wittgenstein.

5.2 Anderson's Account of Wittgenstein

In the wake of the student revolts of the late 1960s a collection of essays, entitled *Student Power*,[12] was published. It contained work by a group of young Marxist intellectuals including one by the editor of the *New Left Review*, Perry Anderson.[13] His essay was an ambitious attempt to give a complete overview of British culture since 1914. The aim was to contribute to a revolutionary culture which would facilitate the emergence of effective class struggle in Britain.

One of the central claims made was that after the First World War Britain's culture was heavily influenced by a wave of immigrants who were fleeing revolution and violence elsewhere in continental Europe. These new immigrants were deeply opposed to revolutionary change and so Anderson characterizes this group entering Britain as 'the white emigration'. The group included Karl Popper, Isaiah Berlin, Ernst Gombrich, Bronislaw Malinowski, and Ludwig Wittgenstein.[14]

In his survey of British culture after 1914 Anderson's section on philosophy focuses on Wittgenstein. The Austrian immigrant is portrayed as a philosopher who fits neatly into the category mentioned above. According to Anderson, Wittgenstein was a 'white', a cultural conservative, and his work was dedicated to undermining the kind of theoretical work that sociologists and Marxists engage in. Wittgenstein dismissed 'general ideas', 'by undermining their status as intelligible discourse altogether'.[15]

---

[11] As I suggested at the outset, I think that the word 'philosophy' can be used to refer to a variety of subject matters and activities, so it is worth making a point of clarification here about what it is that Marxists could gain a better understanding of. I think that Marxists could first gain a better understanding of philosophy as it is done by Wittgenstein by looking at the work of Wittgenstein. That is, they can get a feel for the kind of *elucidatory* philosophy that Wittgenstein and Wittgensteinians engage in. But I think that they also stand to gain a better understanding of other philosopher's work via a better understanding of elucidatory philosophy. Understanding Wittgenstein's work would help Marxists (and others) to better understand the nature of *traditional* philosophical problems and could also help Marxists to produce better *Marxist/emancipatory* philosophy.
[12] Blackburn and Cockburn, *Student Power*.
[13] Anderson, 'Components of the National Culture'.
[14] Ibid., pp. 229–30.
[15] Ibid., p. 232.

The account of Wittgenstein's philosophy continues by characterizing Wittgenstein as an unsystematic empiricist who wanted to simply produce an inventory of things as they are.[16] Wittgenstein was also concerned with concepts, and his aim with regard to concepts was similarly conservative and antitheoretical. According to Anderson, Wittgenstein's view was that 'the meaning of a concept was its conventional use, and the true philosopher was the guardian of conventions'.[17] So, the philosopher's job is to register how things are, both empirically and conceptually, and to try to preserve things as they are.

Anderson describes Wittgenstein as a 'brilliant originator' and yet claims that Wittgenstein's principal achievement was 'to consecrate the banalities of everyday language'.[18] The reason for which the philosopher would want to raise the standing of everyday language against technical philosophical language is not made clear. Nor is it made clear what the philosopher or anybody else is supposed to gain by registering and preserving concepts.

The only quote from Wittgenstein in Anderson's article is from the *Philosophical Investigations*, §124, which concerns the remit of philosophy:

> Philosophy may in no way interfere with the actual use of language; it can in the end only describe it.
>
> For it cannot give it any foundation either.
>
> It leaves everything as it is.[19]

Anderson takes this quote to imply that Wittgenstein opposed change in society and any kind of intellectual innovation.[20]

So, he concludes that Wittgenstein was essentially a conservative, a conformist, and a defender of ruling-class ideology. Even if Wittgenstein had not intended to defend ruling-class ideology, the effect of ordinary-language-worship and defence of common sense is to reinforce ruling-class ideology,

---

[16] Ibid., p. 233.
[17] Ibid., p. 235.
[18] Ibid., p. 236.
[19] L. Wittgenstein, *Philosophical Investigations*, trans. G. E. M. Anscombe, Oxford: Basil Blackwell, 1953.
[20] Anderson, 'Components of the National Culture', p. 236. Incidentally other philosophers have taken this passage to imply that Wittgenstein was politically conservative. For example, H. C. McCauley says that 'it is difficult to see how [...] Wittgenstein could be rescued in a manner capable of enabling his thought to underpin a political philosophy other than conservatism' (in 'Wittgenstein: Philosophy and Political Thought', *The Maynooth Review*, vol. 2, no. 2, November 1976, p. 20).

because 'common sense is the practical wisdom of the ruling class'.[21] Followers of Wittgenstein have naively produced a 'blanket endorsement of the categories of the ongoing society'[22] rather than engaging in a class-conscious, engaged criticism of bourgeois ideology.

Given that Wittgenstein was a great and original thinker why would he and his followers make such naive errors? Anderson gives two explanations. The first is that Wittgenstein was a rich emigrant from continental Europe fleeing from chaos there and so wanted to have a quiet life upon his arrival in England. This explains his tendency towards conservative thought. The second explanation is in terms of Wittgenstein's ignorance. His ignorance of history explains a philosophy of language, which 'presupposes an unchanging corpus of concepts' and the tendency towards an ahistorical and conservative philosophy is reinforced by him lacking 'any notion of contradiction'.[23] Presumably, Wittgenstein's alleged failure could have been avoided if he had read Hegel and Marx and had formulated a dialectical materialist account of linguistic change.[24]

5.3 Problems with Anderson's Account

5.3.1 *Wittgenstein and 'General Ideas'*

One of Anderson's objections to Wittgenstein was that Wittgenstein tried to rule out 'general ideas' as being unintelligible. While it is true that Wittgenstein was very much concerned with intelligibility – with what it makes sense to say – it is not true that Wittgenstein ruled out generalizations or theoretical claims as unintelligible. The claims that 'most people like a good sit down after a long walk' or that 'the dinosaurs died out as a result of a meteor strike' are meaningful and intelligible, although they are not the kinds of claims that concerned Wittgenstein in his philosophical work. Wittgenstein was not concerned with empirical claims as Anderson maintained. He certainly did

---

[21] Anderson, 'Components of the National Culture', p. 237.
[22] Ibid.
[23] Ibid., p. 238.
[24] Incidentally, according to Ray Monk's biography of Wittgenstein he was, to some extent, familiar with Hegel's philosophy. He had read an account of Hegel's dialectical method in C. D. Broad's taxonomy of philosophical styles and said that he preferred Hegel's method to Descartes' ('the dialectical method is very sound and a way in which we do work') (see *Ludwig Wittgenstein: The Duty of Genius*, London: Vintage, 1991, p. 322) and in a conversation with Maurice Drury Wittgenstein said of Hegel: 'Hegel seems to me to be always wanting to say things which look different are really the same. Whereas my interest is in showing that things which look the same are really different' (*Ludwig Wittgenstein*, pp. 536–37).

not want to produce a detailed inventory of things as they are. Philosophy is not an empirical discipline at all, in Wittgenstein's view.[25]

What Wittgenstein *did* want to rule out was theorizing *in philosophy*. Philosophers are engaged in the activity of 'assembling reminders' to dispel conceptual confusions that lead to distinctively philosophical problems.[26] Conceptual problems can be resolved or dissolved in a piecemeal manner as they arise. There is no need for theory in philosophy. In fact, theory is entirely out of place in philosophy, as conceived by Wittgenstein. So, the apparent tension identified by Anderson between theoretical Marxism and anti-theoretical claims made by Wittgenstein dissolves once one recognizes that Wittgenstein was engaged in a quite different sort of task to that engaged in by Marxists. Wittgenstein's elucidatory philosophy does not obviously conflict with Marx's emancipatory philosophy.

There are, however, some genuine tensions between Wittgenstein's philosophy and the claims of some Marxist philosophers. Wittgenstein was opposed to scientism and thought that one source of philosophical confusion was the attempt to construct theories on the model of the sciences where such theories could not be constructed. Wittgenstein also rejected the idea of the unity of the sciences. He did not think, for example, that psychological states were reducible to physical states.[27] To the extent that Marxists accept these approaches/views they are in tension with Wittgenstein's approach. For example, in 'Dialectical Materialism and Science' Leon Trotsky claims that 'materialist psychology has no need of a mystic force – soul – to explain phenomena in its field, but finds them reducible in the final analysis to physiological phenomena' and he connects this with the unity of the sciences. He says that if sociology and psychology were not reducible to 'mechanical properties of elementary particles of matter' then there 'cannot be a finished philosophy linking all phenomena into a single system'.[28]

---

[25] Philosophical problems 'are, of course, not empirical problems; but they are solved through an insight into the workings of our language, and that in such a way that these workings are recognized – despite an urge to misunderstand them. The problems are solved not by coming up with new discoveries, but by assembling what we have long been familiar with.' Wittgenstein, *Philosophical Investigations*, §109.

[26] Wittgenstein, *Philosophical Investigations*, §127.

[27] There is an excellent new collection of essays on Wittgenstein and scientism edited by Jonathan Beale and Ian James Kidd (*Wittgenstein and Scientism*, London: Routledge, 2017).

[28] See http://www.marxists.org/archive/trotsky/1925/09/science.htm; and J. Rees, *The Algebra of Revolution*, London: Routledge, 1998, pp. 276–77. Incidentally, I don't think that there is anything essentially Marxist about defending the idea that sociology and psychology are reducible to physiology or about defending the 'thesis' of the unity of the sciences. The central insights of Marxism can be retained while shedding these elements.

In the *Blue Book* Wittgenstein lists a series of tendencies under the heading of the 'craving for generality' which he says result in philosophical (conceptual) confusion. In addition to the tendency towards scientism ('our preoccupation with the method of science'[29]) Wittgenstein lists other tendencies which he connects to conceptual or philosophical confusions including 'the tendency to look for something in common to all the entities we commonly subsume under a general term'.[30] To the extent that Marxists rule out the possibility of any kind of philosophy that is not theoretical or scientific they are in tension with Wittgensteinian philosophers. Trotsky claims that philosophy 'systematises the generalised conclusions of all sciences'[31] and so it seems that he, at least, failed to recognize the possibility of the kind of philosophy that Wittgenstein and philosophers since him have practiced. As for Anderson, Wittgenstein may well have accused him of having a 'contemptuous attitude towards the particular case'.[32]

5.3.2 *Wittgenstein and the Banal/Common Sense*

Anderson reveals his confusion about Wittgenstein's method when he says that his principal achievement was to 'to consecrate the banalities of everyday language' and accuses him of naively endorsing common-sense views. While it is true that Wittgenstein despised the kind of technical philosophical work found in journals like *Mind*, Wittgenstein's point was not that the same things could be said more clearly in non-technical language or that what people ordinarily said about the issues in question was correct. Wittgenstein thought that previous philosophers' conception of their task was entirely misconceived.

The philosophers' job is not to provide a metaphysical grounding for other regions of thought. Philosophers should not be trying to work out the relation between mind and body. Philosophers working on epistemological problems should not be trying to discover the necessary and sufficient conditions for knowledge and nor should they be trying to provide foundations for knowledge in the face of scepticism. The philosophers' task is not to provide proofs of the existence of God and nor is it their task to try to demonstrate that science has left no room for God. Wittgenstein's originality lay in

---

[29] Wittgenstein, *Blue Book*, p. 18.
[30] Ibid., p. 17.
[31] http://www.marxists.org/archive/trotsky/1925/09/science.htm – Again, I don't think that Marxists have anything to lose in acknowledging the kind of activities that Wittgenstein and his followers have engaged in as legitimate.
[32] Wittgenstein, *Blue Book*, pp. 17–18.

his recognition that these problems were 'pseudo-problems' of a particular sort: the problems would disappear or dissolve once it was recognized that the vexation surrounding them resulted from conceptual confusion rather than from the fact that they were particularly difficult or profound (metaphysical/ epistemological) problems.

A way to dissolve some of these problems is to look at the way that concepts involved in the formulation of the problems are ordinarily used when they are used correctly.[33] Again, Wittgenstein's task here is not an empirical one. He did not want to survey the general population and find out how they ordinarily spoke about such issues – and ordinary *misuses* of concepts could not be used to help solve or dissolve philosophical problems. His point was that we should look at the way certain concepts are used when they are used correctly and that this would reveal that the way that the concepts had been employed in the formulation of the problem were illegitimate.[34]

For example, if we look at the way that the word 'mind' is used (correctly) we can see that it is used in sentences such as 'John couldn't come to the pub this evening because he has got a lot on his mind', 'Sandra was in two minds about taking the philosophy course', and 'that man has got a dirty mind'. In the first case it is clear that we are not committing ourselves to the existence of something that has got a lot of other things on it (like a table that has got a lot of newspapers on it). In the second case it is clear that Sandra is not *in* two things (like the keys that are in a drawer in the front room) and in the third case we are not committing ourselves to the existence of something dirty, other than the man in question. To help make it clearer that when we use the word 'mind' we are not talking about a thing/substance one can rephrase the sentences above so that they do not include the word 'mind'. So, you can say that '*John* is preoccupied with a lot of things and so couldn't come to the pub', '*Sandra* could not decide whether to take the philosophy course or not', and '*that man* is dirty'. Given that in each case the only thing we are speaking of is the person we can come to recognize that use of the term 'mind' is just a convenient way of talking about a person/people and their faculties. Once we have recognized this then we can see that questions like 'what is the mind?' and 'what is the relationship between mind and body?' are at best misleading

---

[33] This is one of several methods used by Wittgenstein. (*PI* §133d, 'There is not a single philosophical method, though there are indeed methods, different therapies, as it were.')

[34] Constantine Sandis makes the distinction between ordinary people's intuitions about linguistic usage (as used by experimental philosophers) and the description of norms found in Wittgenstein very neatly in his paper 'The Experimental Turn and Ordinary Language', *Essays in Philosophy*, vol. 11, no. 2, article 5, pp. 181–96.

and at worst nonsensical, because the mind is not a kind of thing and so is not a kind of thing that might be related to something else.[35]

Wittgenstein didn't want to consecrate ordinary language, although he did think that philosophical confusion could result from venerating 'technical' uses of terms. Given that we can only understand words when they are used in accordance with certain linguistic norms any new use of a familiar word in a different context must be explained. Recent Wittgenstein scholars, for example, have argued that we should not be so overly impressed with neuroscientists that we accept their claims to be using expressions like 'consciousness', 'perception', and 'sensation' in a technical way, when in fact what they are doing (sometimes) is misusing them and creating confusion.[36]

Anderson is also wrong to accuse Wittgenstein of being a 'common-sense' philosopher. In fact, Wittgenstein explicitly disavowed common-sense approaches to philosophy in his lectures and we have no good reason not to take him at his word. Wittgenstein said that 'you must not try to avoid a philosophical problem by appealing to common sense; instead, present it as it arises with most power [...] the common-sense answer in itself is no solution; everyone knows it. One must not in philosophy attempt to short-circuit problems.'[37] In his remarks on epistemological problems, which have been published as *On Certainty*, Wittgenstein attacked G. E. Moore's attempt to use the claims of common sense to undermine scepticism. Instead, Wittgenstein carefully described the use of expressions such as 'knowledge', 'certainty', and 'doubt', with the aim of dissolving the problems.

It is worth noting here that this absolves Wittgenstein of the accusation that he naively accepted ruling-class ideology. Wittgenstein's did not endorse ruling-class ideology in his philosophical work any more than he endorsed any other ideology in it. His work was not concerned with whether the deliverances of common sense support one or another ideology but with particular conceptual problems that have arisen in the history of philosophy.[38]

It is also worth noting, with regard to the question of whether he naively accepted ruling-class ideology, that Wittgenstein took an interest in Soviet Russia and was attracted to the idea of living and working there from about

---

[35] This discussion is derived from Max Bennett and Peter Hacker's discussion of the concept 'mind' in *Philosophical Foundations of Neuroscience*, Oxford: Blackwell, 2003, pp. 104–6.

[36] See Bennett and Hacker, *Philosophical Foundations of Neuroscience*, pp. 74–81.

[37] Alice Ambrose (ed.), *Wittgenstein's Lectures, Cambridge 1932–35*, from the Notes of Alice Ambrose and Margaret Macdonald, Oxford: Blackwell, 1979, p. 109.

[38] It is also worth noting that Wittgenstein did not just examine 'ordinary language' as opposed to technical language. For example, Wittgenstein discusses the theory of Dedekind's cut in *Remarks on the Foundations of Mathematics*, Oxford: Blackwell, 2001 [1956], IV, pp. 29–40.

1922 onwards. According to John Maynard Keynes Wittgenstein was among those who 'seek for something good in Soviet Russia'.[39] In the 1930s a friend of Wittgenstein's, George Thomson, said that Wittgenstein's political awareness was growing and that 'he was alive to the evils of unemployment and fascism and the growing danger of war'. According to Thomson Wittgenstein's attitude towards Marxism was that 'he was opposed to it in theory, but supported it in practice'. As Ray Monk points out in his biography of Wittgenstein, this accords with Wittgenstein's own claim that 'I am a communist, *at heart*' and with the fact that Wittgenstein's friends included the Marxist Piero Sraffa, among others.[40] Wittgenstein held Sraffa's opinion in the highest regard when it came to political matters. Wittgenstein remained sympathetic towards Soviet Russia in the 1930s and said that 'if anything could destroy my sympathy with the Russian regime it would be the growth of class distinctions'.[41] While this isn't clear evidence that Wittgenstein was a Marxist – I don't think that he was – it at least strongly suggests that Wittgenstein did not lap up the 'ruling ideas' in Britain at the time unquestioningly.

5.3.3 *Registering/Preserving Concepts*

Anderson asserts that Wittgenstein thought that one of the philosophers' tasks was to produce a catalogue of concepts as they stand and to keep concepts that way. A problem with Wittgenstein's theory of language, as Anderson saw it, was that it 'presupposes an unchanging corpus of concepts'. It is not clear where Anderson has gained this impression of Wittgenstein's views about the duties of the philosopher from but, as mentioned earlier, he cites *Philosophical Investigations* §124 in support of his account and so perhaps Anderson's interpretation is a result of misreading this passage.

A first problem to note with Anderson's account is that Wittgenstein did not propound a theory of language and so his 'theory' cannot have presupposed anything. Anderson himself criticizes Wittgenstein for failing to generate 'general ideas' in the way that philosophers of the past did (see the discussion of general ideas above). The second problem is that Wittgenstein *did* recognize that conceptual change occurred and in fact Wittgenstein can be credited with giving a very sophisticated account of conceptual change. For example, in *Philosophical Investigations* §23 Wittgenstein says that 'this diversity [of sentences] is not something fixed, given once for all; but new types of language, new language-games, as we may say, come into existence, and others become

---

[39] See Monk, *Ludwig Wittgenstein*, p. 248.
[40] Ibid., p. 343.
[41] Ibid., p. 353.

obsolete and get forgotten'.[42] In *On Certainty* §65 he says that 'when language-games change, then there is a change in concepts, and with the concepts the meanings of words change'. In talking about 'hinge propositions' (*OC* §96) Wittgenstein says, 'It might be imagined that some propositions, of the form of empirical propositions, were hardened and functioned as channels for such empirical propositions as were not hardened but fluid; and that this relation altered with time.' Nowhere in *On Certainty*, or anywhere else, does Wittgenstein say that conceptual change is a bad thing or that it should be prevented.

Third, it is worth looking again at §124 to see that it gives no support to Anderson's account:

> Philosophy may in no way interfere with the actual use of language; it can in the end only describe it.
>
> For it cannot give it any foundation either.
>
> It leaves everything as it is.[43]

This passage does not say, or imply, that the uses of expressions will not change or that they should not change. Wittgenstein's point is that the philosopher's task is not to come up with new concepts but to examine the uses of the concepts which are causing confusions in philosophical problems.[44] It is also worth noting that Wittgenstein is talking here about what *philosophy* may or may not do. Wittgenstein was not opposed to scientists (or anybody else) formulating new concepts, as long as those concepts played a role in the persons' work or life.[45]

Finally, it is worth noting that endorsing a set of concepts (whatever that might amount to) is not the same thing as endorsing an ideology. Ideological convictions of various sorts can be expressed in a language but the language

---

[42] Wittgenstein, *Philosophical Investigations*.

[43] Ibid.

[44] This is not the only task of philosophers, in Wittgenstein's view. Wittgenstein thought that there was a variety of different kinds of philosophical problems and proposed a variety of methods in dissolving them. See *PI* §133d, 'There is not a single philosophical method, though there are indeed methods, different therapies, as it were.'

[45] However, scientists have a habit of misusing ordinary concepts without giving them a clear new technical use and they can generate conceptual confusion in doing so. The Wittgensteinian philosopher Peter Hacker and the neuroscientist Max Bennett give an excellent account of philosophical confusions in neuroscience in their *Philosophical Foundations of Neuroscience*. Wittgenstein himself postulated new concepts and provided technical definitions of terms that have an ordinary use, e.g. 'language games', 'family resemblances', 'nonsense', 'forms of life', but did not vacillate between ordinary and technical uses or fail to explain these new terms in a way that would generate philosophical confusions.

itself is not an ideology. It is fair to say that people might try to redefine terms with ideological goals in mind (e.g. the ruling class might try to define class in cultural terms as a way of preventing people from identifying themselves with people with common economic interests) – but one can recognize this without coming into conflict with Wittgenstein's conception of conceptual change.

5.4 Callinicos

Alex Callinicos, in his book *Marxism and Philosophy*,[46] makes a noble attempt to engage with the analytic tradition in philosophy from a Marxist perspective. He describes Anderson's treatment of Wittgenstein as 'grossly unfair'.[47] However, Callinicos does not make it clear exactly how he thinks Anderson's treatment of Wittgenstein misrepresented Wittgenstein and he repeats many of the same criticisms of Wittgenstein that Anderson made. For example, Callinicos describes mainstream Anglo-Saxon philosophy, with Wittgenstein presumably included, as 'bourgeois thought', and says that 'many of the charges made by Anderson and others against mainstream Anglo-Saxon philosophy can be justified' and he mentions Frege and Wittgenstein as exemplars of this tradition.[48] Like Anderson, Callinicos objects to anti-theoretical aspects of Wittgenstein's work,[49] claims that analytic philosophy (presumably including Wittgenstein) ignores history,[50] suggests that analytic philosophers generally fail to consider conceptual change,[51] and objects to the 'apologetic cult of common sense'[52] found among ordinary language philosophers (inspired by Wittgenstein).

Callinicos criticizes the idea that philosophical views can be dissolved through analysis of ordinary language by saying that 'every major scientific discovery – those of Copernicus, Galileo, Newton, Marx, Darwin, Freud and Einstein in particular – involved a challenge to common sense. Our everyday beliefs are in part the product of these breakthroughs; to make them the benchmark by which to judge new theories would be to place a halter on scientific progress.'

It has already been pointed out that Wittgenstein was opposed to the idea that philosophers could simply cite common sense as a means of disposing of philosophical problems. It should also be clear that Wittgenstein acknowledged conceptual change. In particular, Wittgenstein was well aware

---

[46] A. Callinicos, *Marxism and Philosophy*, Oxford: Oxford University Press, 1985.
[47] Ibid., p. 4.
[48] Ibid., pp. 6–7.
[49] Ibid., p. 141.
[50] Ibid., p. 148.
[51] Ibid., p. 149.
[52] Ibid., pp. 149–50.

of conceptual innovation in the sciences. Wittgenstein thought carefully about the new terminology introduced by Freud and Wittgenstein's philosophy was influenced by the conceptual innovator and scientist Heinrich Hertz. It should also be clear from what has been said before about Wittgenstein's methods that he did not think that philosophy involved cataloguing our everyday beliefs and did not claim that our everyday beliefs should be the benchmark against which we judge scientific theories. Finally, it is also worth making the point that Wittgenstein did not engage in analysis of ordinary language but in the clarification or elucidation of the uses of ordinary language.[53]

Far from placing a halter on scientific progress Wittgenstein's philosophical methods provide a means for getting rid of conceptual confusions which get in the way of it. Misconceived experiments involving conceptual confusions can prove to be a waste of time for scientists. For example, in the *Philosophical Investigations* Wittgenstein remarks that 'only of a living human being and what resembles (behaves like) a living human being can one say: it has sensations; it sees; is blind; hears; is deaf; is conscious or unconscious'.[54] An implication of this is that parts of human beings that do not resemble human beings, such as their brains, cannot be said to be conscious, to think, to perceive, or to decide. This is a matter of what makes sense and not an empirical matter. However, many scientists have succumbed to the temptation to commit what has been called the 'mereological fallacy',[55] the fallacy of ascribing psychological predicates to parts of human beings – in particular, their brains.

A famous incidence of this is Benjamin Libet's claim that the brain of a person decides to act before the person acts. This, nonsensical, claim has been taken as the basis for further scientific experimentation and has even been cited by philosophers as evidence that freedom of choice is an illusion.[56] Jeff Miller and Judy Travena take themselves to have demonstrated that Benjamin Libet's conclusion, that voluntary movements are initiated unconsciously, is false.[57] They take themselves to have undermined his work by conducting

---

[53] Constantine Sandis reminded me of this point.

[54] Wittgenstein, *Philosophical Investigations*, §281.

[55] Bennett, and Hacker, *Philosophical Foundations of Neuroscience*, pp. 68–107.

[56] E.g. the Marxist philosopher Slavoj Žižek says that 'even though brain scientists point out that freedom of choice is an illusion – we experience ourselves as free [...] Recent research has already moved much further than Benjamin Libet's classic experiment from the 1980s, which demonstrated that our brain makes a decision around three tenths of a second before the brain's owner becomes aware of it' (in S. Žižek, *First as Tragedy Then as Farce*, London: Verso, 2009).

[57] J. Travena and J. Miller, 'Brain Preparation before a Voluntary Action: Evidence against Unconscious Movement Initiation', *Consciousness and Cognition*, vol. 19, no. 1, March 2010, pp. 447–56.

empirical experiments themselves. However, a grammatical or conceptual error cannot be undone by scientific experiment and moreover their own conclusion, that 'electrophysical signs' only indicate that the brain is paying attention and not that a decision has been made, commits the same grammatical error that Libet himself committed (i.e. the mereological fallacy). It is people who pay attention to things, not brains (this is a grammatical observation and not an empirical one), and so a brain can no more pay attention than it can make decisions.

Callinicos objects to anti-theoretical elements in Wittgenstein's thought in a slightly different way to Anderson. Callinicos attacks Wittgenstein's remarks about meaning and use as a way of defending the notion that we can and should develop a theory of language. Callinicos suggests that some Marxists might raise objections to the very idea of a systematic theory of meaning, taking Wittgenstein's 'slogan' 'the meaning of a word is its use in the language'[58] to imply that 'words and sentences acquire a meaning only in the specific context of their use'.[59] Callinicos takes it that this objection to developing a theory of language has been dealt with decisively by Michael Dummett in his book *Truth and Other Enigmas* where he says,

> The fact that anyone who has a mastery of any given language is able to understand an infinity of sentences, an infinity which is, of course, principally composed of sentences which he has never heard before [...] can hardly be explained otherwise than by supposing that each speaker has an implicit grasp of a number of general principles governing the use in sentences of words of the language [...] It is hard to see how there can be any theoretical obstacle to making those principles explicit; and an explicit statement of those principles an implicit grasp of which constitutes mastery of the language would be, precisely, a complete theory of meaning for the language.[60]

So, Callinicos thinks that we should develop a theory of language and he thinks that an important aspect of language to acknowledge in developing such a theory would be Frege's distinction between the sense of a sentence and its force. The thought expressed by a sentence is its sense. But we can express thoughts without asserting them or judging that they are the case. We should distinguish the thought expressed from the force with which a sentence is uttered, that is, whether we *assert* the thought, *judge* the thought to be

---

[58] Wittgenstein, *Philosophical Investigations*, §43.
[59] Callinicos, *Marxism and Philosophy*, p. 141.
[60] M. Dummett, *Truth and Other Enigmas*, London: Duckworth, 1978, p. 451.

true, issue an *imperative* involving the thought, or ask a question involving the thought (utter it with *interrogative* force).

However, there are several problems with Callinicos's and Dummett's arguments here. One thing to note initially is that it is a misconstrual of Wittgenstein's remark to describe it as a slogan. The remark quoted by Callinicos is part of a longer passage where Wittgenstein says that in a 'large class of cases [...] though not all' 'meaning' can be explained by saying that 'the meaning of a word is its use in the language'.[61] The passage is meant as an explanation of meaning of the word 'meaning', and so it is meant as a grammatical claim, a claim about the grammar of the word 'meaning'. It is a description of the grammar of an expression – 'meaning' – and so not a slogan. The second thing to note is that what is said in §43 does not imply that 'words and sentences acquire a meaning only in the specific context of their use'. As just noted, Wittgenstein is clear that there are cases where 'meaning' cannot be explained in terms of use ('large class of cases [...] though *not all*') and it is also not clear that even in the cases where the meaning of a word *is* its use that this means 'use on a particular occasion'.[62]

It might be thought that the argument against Callinicos thus far only adds to his case because it dismantles the argument against the possibility of a theory of language that he raises. The argument in *favour* of a theory of language is in the passage Callinicos cites from Dummett. However, Dummett's argument does not establish the conclusion that Callinicos wants. A statement of the 'general principles governing the use in sentences of words of the language' (the rules of language) is no more a theory than a statement of the rules of chess is a theory of chess. It might aid our understanding to be presented with a list of rules but a list of rules does not constitute a theory. It might be objected that the rules of a single game, chess, are not analogous to the rules of a language but to the rules of a language game (or a region/segment of language). However, adding the rules of more games would not make the product any more theoretical. A statement of the rules of all existing games would not be a theory of games and similarly a statement of the rules of all language games would not be a theory of language. Callinicos's and Dummett's confusion here is an example of more general confusion in philosophy about

---

[61] Wittgenstein, *Philosophical Investigations*, 4th edition, §43.
[62] There are some excellent discussions of meaning and use in *The Later Wittgenstein on Language*, edited by Daniel Whiting. Whiting's own introduction contains a sharp discussion of meaning and use and the first two essays in the collection are also focused on this issue (see D. Whiting 'Introduction'; P. Horwich, 'Wittgenstein's Definition of Meaning as Use'; and P. M. S. Hacker, 'Meaning and Use', in D. Whiting (ed.), *The Later Wittgenstein on Language*, Basingstoke: Palgrave MacMillan, 2010).

the difference between grammatical or conceptual investigations on the one hand and theoretical or empirical investigations on the other.

Moreover, it is unfortunate that Callinicos does not consider Wittgenstein's remarks in response to Frege, since they undermine the claim that his distinction between sense and force might form a significant part of a theory of language. In §22 of Wittgenstein's *Philosophical Investigations*, for example, he says,

> Frege's opinion that every assertion contains an assumption, which is the thing that is asserted, really rests on the possibility, found in our language, of writing every assertoric sentence in the form 'It is asserted that such-and-such is the case'. – But 'that such-and-such is the case' is *not* a sentence in our language – it is not yet a *move* in the language-game. And if I write, not 'It is asserted that [...]' but 'It is asserted: such-and-such is the case', the words 'It is asserted' simply become superfluous.
>
> We might very well also write every assertion in the form of a question followed by an affirmative expression; for instance 'Is it raining? – Yes!' Would this show that every assertion contained a question?[63]

So, Callinicos, employing an argument from Dummett, has not established that a theory of language is possible or desirable. If what we are after is an account of what language *is* then what we want is not a theory but a clarification of the meaning of expressions such as 'language', 'meaning', and 'proposition' and this is something that Wittgenstein in the *Philosophical Investigations* offers.[64] In asking what language is we are asking what 'language' means and we should not expect an answer which specifies an essential feature of language. This grasping after essences is something that has led philosophers astray on all kinds of questions. As Wittgenstein says, 'When philosophers use a word – "knowledge", "being", "object", "I", "proposition/sentence", "name" [and we could add 'language'] – and try to grasp the *essence* of the thing: one must always ask oneself: is the word ever actually used in this way in the language in which it is at home? – What *we* do is to bring words back from their metaphysical to their everyday use.'[65] Callinicos, as a Marxist sensitive to the changing nature of language, should appreciate that a theory of sense

---

[63] Wittgenstein, *Philosophical Investigations*, 4th edition, §22.
[64] See, e.g. §§65–66 of the *Philosophical Investigations* and many of the passages leading up to them. Wittgenstein also asks the question 'what is the meaning of a word?' at the beginning of *The Blue Book* (L. Wittgenstein, *The Blue and Brown Books*, Oxford: Basil Blackwell, 1958, pp. 1–5).
[65] Wittgenstein *Philosophical Investigations*, 4th edition, §116.

and force along Fregean lines would struggle to get to grips with the open-endedness and ever-changing diversity of language. Words and sentences are comparable to *tools* and new tasks, new activities, call for new tools, or adaptation of tools to those new activities.[66]

5.5 What Do Marxists Stand to Gain from a Better Understanding of Wittgenstein?

I hope that in the foregoing discussion I have demonstrated that Marxists should not be put off reading Wittgenstein by accusations that he is a naive supporter of ruling-class ideology. The criticisms made of Wittgenstein by Anderson and Callinicos reveal some confusion from them about what Wittgenstein's philosophy involved and what it might hope to achieve.

In terms of what Marxists could gain from an appreciation of Wittgenstein's philosophy, I think that they could gain what everyone else stands to gain, namely a clearer picture of the nature of the problems handed down to us by traditional philosophers such as Descartes, Hume, and Kant, and a sense of how problems that are the upshot of conceptual confusions might be dissolved.[67] Dissolving conceptual confusions is not just a matter of playing around with words but has practical consequences for scientists devising experiments and for those who want to understand human action (including Marxists).

In *Marxism and Philosophy* Callinicos welcomes the move away from 'complacent lexicography' 'towards epistemological and metaphysical issues of substance'[68] that has occurred in analytic philosophy since the 1970s. He approves of attempts by analytic philosophers, such as Donald Davidson, to construct a systematic theory of meaning. With a clearer understanding of Wittgenstein Callinicos might not have been so tempted to dismiss the philosophy of the

---

[66] Ibid., §23.
[67] One reason that Wittgenstein is held in such high regard is that he had something to say about an incredible range of philosophical issues. For example, Wittgenstein makes remarks on the problem of other minds (*Blue Book*, p. 46; *Philosophical Investigations*, §253–63), the referential/Augustinian theory of meaning (*Philosophical Investigations*, §§1–64), the nature of philosophy (*Philosophical Investigations*, §§89–133), religious belief ('Lectures on Religious Belief', in *Lectures and Conversations on Aesthetics, Psychology and Religious Belief*), early modern conceptions of language and meaning (*PI* §§189–202, §§253–63), Platonism in mathematics (*Tractatus Logico-Philosophicus*, 6.2–6.241, *Remarks on the Foundations of Mathematics*, 363, 425, 431), logic (*Tractatus Logico-Philosophicus*, *RFM*, 98–99), scepticism and G. E. Moore's 'common-sense' response to it (*On Certainty*), epistemology more generally (*On Certainty*), Augustine's conception of time (*Blue Book*, p. 26), realism, solipsism, and idealism (*Blue Book*, pp. 57–59), and many more.
[68] Callinicos, *Marxism and Philosophy*, p. 5.

mid-twentieth century as 'complacent lexicography', and would be less inclined to welcome a return to philosophy of the sort that Wittgenstein had opposed.

Marxists might also be drawn to Wittgenstein because there are certain similarities between Marx and Wittgenstein. Both philosophers saw themselves as doing something which went beyond philosophy as it had been done previously. Both opposed modern philosophy (Descartes and post-Descartes) in the way that it separated mind from action. Wittgenstein's discussion of language in his later work points out internal connections between language and human behaviour and Wittgenstein emphasizes that language is embedded in various practices that human beings engage in. For Marx the problem is the detachment of moral, political, and economic theory from what is going on in the world and in particular its detachment from human activity. So, both are opposed to speculative philosophy detached from discussion of human activity, albeit for different reasons.

Wittgenstein and Marx were both sensitive to the importance of (social) context. In dissolving philosophical problems Wittgenstein often asks us to imagine the circumstances in which uttering a certain sentence would make sense.[69] He spends quite a lot of time constructing 'language games' to illustrate the variety of uses of words in certain contexts.

Marxists are sensitive to the context in which utterances are made for a variety of reasons – motivated by slightly different interests to Wittgenstein. For example, one reason that it might not be a good time to focus energies on criticizing Islam is that the situation at present is such that Muslims are being used as scapegoats in the 'war on terror'. They are experiencing unwarranted criticism from governments and the media in the United States and across Europe. Another example is the case of free speech. One reason that free speech doesn't extend to being able to say whatever you want, wherever you want, whenever you want is that there are contexts in which it is clear that you shouldn't say certain things – for example, 'Fire!' in a theatre.[70] This kind of

---

[69] E.g. *Philosophical Investigations*, §117: 'If, for example, someone says that the sentence "this is here" (saying which he points to an object in front of him) makes sense to him, then he should ask himself in what special circumstances this sentence is actually used. There it does make sense'; and *On Certainty*, §10:

'I know that there's a sick man lying here', used in an *unsuitable* situation, seems not to be nonsense but rather seems matter-of-course, only because one can fairly easily imagine a situation to fit it, and one thinks that the words 'I know that […]' are always in place where there is no doubt, and hence even where the expression of doubt would be unintelligible.

[70] Apparently this example was first used by Justice Oliver Wendell Holmes Jr. in stating his opinion in the case *Schenk v. United States* (1919) – 'The most stringent protection of free speech would not protect a man in falsely shouting "fire" in a theatre and causing a panic.'

point could be used to criticize certain liberals (i.e. those who hold that people should be able to say whatever they want whenever they want) whose political philosophy is too detached from what is going on in the world.

In conclusion then, I think that it is fair to say that Marxists stand to gain from developing an appreciation for philosophy as Wittgenstein conceived it. I also think that Wittgensteinians stand to gain something from looking beyond the dissolution of philosophical problems à la Wittgenstein towards the kind of analysis of economics, society, and politics offered by Marxists. Although there may be some genuine tensions between the two approaches there is no barrier in place stopping Marxists from taking on board arguments such as those that have been called 'the private language argument' and there is no particularly Wittgensteinian reason why Wittgensteinians shouldn't become involved in workers' struggles with the aim of creating a classless society.

Chapter 6

EAGLETON'S WITTGENSTEIN

6.1 Marx and Wittgenstein

Karl Marx is rightly regarded as one of the most important philosophers of the nineteenth century.[1] His work encouraged the growth of socialist and communist parties and inspired revolutions in the twentieth century. Marx and Engels's *Communist Manifesto* has sold more copies than *50 Shades of Grey*. In fact, the only book to have sold more copies is *the Bible*.[2] With capitalism having recently been in a deep economic crisis around the world, trust in mainstream economists is dwindling and a new generation is turning to Marx for answers. David Harvey's lectures on Marx's *Capital* are being viewed by hundreds of thousands of people via the internet and sales of the book itself are up.[3] Since Syriza's victory in the Greek election of January 2015 the 'erratic Marxist', and finance minister, Yanis Varoufakis, has become a regular feature on the news. Historians, political theorists, and philosophers who are opposed to Marx's thought cannot afford to ignore it.

Similarly, Wittgenstein is regarded by many as the greatest philosopher of the twentieth century. Bertrand Russell, writing in 1959, said that 'during the period since 1914 three philosophies have successively dominated the British philosophical world, first that of Wittgenstein's *Tractatus*, second that of the Logical Positivists, and third that of Wittgenstein's *Philosophical Investigations*'.[4] Peter Hacker, commenting on this assessment, suggests that 'Wittgenstein bestrides fifty years of twentieth century analytic philosophy somewhat as

---

[1] E.g. Victor Ferkiss, in his book *Nature, Technology and Society* (New York: New York University Press, 1993), says that 'without question, the most important political thinker in the modern world has been Karl Marx (1818–1883)' (p. 105), and Allen W. Wood describes Marx as 'one of the nineteenth century's greatest philosophers' (in *Karl Marx – Arguments of the Philosophers*, 2nd edition, Routledge: London, 2004, p. xi).

[2] S. Jeffries, 'Why Marxism Is on the Rise Again', in *The Guardian*, 4 July 2012, https://www.theguardian.com/world/2012/jul/04/the-return-of-marxism (accessed 23 July 2019).

[3] Ibid.

[4] B. Russell, *My Philosophical Development*, London: Allen and Unwin, 1959, p. 216.

Picasso bestrides fifty years of twentieth century painting'.[5] His work has influenced the course of psychology, sociology, and cultural theory as well as philosophy and it has inspired poetry, novels, and films.

However, given the enormous influence of these two thinkers it is surprising that little has been written about the commonalities in their thought or about the possibility that the two philosophies might be mutually enriching.[6] It is not that commonalities do not exist.[7] Gavin Kitching, in his introduction to a collection of essays about Marx and Wittgenstein, claims that both Wittgenstein and Marx reject the idea that language 'pictures' reality, oppose the idea that in studying society we study something essentially non-linguistic, and reject the dualisms of observer-observed and subject-object.[8] Others have pointed out that Marx and Wittgenstein both evoke natural history,[9] that they both think that philosophers need to entirely reconceive their task,[10] and that both philosophers are particularly sensitive to social context.[11]

---

[5] P. M. S. Hacker, *Wittgenstein's Place in Twentieth Century Analytic Philosophy*, Oxford: Blackwell, 1996, p. 1.

[6] There are a few notable exceptions: A. R. Manser, in his inaugural lecture at Southampton University, compared Wittgenstein and Marx and concluded that there are similarities in terms of Marx and Wittgenstein's relationships to the philosophers who have gone before them. Wittgenstein and Marx are both 'end of philosophy' philosophers (published as A. R. Manser, *The End of Philosophy: Marx and Wittgenstein*, Southampton: Camelot Press, 1973). Other books on the topic include Susan Easton's *Humanist Marxism and Wittgensteinian Social Philosophy*, Manchester: Manchester University Press, 1983; David Rubinstein's *Marx and Wittgenstein: Social Praxis and Social Explanation*, London: Routledge, 1981; and a collection of essays edited by Gavin Kitching and Nigel Pleasants – *Marx and Wittgenstein: Knowledge, Morality and Politics*, London: Routledge, 2002. Pedro Karczmarczyk has also recently suggested that there are similarities between Wittgenstein's thought and Althusser's claims about ideology (in 'Althusser and Wittgenstein: Ideology and Therapeutic Analysis of Language', *Rethinking Marxism*, vol. 25, no. 4, pp. 534–48.

[7] T. P. Uschanov has argued that one reason why Marxist philosophers and social theorists more generally have ignored or misrepresented Wittgenstein's views is the influence of Ernest Gellner's book *Words and Things*, which may well be true. See, 'Ernest Gellner's Criticisms of Wittgenstein and Ordinary Language Philosophy', in *Marx and Wittgenstein: Knowledge, Morality and Politics*, London: Routledge, 2002, pp. 23–46.

[8] G. Kitching, 'Introduction', in *Marx and Wittgenstein: Knowledge, Morality and Politics*, London: Routledge, 2002, p. 3.

[9] T. Schatski, 'Marx and Wittgenstein: Natural Historians', in *Marx and Wittgenstein: Knowledge, Morality and Politics*, London: Routledge, 2002, pp. 49–62.

[10] See, e.g. Manser, *The End of Philosophy*.

[11] See, e.g. Rubinstein, *Marx and Wittgenstein*.

6.2 The Marxists are Racing Motorists

The recent publication, for the first time, of several of Rush Rhees's notes on conversations with Wittgenstein[12] might prompt a re-evaluation of the relationship between Wittgensteinian and Marxist thought. The notes document some remarks made by Wittgenstein about Marxist philosophy, anarchism, and fascism as well as interesting material about psychological notions, the problem of free will, and philosophical methodology.

On 8 April 1947, Wittgenstein discussed the relationship between science and philosophy with Rhees. Philosophy, as Wittgenstein conceived it, is a contemplative activity unlike the activities of science. Scientists, absorbed in the activities of science, do not contemplate science in the way that philosophers do and given that they do not contemplate alternative kinds of investigation they tend to be dismissive of other, non-causal, kinds of investigation. Rhees reports that Wittgenstein said that 'for the scientist any suggestion of a *Betrachtung* [investigation] which abandons measurement & causality is a backsliding into something more primitive [...] and so something to be *ashamed* of. Or at any rate that science is the *fruition* of which any other view is an inadequate anticipation (*Vorstufe* [preliminary stage]).'[13]

According to Rhees, Wittgenstein compared scientists to professional racing drivers, who attempt to break speed records. The racing driver is totally preoccupied breaking speed records and must dedicate their life to the task. They cannot seriously contemplate an alternative take on things which has it that breaking speed records is unimportant and that there could be a world where nobody attempts to break speed records. Rhees reports that Wittgenstein said that 'that sort of consideration must be foreign to the racing motorist. And the scientist in the same way. (The scientist would regard it as reactionary. So the Marxists would regard it too. For the Marxists are racing motorists.)'[14]

It seems clear that this is not a wholly negative appraisal of Marxism. Although Wittgenstein suggests that scientists are blinkered in their work, he does not suggest that people should not engage in scientific activity. So, it is not clear from these remarks that Wittgenstein thought that people should not engage in Marxist activity. Dedication to a project is not necessarily a bad thing. There is, however, the implication that Marxists are blinkered, in a similar way to scientists, to alternative kinds of investigation.

---

[12] R. Rhees, L. Wittgenstein, and G. Citron (eds), 'Wittgenstein's Philosophical Conversations with Rush Rhees (1939–50): From the Notes of Rush Rhees', *Mind*, vol. 124, no. 493, January 2015.
[13] Ibid., p. 38.
[14] Ibid.

This is somewhat unfair. It is not true that Marxists have failed to recognize a variety of kinds of investigation (and nor is it true that all scientists are blinkered in the way that Wittgenstein suggests). However, this does not mean that there is nothing to this analogy. Marxists have sometimes failed to recognize alternative kinds of investigation and should be wary of assimilating all kinds of explanations of social events and activities to causal or scientific explanations. In this chapter I want to examine a particular instance of a somewhat blinkered Marxist take on alternatives, namely Terry Eagleton's take on Wittgensteinian philosophical method.

6.3 Eagleton

Terry Eagleton wrote the script for the film *Wittgenstein*[15] and he has clearly both engaged with Wittgenstein's texts and tried to develop an understanding of Wittgenstein as a person. Wittgenstein's influence can be seen in Eagleton's work. In *Ideology: An Introduction*, for example, it can be seen in Eagleton describing 'ideology' as a family resemblance concept,[16] his use of the notion of a 'form of life',[17] and in some of his discussions of epistemological matters.[18] It can also be seen, more explicitly, in the fact that Eagleton makes reference, approvingly, to Wittgenstein's work in the course of making his own arguments in several of his books.[19]

---

[15] D. Jarman (dir.), *Wittgenstein* [Film], Japan/UK: BFI Production/Bandung Productions/Channel Four Films/Uplink Co., 1993. Eagleton's script for the film was published in the same year: T. Eagleton, *Wittgenstein: The Terry Eagleton Script, The Derek Jarman Film*, London: British Film Institute, 1993. For a critical take on Jarman's film and Eagleton's script see Colin McGinn's article in *New Republic*, 'Soul on Fire', vol. 210, no. 25, 20 June 1994, pp. 34–39.

[16] T. Eagleton, *Ideology: An Introduction (New and Updated Edition)*, London: Verso, 2007, p. 193.

[17] Ibid., pp. 27–29, 51, 171.

[18] The following passage, from *Ideology: An Introduction*, is reminiscent of Wittgenstein's distinction between a mistake and a mental disturbance (see *On Certainty*, §§67–75, §647): 'There is a difference between being mistaken and being deluded: if someone lifts a cucumber and announces his telephone number we may conclude that he has made a mistake, whereas if he spends long evenings chatting vivaciously into a cucumber we might have to draw different conclusions' (Eagleton in *Ideology: An Introduction*, pp. 26–27).

[19] See, e.g. Eagleton, *Ideology: An Introduction*, pp. 88, 168, 193; *The Meaning of Life: A Very Short Introduction*, Oxford: Oxford University Press, 2008, pp. 3–7, 47, 50–51, 77, 78, 93–94 (first published in 2007); *Why Marx Was Right*, New Haven, CT: Yale University Press, 2011, p. 144; and *Reason, Faith, and Revolution*, New Haven, CT: Yale University Press, 2009, pp. 53, 80, 124, 130. More recently Eagleton has tried to combine the

Wittgenstein, as Eagleton acknowledges, is widely regarded to be the greatest philosopher of the twentieth century.[20] Given that social theorists and political theorists often engage in philosophical discussions regarding theory, epistemology, and mind, it is important that they engage with Wittgenstein's thought and try to come to a correct understanding of it. Eagleton is a prominent social theorist who straddles many disciplines in his work – literary theory, philosophy, sociology, economics, and politics. My contention in this chapter will be that his interpretation of Wittgenstein is, in some respects, defective, and that he exhibits something like the blindness of the racing motorist.

My focus will be on Eagleton's interpretation of Wittgenstein's later philosophy in his article 'Wittgenstein's Friends' and also in his recent book *Materialism*, since these are the texts in which Eagleton presents a prolonged discussion of Wittgenstein's later work.[21] I'll start by outlining Eagleton's take on the question of whether Wittgenstein is conservative or reactionary and will then examine Eagleton's interpretation critically. Along the way I will explain why I think Eagleton's interpretation is preferable to some other Marxist's interpretations, namely Perry Anderson's and Alex Callinicos', whose work was examined in the last chapter, but I will nonetheless conclude that ultimately Eagleton's interpretation is unsatisfactory in various respects.

6.4 Eagleton's Account

6.4.1 *Eagleton's Defence of Wittgenstein against the Charge of Conservatism*

Eagleton commences his essay 'Wittgenstein's Friends' by noting similarities between Wittgenstein's writing and the writings of post-structuralists and deconstructionists. Many of those who have been inspired by Wittgenstein 'have lost that distinctively European timbre, that dimension of sheer strangeness and intractability'.[22] Eagleton also compares Wittgenstein's *Philosophical Investigations* to the Socratic dialogues of Plato: 'The *Investigations* are a voice in dialogue with itself and an implied other, digressing and doubling back, so that the reader is not supplied with a ready-made truth as in the monologism of

---

insights of Marx and Wittgenstein in his account of materialism (see *Materialism*, New Haven: Yale University Press, 2017).

[20] Eagleton, *The Meaning of Life*, p. 5.
[21] T. Eagleton, 'Wittgenstein's Friends', *New Left Review*, vol. 135, September–October 1982, republished in T. Eagleton, *Against the Grain: Selected Essays*, London: Verso, 1986, pp. 99–130; and Eagleton, *Materialism*.
[22] Eagleton, 'Wittgenstein's Friends', in *Against the Grain*, p. 99.

Russell.'[23] The peculiar numbered paragraphs of the *Philosophical Investigations* incorporate 'jokes, aphorisms, unanswered questions, parables, exclamations and wonderings aloud'.[24] We need not worry ourselves here about just how close Wittgenstein is in style to post-structuralists, deconstructionists, or Plato. Eagleton is right to point out that Wittgenstein is stylistically different to many of those who have followed in his footsteps. Wittgenstein's writing *is* unusual and it is important for interpreters of the *Philosophical Investigations* to recognize that it is not simply made up of a series of assertions that Wittgenstein wants to make. Many of the sentences in the *Investigations* are not sentences that Wittgenstein would want to affirm and it takes some thought to decide which among them represent Wittgenstein's perspective on things.

It is perhaps due to Eagleton's sensitivity to the fact that the *Investigations* is not intended to present us with a series of 'ready-made truths' that he does not fall into the error of accusing Wittgenstein of conservatism by looking at his remarks in isolation and taking them at face value. Marxist philosophers, with their interest in radical change, are naturally drawn, with a critical eye, to Wittgenstein's proclamation that 'philosophy [...] leaves everything as it is'.[25] As we have seen in previous chapters, several philosophers and political theorists have taken this as a clear demonstration of Wittgenstein's conservatism.[26] But given that Wittgenstein's later writings often involve discussion with an interlocutor and given that his writings do not just consist of assertions we should, at the very least, look at the context of the remark and think about (i) whether Wittgenstein wants to assert that philosophy leaves everything as it is and (ii) what attitude Wittgenstein is taking up to this claim. Does he, for example, think that it is regrettable that philosophy leaves everything as it is?

Eagleton takes it that Wittgenstein does want to affirm the claim but, unlike Anderson and Callinicos, Eagleton does not take this to demonstrate that Wittgenstein was conservative. Eagleton's take on what Wittgenstein says in §124 is that Wittgenstein thinks it is regrettable that philosophy leaves everything as it is and that is why Wittgenstein recommended that his acolytes abandon philosophy. Wittgenstein's attitude towards philosophy in this

---

[23] Eagleton, *Against the Grain*, p. 118.
[24] Ibid.
[25] L. Wittgenstein, *Philosophical Investigations*, 4th edition, Oxford: Blackwell, 2009, §124.
[26] Perhaps most famously J. C. Nyiri has argued in a series of articles that the tone and content of Wittgenstein's writings as well as Wittgenstein's historical circumstances lend support to the view that there are 'family resemblances' between Wittgenstein and conservative philosophers. See, e.g. 'Wittgenstein's Later Work in Relation to Conservatism', in B. McGuiness (ed.), *Wittgenstein and His Time*, Oxford: Blackwell, 1981, p. 44. Others arguing for this view of Wittgenstein include Perry Anderson, Alex Callinicos, Ernest Gellner, and H. C. McCauley.

passage is 'not after all very different from that of Marx's eleventh thesis on Feuerbach',[27] Eagleton says. It is open to both Marx and Wittgenstein to want radical change despite their somewhat dismissive attitudes towards the philosophy that has gone before them. A desire for radical change is also consistent with low hopes for philosophy in the future.

But there is another passage in Wittgenstein's *Philosophical Investigations* that has fed the charge that Wittgenstein is a conservative philosopher. In §226 Wittgenstein says that 'what has to be accepted, the given, is – so one could say – forms of life'.[28] This can be interpreted as conservative for more than one reason. First of all, it might be taken to mean that we have to accept the ways of living and the institutions that we are presented with and second Wittgenstein could be accused of making forms of life other than one's own immune from criticism by suggesting that those engaged in other forms of life operate with different concepts and so any attempt to criticize another form of life will inevitably just end up talking past the target of the criticism.[29]

Eagleton takes on the first of the criticisms by arguing that 'there is no reason why what has to be accepted are *these particular* forms of life, and [...] little reason to believe that Wittgenstein himself was in the least content with his own society'.[30] So Wittgenstein is not giving expression to conservatism here. In fact, one might argue, as Eagleton suggests, that 'if deep-seated conceptual change is to be possible it can only be the result of transformations in forms of life'.[31] If this was Wittgenstein's position then he could be rescued from the charge of conservatism by saying that although he thought philosophy leaves everything as it is he nonetheless thought that change was possible and it is open to him to think that change is desirable. Change wouldn't come through philosophy but through dramatically transforming forms of life. In fact Wittgenstein said something like this himself when he said that 'the sickness of a time is cured by an alteration in the mode of life of human beings, and it was possible for the sickness of problems to get cured only through a changed mode of thought and life, not through a medicine invented by an individual'.[32]

---

[27] Eagleton, 'Wittgenstein's Friends', in *Against the Grain*, p. 100.
[28] Ibid.
[29] Nyiri makes this argument in 'Wittgenstein's Later Work in Relation to Conservatism' (p. 58), as does Ernest Gellner (see *Reason and Culture*, Oxford: Blackwell, 1992, p. 120) and David Bloor (see *Wittgenstein: A Social Theory of Knowledge*, London: Macmillan, 1983, p. 161). I will not respond to this criticism here. My aim in this chapter is to engage with Eagleton's arguments in particular.
[30] Eagleton, 'Wittgenstein's Friends', in *Against the Grain*, p. 107.
[31] Ibid., p. 100.
[32] L. Wittgenstein, *Remarks on the Foundations of Mathematics*, Oxford: Blackwell, revised edition, 1978, part II, §23.

Additionally, there is evidence from the recently published conversations with Rush Rhees that Wittgenstein thought that changes in people's ideas might come through changes in society. According to Rhees Wittgenstein was dismissive of the idea that fascism could be combatted by combatting loose thinking, 'as though you could *persuade* people to be logical in their thinking'.[33] Wittgenstein apparently regularly spoke to Rhees about how he thought that anti-Semitism had disappeared as a result of a 'change in the form of society' in Russia. Rhees opines, 'I think he believed that the central place of manual labour and the vanishing of the prestige which money gives [with us] was one main factor in this.'[34]

Eagleton defends Wittgenstein against accusations of conservatism from yet another angle by pointing to Wittgenstein's personal relationships with various left-wing thinkers (the *friends* from the title of his essay). This, of course, is no proof that Wittgenstein was left-wing himself, but it does take the sting out of criticisms of Wittgenstein which try to paint him as conservative by citing his historical circumstances and relationships. As mentioned in previous chapters, among Wittgenstein's friends were people like Nikolai Bakhtin, a classics lecturer at Birmingham University, described by Fania Pascal as a 'fiery communist';[35] George Thomson, another Marxist classics lecturer at Birmingham who had a role in shifting Bakhtin's politics to the left; and Pierro Sraffa, an economist who was friends with the Marxist Antonio Gramsci and who Wittgenstein credits as being the stimulus for 'the most fruitful ideas' of the *Philosophical Investigations*.[36]

We also know, from accounts given by these friends of Wittgenstein, that he personally expressed some sympathy for left-wing stances. As Eagleton notes, George Thomson claimed that Wittgenstein 'was opposed to [Marxism] in theory, but supported it to a large extent in practice'.[37] In his biography of Wittgenstein Ray Monk adds that 'this chimes with a remark Wittgenstein

---

[33] Rhees, Wittgenstein, and Citron (eds), 'Wittgenstein's Philosophical Conversations with Rush Rhees (1939–50), p. 58.

[34] Ibid., p. 59 (the words in square brackets are unclear in Rhees's notes).

[35] F. Pascal, 'A Personal Memoir', in Rush Rhees (ed.), *Recollections of Wittgenstein*, revised edition, Oxford: Oxford University Press, 1984, p. 14.

[36] Wittgenstein, *Philosophical Investigations (Preface)*, p. 4 (in the revised 4th edition by P. M. S. Hacker and Joachim Schulte).

[37] Eagleton, 'Wittgenstein's Friends', in *Against the Grain*, p. 194n70 (the claim from Thomson originally appeared in G. Thomson, 'Wittgenstein: Some Personal Recollections', *Revolutionary World*, vols. 37–39, Amsterdam, 1979). Eagleton also emphasizes Wittgenstein's relationships with left-wing friends and their influence on him in chapter 5 of his recent book *Materialism* (2017). He describes Wittgenstein as 'a Stalinist of sorts' in that book (p. 130) and also as a conservative, traditionalist, *Kulturkritiker* (p. 134).

once made to Rowland Hutt [...] "I am a communist, *at heart*" '. Monk also draws on Thomson's account to demonstrate that in the 1930s Wittgenstein was keen on the idea of full employment and alert to the dangers of fascism. He concludes that 'there is no doubt that during the political upheavals of the mid-1930s Wittgenstein's sympathies were with the working class and the unemployed, and that his allegiance, broadly speaking, was with the Left'.[38]

6.4.2 *Eagleton's Criticism of Wittgenstein*

Despite building up a defence of Wittgenstein against the charge of conservatism from several angles Eagleton ultimately argues that Wittgenstein is 'reactionary' and argues that Marxist theories have certain advantages over Wittgenstein's take on language and philosophy.[39] This, I think, mirrors the scientist's idea that forms of investigation that do not involve measurement and reference to causality are 'primitive' in Wittgenstein's example of the scientists and the racing motorists. Eagleton thinks of Wittgensteinian 'explanation' as in competition with Marxist explanation and thinks that it comes off the worst for it.

Although Eagleton doesn't fall into the traps of attributing a conservative ideology to Wittgenstein on the basis of §124 and §226 (discussed in Section 6.2.1), he does say that there is something to the idea that §124 ('philosophy [...] leaves everything as it is') is 'an index of social and intellectual reaction, a complacent consecration of existing "language games"'.[40] Later Eagleton claims that 'the criticism that Wittgenstein consecrates the linguistic status quo' is 'accurate in one sense'.[41] Exactly in what sense Wittgenstein consecrates the linguistic status quo is left unclear but Eagleton ultimately argues that Wittgenstein is 'reactionary' because, unlike Marxists, he does not recognize that metaphysics is at home in the everyday.[42] Wittgenstein suggests

---

[38] R. Monk, *Ludwig Wittgenstein: The Duty of Genius*, London: Random House, 1990, p. 343.

[39] In his book *Ludwig Wittgenstein*, Edward Kanterian argues that 'to claim, as Terry Eagleton has done, that Wittgenstein's ideas were somehow related to the Marxist aesthetics of Mikhail Bakhtin via this broad affinity with brother Nikolai is to overlook subtle and not so subtle differences between Wittgenstein and Marxist thought' (p. 160). While I agree with Kanterian that there are significant differences between Wittgensteinian and Marxist philosophy, my aim here will be to demonstrate that the two philosophies are not so incompatible as Eagleton thinks.

[40] Eagleton, 'Wittgenstein's Friends', in *Against the Grain*, p. 100.

[41] Ibid., p. 104.

[42] Eagleton makes a similar criticism in his book *Walter Benjamin or towards a Revolutionary Criticism*, London: Verso, 1981, p. 153: 'Benjamin's case is as complex as that of another Jewish philosopher, Ludwig Wittgenstein, who similarly returns language to social practice at the same time as too complacently endorsing existing practices.'

that metaphysical problems can be dissolved by 'bring[ing] words back from their metaphysical to their everyday use' which Eagleton interprets as 'referring of beliefs and discourses to social activity'.[43] But Eagleton thinks that Wittgenstein is mistaken if he thinks that 'such referring constitutes a liberation from the metaphysical'.[44]

Why does Eagleton doubt that Wittgenstein's methods can liberate us from metaphysics? In discussing one of the metaphysical 'pictures' of the *Tractatus*, the idea of the 'crystalline purity of logic', Wittgenstein compares the picture to a pair of glasses distorting our vision. What we need to do, according to Wittgenstein, is to take the glasses off.[45] We need to return to the 'rough ground' of ordinary language to dissolve metaphysical problems.[46] But Eagleton detects a tension here in Wittgenstein's thought. On the one hand Wittgenstein wants us to look to everyday uses of words to dissolve metaphysical problems but on the other he wants to say that metaphysical mystification arises out of ordinary language, 'out of the very structures of our grammar'.[47] But if the problems are problems in ordinary language then how can returning to language help to solve the problems? If the 'glasses' belong to ordinary language then how can we take them off? Eagleton concludes that, despite having some insight into philosophical questions, Wittgenstein's '"popular" language remains largely metaphysical'.[48]

In order to get past this stumbling block Eagleton thinks that Wittgenstein can learn from Marxists. If metaphysics is at home in everyday language then what is needed is a transformation of the everyday. Marx was right to claim that 'the point is to change [the world]'. Eagleton also thinks that Wittgenstein could learn from Marxists that metaphysical problems are not always rooted in language. According to Eagleton, 'For Wittgenstein, metaphysical mystifications seem to arise for purely linguistic reasons – from "a tendency to sublime the logic of our language".'[49]

Eagleton provides an example of where he thinks Wittgenstein's appeal to ordinary language runs into trouble in §120 of the *Philosophical Investigations*:

> You say: the point isn't the word but its meaning and you think of the meaning as a thing of the same kind as the word, though also different

---

[43] Eagleton, 'Wittgenstein's Friends', in *Against the Grain*, p. 107.
[44] Ibid.
[45] Wittgenstein, *Philosophical Investigations*, §103.
[46] Ibid., §107.
[47] Eagleton, 'Wittgenstein's Friends', in *Against the Grain*, p. 108.
[48] Ibid., p. 111.
[49] Ibid., p. 107.

from the word. Here the word, there the meaning. The money, and the cow one can buy with it. But contrast: money and its use.[50]

Here Eagleton thinks that Wittgenstein escapes from one philosophical problem (conceiving the meanings of words as entities) but runs into another (thinking that the value of money derives from its uses). But it isn't obvious that Wittgenstein does do this. As a Marxist, presumably Eagleton's point is that the value of money is to be thought about in terms of it being a commodity. Eagleton emphasizes money's role in extinguishing differences. Money is the 'universal equivalent' that extinguishes qualitative differences between commodities. However, according to Eagleton, Wittgenstein makes the mistake of stressing the various things you can do with money and so obscures this role. Wittgenstein makes the mistake of 'trusting to money as *difference*'.[51]

6.5 Problems with Eagleton's Account

6.5.1 *Wittgenstein and Money*

Eagleton criticizes Wittgenstein for entangling himself in metaphysical mysteries by suggesting that the value of money derives from its uses. However, nothing that Wittgenstein says in §120 (see above) implies or even more loosely suggests that this is Wittgenstein's position. One can hold that (i) the meanings of words are not entities, (ii) that it is useful to think about meaning in terms of the use of a word,[52] (iii) that money can be used to buy many things, and (iv) that the value of money derives from something other than its uses perfectly consistently.

Wittgenstein is not getting entangled in any kind of metaphysical mystery at all here. It would be peculiar for Marxists to deny that money can be used to buy cows and a great many other things, as there is nothing nonsensical or 'metaphysical' about this claim. It is true that Wittgenstein emphasizes the uses of money in §120 rather than examining the question of the value of money from a Marxist perspective but it is worth remembering that the point of §120 is not to say something revealing about money but to make a point about the meanings of words. Right at the beginning of the *Investigations* Wittgenstein

---

[50] Wittgenstein, *Philosophical Investigations*, §120.
[51] Eagleton, 'Wittgenstein's Friends', in *Against the Grain*, p. 122.
[52] To be clear, Wittgenstein does not *identify* meaning and use. As was pointed out in the previous chapter, what Wittgenstein said was that 'for a *large* class of cases of the employment of the word "meaning" – though not for all – this word can be explained in this way: the meaning of a word is its use in the language'. *Philosophical Investigations*, 4th edition, §43.

launches an attack on the 'Augustinian' theory of language, which includes the idea that 'every word has a meaning. This meaning is correlated with the word. It is the object for which the word stands.'[53]

Wittgenstein's association of meaning with use in §120 can be viewed as a response to the Augustinian theory. It certainly provides an alternative way of viewing meaning and it is our ordinary way of talking and thinking about meaning. But to what end? The immediate context of the remark is a series of remarks about the nature of philosophy. The remark about philosophy leaving everything as it is (§124) appears on the next page. Also close by is another remark that Eagleton thought was problematic, namely §116, which includes the sentence: 'What we do is to bring words back from their metaphysical to their everyday use.' A proper understanding of these remarks and the other remarks about philosophy show that Eagleton's understanding of Wittgenstein is problematic.

6.5.2 *Language and Metaphysics*

Immediately before the remark about bringing words back to their everyday use (§116) Wittgenstein says, 'When philosophers use a word – "knowledge", "being", "object", "I", "proposition/sentence", "name" – and try to grasp the *essence* of the thing, one must always ask oneself: is the word ever actually used in this way in the language in which it is at home?'[54] Now, given that in §43 of the *Philosophical Investigations* Wittgenstein had suggested that 'meaning' and 'use' are employed in the same way in a large class of cases it seems clear that Wittgenstein is here (in §116) making a point about the meanings of words like 'knowledge' and 'object'. These are words that philosophers very often concern themselves with, in epistemology and metaphysics, respectively, and they are words that philosophers are keen to get clear about the meaning of because in order to solve or dissolve philosophical problems about them we must first be clear about what the words mean. Wittgenstein's suggestion is that we will not get clear about the meaning of words by always assuming that we must find some kind of common *essential* feature of the things referred to by the word. If we want to get clear about the meaning of 'knowledge' and 'object' we should look at how the words are actually used and it may be that they aren't used to refer to a set of things with a common feature. So, what Wittgenstein is doing in §116 is suggesting a way of going about doing philosophy.

---

[53] Wittgenstein, *Philosophical Investigations*, §1.
[54] Ibid., §116.

One thing to notice about this point is that the words Wittgenstein is talking about are commonly used ordinary words, for the most part. People very often use the word 'I', they often talk about what they know and what they don't know, and they often use and talk about names. This shows that, contra Eagleton, Wittgenstein *did* recognize that metaphysics has a home in the everyday (or at least that everyday words often crop up in philosophical problems).[55] This is something that Eagleton himself must acknowledge in order to criticize Wittgenstein for suggesting that returning to everyday use to dissolve metaphysical problems conflicts with his claim that metaphysical problems arise out of ordinary language (I'll return to this criticism in the next section).

A second thing to notice about this point is that it helps to contextualize Wittgenstein's remark about the use of money in §120. The context of that remark helps us to see that it is not only a response to the Augustinian theory but also a remark about how to go about dealing with philosophical problems. Philosophers have been vexed for centuries trying to understand words like 'knowledge' and 'mind' in terms of their essential features or in terms of some kind of entity corresponding to them. What we can do to overcome that vexation is to approach the problems differently. If we want to get clear about what 'knowledge' means or about what 'mind' means we should think about how those terms are ordinarily used. Wittgenstein can be seen as recommending that instead of looking for an entity corresponding to words like 'mind' we should look at 'what can be done with'[56] words like 'mind'.

Before moving on to look at Eagleton's suggestion that there is a tension in Wittgenstein's thought regarding the everyday it is worth quickly setting aside Eagleton's claim that Wittgenstein mistakenly thought that all metaphysical

---

[55] Andrew Lugg makes a similar criticism of Eagleton's interpretation of Wittgenstein in his 'Was Wittgenstein a Conservative Thinker?' (*Southern Journal of Philosophy*, vol. XXIII, no. 4 (1985)) where he argues,

> This [Eagleton's] criticism [...] labours under the difficulty that Wittgenstein does not afford 'the everyday' the privileged position that he is thought to afford it. He does not think that common sense provides us with an alternative, more adequate theory of how things are, only that the poverty of philosophical ideas concerning human thought and behaviour can be exposed by examining how we actually think and behave. (p. 469)

> Lugg is correct, I think, in saying that Wittgenstein does not just counterpose common sense to philosophical metaphysics, but his account of what Wittgenstein actually does is slightly different to mine here (Lugg suggests that what Wittgenstein does is to 'adduce facts about our mental life' and to 'confront theory with practice, what we think people do with what they actually do' (p. 469)).

[56] Wittgenstein, *Philosophical Investigations*, §120.

muddles have their source in language. This can be easily disposed of by looking at some of the remarks that Wittgenstein made about the sources of philosophical error. In the *Blue Book* we find that Wittgenstein says that 'our preoccupation with the method of science' results in philosophical errors. 'Philosophers constantly see the method of science before their eyes, and are irresistibly tempted to ask and answer questions in the way that science does. This tendency is the real source of metaphysics, and leads the philosopher into complete darkness.'[57] In the *Philosophical Investigations* Wittgenstein suggests that trying to treat logic like a natural science leads to problems (§81, §89), that treating philosophical questions about time as scientific questions leads to error (§89), and that philosophical questions more generally are not like scientific ones (§109).

6.5.3 *The 'Glasses' Metaphor*

What about the supposed tension between the claim that philosophical problems originate in ordinary language and the claim that we should 'take off the glasses' and 'return to the rough ground'? Recall that Eagleton criticized Wittgenstein for claiming on the one hand that (i) philosophical problems can be dissolved by looking carefully at our ordinary ways of using (often ordinary) words but on the other hand claiming that (ii) metaphysical problems arise out of ordinary language. It seems that we cannot solve problems by looking at ordinary language if the problems originate in features of our ordinary language. Did Wittgenstein really hold both of these positions? If so, then is the tension really as problematic as Eagleton claims?

We've already seen in §116 that Wittgenstein wants to claim that we should 'bring words back from their metaphysical to their ordinary use' in order to deal with philosophical problems. So, it seems clear enough that he is committed to the view that we can dissolve philosophical problems by looking carefully at our ordinary use of words like 'knowledge' and 'being'. In §111 Wittgenstein says that the 'disquietudes' of philosophy 'are as deeply rooted in us as the forms of our language' and then in §112 Wittgenstein says that 'a simile that has been absorbed into the forms of our language produces a false

---

[57] L. Wittgenstein, *The Blue and Brown Books*, New York: Harper & Row, 1958, p. 18. Andrew Lugg also takes Eagleton to task on this point drawing on the same part of the *Blue Book* in his 'Wittgenstein and Politics: Not Right, Left or Center' (in *International Studies in Philosophy*, vol. XXXVI/I, 2004, pp. 61–79): 'Wittgenstein […] frequently reminds us that we are apt to accept views that are wrong, misguided or incoherent for other than "purely linguistic reasons". It is not for nothing that he deplores our "craving for generality" and notes that we frequently embrace explanations for their "charm"' (p. 67).

appearance which disquiets us'. Furthermore, elsewhere in his later work (in what has now been published as the *Big Typescript*) Wittgenstein explained why it is that philosophical questions had continued to perplex us since the time of Plato:

> The reason is that our language has remained the same and always introduces us to the same questions. As long as there is a verb 'to be' which seems to work like 'to eat' and 'to drink'; as long as there are adjectives like 'identical', 'true', 'false', 'possible'; as long as people speak of the passage of time and of the extent of space, and so on; as long as this happens people will always run up against the same teasing difficulties and will stare at something which no explanation seems to remove.[58]

So, it seems clear that Eagleton is correct that there is at least the appearance of tension here. Philosophical problems are solved in ordinary language but also originate there. Does this mean that metaphysics cannot be abolished using Wittgenstein's methodologies as Eagleton claims? Is transforming our practical life the only possible solution as some Marxists have claimed?

6.5.4 *Abolishing Metaphysics*

One point that could be made in response to Eagleton's criticism is that it is perfectly possible for one thing to contain both puzzles *and* their solutions and for it to leave us satisfied with having solved the problems. There are books that contain both puzzles (e.g. crossword puzzles or riddles) and their solutions and we can work our way through the puzzles to our satisfaction and check our answers against the solutions given in the back of the book. These books might leave us puzzled but they need not. We might then wonder whether the philosophical problems that misleading features of our language tempt us into are analogous to the puzzles in a puzzle book. There are certainly ways in which philosophical problems are different. The problems found in a puzzle book are usually formulated in sentences that make sense. However, according to Wittgenstein philosophical problems 'arise when language is, as it were, idling, not when it is doing work'.[59] In §38 of the *Philosophical Investigations* Wittgenstein makes the same sort of point when he says that these problems arise 'when language goes on holiday'.[60] When we twist a concept out of shape

---

[58] L. Wittgenstein, *Big Typescript: TS 213*, trans. C. Grant Luckhardt and Maximilian E. Aue, Chichester: Wiley-Blackwell, 2005 (BT 424).
[59] Wittgenstein, *Philosophical Investigations*, §132.
[60] Ibid., §38.

so that it is not being put to work any more it is not being used in a way such that what we are saying makes sense (it is not being used at all). When philosophers are vexed by metaphysical problems they have been tempted into saying things that do not make sense. Moreover, as Wittgenstein said in the passage cited from the *Big Typescript* above, philosophical problems tend to reoccur because the misleading features of language remain.

However, despite the fact that language continues to contain misleading features, Wittgenstein has some confidence that philosophical problems can be overcome. In the collection of remarks that have been published as *Culture and Value* we find that Wittgenstein said that although 'language sets everyone the same traps; it is an immense network of easily accessible wrong turnings', this does not mean that we have to keep on falling into the traps. We might be tempted to speak nonsense but we are not compelled to. Wittgenstein's task, as he saw it, was to 'erect signposts at all the junctions where there are wrong turnings so as to help people past the danger points'.[61] What this means is that in order to dissolve philosophical problems we must remind people of how the concepts that are misused[62] in philosophical problems are in fact correctly used. These 'reminders' are the signposts that help us to get past the 'danger points'. This suggests that Eagleton is mistaken to criticize Wittgenstein for seeing ordinary language as both a source of problems and the solution to problems. There is no inconsistency in saying that philosophical or metaphysical problems arise when we get confused about the use of ordinary concepts and that the solution is to return to ordinary language (i.e. to look carefully at how the concepts are used correctly).[63]

Eagleton himself gives an example of where Wittgenstein spots a wrong turning and helpfully erects signposts. Commenting on §246 of the *Philosophical*

---

[61] L. Wittgenstein, *Culture and Value*, Oxford: Blackwell, 1980, §18.

[62] Misused or not used at all – 'idling'/'on holiday'.

[63] My response to Eagleton here is slightly different to the one that Andrew Lugg makes in his 'Was Wittgenstein a Conservative Thinker?'. I want to suggest that we can remove the metaphorical glasses, as Wittgenstein suggests, whereas Lugg says that

> it may be true that one can only survey human practices as though through a pair of spectacles, but to say that such practices can never be surveyed without distortion is like saying that spectacles can never improve sight. As I understand Wittgenstein, his view is not that descriptions of practices can be given in a 'theory neutral' manner but only that there is a distinction to be drawn between ideological and nonideological descriptions. (pp. 469–70)

> It suggests that Lugg thinks that the glasses cannot be removed but that they can be adjusted so as not to distort what is seen through them. It could be that there is no disagreement here, depending on whether the glasses are taken to be language in its entirety or a distorting ideal.

Investigations Eagleton says, 'I cannot say, "I can know that I am in pain but can only guess that you are," since as Wittgenstein comments the sentence "I know that I am in pain" is meaningless. I can be as certain of someone else's sensations in certain circumstances as I am of any fact.' What is the 'wrong turning' that has been taken here and what are Wittgenstein's 'signposts'? It is a mistake (a wrong turning) to think that in saying 'I know that I am in pain' I am saying something just like 'I know that I am in Europe', while in Istanbul. We are misled into thinking that we know when we are in pain by the fact that ignorance is excluded, as is doubt. If I cannot doubt that I am in pain and I am not ignorant of the fact then surely I *know* that I am in pain when I am in pain. But in this case ignorance is logically or grammatically excluded. There is *no such thing* as being in pain but being ignorant of it. The sentence 'I am in pain but I doubt that I am' does not make *sense*. One of Wittgenstein's 'signposts' here, his reminder of correct ordinary use of the term 'pain', is his point that 'it makes sense to say about other people that they doubt whether I am in pain; but not to say it about myself'. And if doubt and ignorance are *logically* excluded, then so is knowledge. The claim that 'I know that I am in Europe', unlike 'I know that I am in pain', is a genuine case of knowledge because it is possible for me to doubt that I am in Europe (when I am in Istanbul and unsure of where the continental border lies) and I can resolve my doubt by, for example, consulting a map.[64]

6.5.5 *How Should We Interpret §124?*

Given what has been said above about Wittgenstein's conception of philosophy we can return to Wittgenstein's claim that 'philosophy [...] leaves everything as it is' (*PI*, §124) and see it in a new light that reveals a problem with Eagleton's interpretation of it. Eagleton compares Wittgenstein's claim with Marx's eleventh thesis on Feuerbach, where Marx says, 'The philosophers have only interpreted the world, in various ways; the point is to change it.'[65] What is it that Marx and Wittgenstein thinks changes (or remains unchanged)? In Marx's case he wants to criticize the philosophy that has gone before him for merely interpreting *the world* and not changing

---

[64] Wittgenstein puts up another signpost in §246 when he points out that 'I cannot be said to learn of [my sensations]. I have them.' And, as Peter Hacker points out, 'It makes sense to talk of knowing where it also makes sense to talk of finding out, coming to know, or learning' (in *Wittgenstein*, London: Phoenix, 1997, p. 28).

[65] K. Marx, 'Theses on Feuerbach', Thesis 11, 1845, in Karl Marx, *The German Ideology*, 2nd edition, edited and introduced by C. J. Arthur, London: Lawrence & Wishart, 1974, p. 123.

it (*the world*). Marx is urging us to take action to change our surroundings rather than just sitting in an ivory tower writing and thinking about them. However, Wittgenstein's complaint about past philosophers is not that they have misinterpreted *the world* but that they have failed to use concepts correctly and so have ended up confused. His proposed solution is to remind us of the correct use of the concepts that are causing confusion. I suggest that when Wittgenstein says that philosophy leaves *everything* as it is that he means that it leaves everything *in its domain* as it is, namely the concepts that philosophers are confused about. His point is not that concepts should be preserved as they are, as Perry Anderson has argued,[66] but that it is not philosophy's job to alter concepts in a way that seems to suit philosophers' inclinations (and thus end up speaking nonsense).

What this means is that Eagleton's interpretation of §124 is off the mark. Eagleton is wrong to think that in order for Wittgenstein to be absolved of the charge of conservatism that he must think it is regrettable that philosophy leaves everything as it is.[67] What Eagleton gets right is that Wittgenstein really did want to assert that philosophy leaves everything as it is. But this is not a conservative position. It is not asserting either that concepts should not be subject to radical change or that the world should not be subject to radical change. What Wittgenstein is saying in §124 is that philosophers should not alter concepts in such a way that they are no longer doing work – such that they are idling or on holiday – because doing this is a wrong turn off in the direction of nonsense.

6.5.6 *Materialism, Metaphysics, and Religion*

In his recent book *Materialism* Terry Eagleton again gives a detailed, largely sympathetic, account of Wittgenstein's later philosophy but he nonetheless remains unconvinced that Wittgenstein came up with adequate ways of getting rid of metaphysics. There are references to Wittgenstein throughout the book and the final chapter of it focuses on the later Wittgenstein's philosophy. Eagleton clearly finds Wittgenstein's account of language compelling: an account which connects our uses of language with the kind of creature that we are and which sees language as being 'woven into our practical existence'.[68]

---

[66] See Chapter 5 of this book.
[67] This leaves open the possibility that Wittgenstein nonetheless thought that it is shame that *the world* is the way that it is.
[68] Eagleton, *Materialism*, p. 122.

He describes Wittgenstein's later thought, in terms which Marxists might find congenial, as 'broadly materialist'.[69] He presents a sympathetic account of Wittgenstein's notion of grammar and the autonomy of grammar and defends Wittgenstein against the charge of linguistic idealism.[70] Eagleton also defends Wittgenstein against the charge that he is a naive defender of common sense (which we saw Anderson and Callinicos making in the last chapter).[71]

However, although Eagleton finds much of value in Wittgenstein his account is not entirely uncritical. He thinks that Wittgenstein's philosophical approach is limited in certain ways and mistaken in others. Eagleton says that 'Wittgenstein's conservatism does indeed place limits on his thought. It is not true, as he claims, that to resolve our problems we simply need to rearrange what we already know. Indeed it is blatantly, laughably false [...] There is a glibness about such talk which grates.'[72] Eagleton compares Wittgenstein with Marx and thinks that whereas Marx gave us a sophisticated and useful account of ideology, 'there is no concept of ideology in Wittgenstein's work'.[73] Wittgenstein misses what philosophers like Marx and Habermas capture, namely the relationship between ideological distortions and power. Eagleton identifies 'bourgeois individualism' as being a source of the metaphysical 'delusions' that Wittgenstein examined and suggests that socialism is a solution. However, Eagleton thinks that Wittgenstein's manner of philosophizing and Marxist critique of ideology are the same kind of thing. Both are activities aimed at demythologizing or at getting rid of mystification. What Wittgenstein wanted to do was to overcome the delusions or the false consciousness that our language inclines us towards.[74]

Much of what Eagleton says about Wittgenstein in *Materialism* is correct but his criticisms of Wittgenstein do not hit their target. When Eagleton says that it is 'blatantly false' that we can resolve our problems by rearranging what we already know he presumably has §109 of Wittgenstein's *Philosophical Investigations* in mind. There Wittgenstein says that 'the problems are solved, not by coming up with new discoveries, but by assembling what we have long been familiar with'.[75] What are the problems that Wittgenstein is referring

---

[69] Ibid. I would not describe Wittgenstein as a materialist myself but Eagleton is undoubtedly right that Marx and Wittgenstein have things in common and that the Marxist and Wittgensteinian traditions can learn from one another.

[70] Ibid., pp. 122–26.

[71] Ibid., pp. 143–44.

[72] Ibid., pp. 137–38.

[73] Ibid., p. 140.

[74] Ibid., p. 145.

[75] Wittgenstein, *Philosophical Investigations*, 4th edition, §109. In Anscombe's earlier translation Wittgenstein's words are translated as 'The problems are solved, not by giving new information, but by arranging what we have always known' (Wittgenstein's original

to here? The problems that he has discussed in the *Investigations* up to this point are problems like 'what is the meaning of the word five?' (§1), 'what is a question?' (§24), 'what is the relation between a name and the thing named?' (§37), 'what is an element of reality?' (§59), 'what is language?' (§65, §92), 'what is common to all the activities we call games?' (§66), 'what is time?' (§89), 'what is a proposition?' (§92), and 'what is a word?' (§108).

Now, it is blatantly false that we can solve *all* of our problems by rearranging what we already know. Some problems involve conducting experiments or finding out new things. Some problems involve investigation. Some involve practical action. But it is clear that the kind of problems that involve empirical investigation or experiment are not the kind of problems that Wittgenstein has in mind. It is also clear that he is not trying to work out how to get across a river or how to get away from a rampaging bull or something of that sort. Nor is he concerned with problems about, say, how best to organize society. His concerns are with problems about meaning, language, thought, and reality. He is concerned with problems that have been called metaphysical problems, epistemological problems, problems from the philosophy of mind, and problems from the philosophy of language. But if these are the problems Wittgenstein is dealing with when he talks about 'the problems' that are solved by assembling what we have long been familiar with then it is not 'blatantly false' that we can solve them by arranging what we know. Wittgenstein makes a good case that what is needed in order to resolve these questions is for us to look carefully at the things we say when we use the relevant expressions and to give a synoptic overview of relationships between them (words like 'word', 'proposition', 'language', 'meaning', 'question', etc.).

In §89 of the *Investigations* Wittgenstein looks at Augustine's question 'what is time?' and Augustine's remark about the question that 'if no one asks me [what time is] I know, but if I want to explain it to someone who asks, I do not know'. Wittgenstein makes the observation that Augustine's remark could not be made about a question of natural science, such as 'what is the specific gravity of hydrogen?', and he remarks that 'something that one knows when nobody asks one, but no longer knows when one is asked to explain it, is something that has to be *called to mind*'. Competent language users are able to talk about time. They can tell somebody what time it is. They can use devices to time the activities they engage in (e.g. use a stopwatch to determine how long somebody has been running for). They can coordinate their activities by arranging to do things at a certain time in a certain place. They are usually able to, say, arrive at work on time. But when asked 'what is time?' in a philosophy class they might be

---

German version of the sentence: 'Die Probleme werden gelöst, nicht durch Beibringen neuer Erfahrung, sondern durch Zusammenstellung des längst Bekannten').

puzzled. The solution is to look carefully at familiar expressions and activities involving time and to assemble those in such a way as to bring about clarity. It is to remind ourselves of things that we are already familiar with.[76]

This philosophical method (or set of methods) is controversial. Not every philosopher will accept that philosophical problems in metaphysics, epistemology, and the philosophy of language are to be solved by producing a synopsis of familiar linguistic rules and reminders of the kinds of activities we engage in involving the concept we are confused about. Nonetheless, it should be clear that it is not 'blatantly false' that this is the way to go about solving philosophical problems. Eagleton himself acknowledges the power of this philosophical approach when he looks at Wittgenstein's reminders concerning our use of the concepts 'knowledge' and 'pain': reminders about the use of those expressions which we, as competent language users, are familiar with and which help us to overcome philosophical confusion.[77]

Eagleton claims that Wittgenstein is limited in that he does not acknowledge connections between ideology, mystification, and power in the manner of Habermas or Marx. While it is true that Wittgenstein does not discuss ideology and power relations it is not clear that it is a limitation of Wittgenstein's philosophy. In their approaches to metaphysics and ideology there are clear differences between Marx and Wittgenstein. Marx was a part of the philosophical tradition which saw philosophy as a cognitive discipline whereas Wittgenstein saw philosophy's aim as being clarity and understanding.[78] Marx

---

[76] There is a good discussion of Augustine's philosophical confusions concerning time in Severin Schroeder's book about Wittgenstein. He also discusses Wittgensteinian responses to those concerns in that book (see S. Schroeder, *Wittgenstein*, Cambridge: Polity, 2006, pp. 158–59).

[77] Eagleton discusses knowledge of other people's pain and what we say about our own experience of pain on page 135 of *Materialism*. His discussion is based on §246 of Wittgenstein's *Philosophical Investigations*. In Section 6.5.4 of this chapter I examine this passage from Wittgenstein's work as well as Eagleton's own earlier discussion of the example in 'Wittgenstein's Friends'.

[78] There are passages in *Materialism* which suggest that Eagleton thinks Wittgenstein's aim is to get at the truth (but in a roundabout way). For example, Eagleton says that 'Wittgenstein sees the task of the philosopher not as delivering the truth head-on' (p. 144) and later says that for Wittgenstein 'it is because the truth is so obvious that we fail to notice it' (whereas in Marx's case 'the obvious is the very homeland of ideology') (p. 147). However, in the passage in the *Investigations* where Wittgenstein says something similar to this (§129) he makes no mention of truth. He says that 'the aspects of things that are most important for us are hidden because of their simplicity and familiarity (One is unable to notice something – because it is always before one's eyes)' but Wittgenstein is clear that the enquiry he is engaged in is not empirical but is concerned with 'the workings of our language' (§109) – with grammar or with what *makes sense*.

wanted to unmask the illusions that we are tempted by as a result of being alienated under capitalism and he saw those illusions as often being in the service of power. If you clear away the class system and its relationships of power and produce a society where people are equal then the accompanying illusions will disappear along with the system. On the other hand, Wittgenstein, although he talks in a similar way about 'illusions', is primarily concerned with *grammatical* illusions. Philosophers have been under the impression that they are involved in a profound search for truth about the essential nature of things. For example, in his own earlier philosophy Wittgenstein had thought of reality as composed of simple (unanalysable) elements such as the colour red. In the *Investigations* he notes that metaphysicians (such as himself in his own earlier work) have been tempted to say such things as that 'simples (like redness) are indestructible'. However, in his later philosophy Wittgenstein rejects this approach and argues that statements like 'redness is indestructible' are metaphysical statements and metaphysical statements are either confused formulations of grammatical propositions or nonsense and in neither case can they be true or false. We might say that it is part of the grammar of the word 'red' that nothing counts as destroying red or that it is nonsense to say that 'redness might be destroyed' (or that it is indestructible).[79] What metaphysicians do is confuse factual and conceptual investigations. In making metaphysical statements they think of what they are saying as being about the world (factual) *and* as being necessarily true (conceptual).[80]

When Marx speaks of illusions he is not talking about the illusion that something (e.g. a claim about something necessarily existing) makes sense but the illusion that something is *true*. His claim is that ideology deals in falsehoods, not that it deals in nonsense. Politicians, priests, and others in powerful positions tell us things that are false in order to shore up their own position in society, to retain their power and their privileges. To be sure, they might not recognize what they are saying as being false themselves. They might actually buy into the ideology that they promote, and the preservation of power

---

[79] The discussion of redness is in §§55–60 of the *Philosophical Investigations*. Elsewhere in the *Investigations* Wittgenstein says that 'Language is something unique' is a superstition produced by grammatical illusions (§110), and that the private exhibition of pain is an illusion (§311). Robert Arrington gives a very clear explanation of §58 from the *Philosophical Investigations* in his paper 'Theology as Grammar' (p. 170). There he says, '"Red exists" is [...] nonsense if it is taken to be a factual claim. But "Red exists" might have a use and hence a meaning: it might be taken to say that "red" has a meaning. In other words it might be used to license or authorise the use of the term "red" in our ordinary empirical discourse.'

[80] See L. Wittgenstein, *Zettel*, where he says, 'The essential thing about metaphysics: it obliterates the distinction between factual and conceptual investigations' (§458).

is not the only reason behind the spreading of false ideologies. The point is that Marx is primarily concerned with guiding us towards truths about reality and to the recognition of mechanisms for promoting falsehood and illusion. Marx claims that the task of history is 'to establish the truth of this world' and philosophy's task is 'in the service of history' and that task is 'to unmask human self-alienation in its *secular forms* once its *sacred* form has been unmasked'.[81]

It is interesting that Eagleton lists 'God' and 'Geist' among possible metaphysical foundations when he discusses metaphysics in *Materialism*. This is of interest, in part, because Wittgenstein, in his later work, does not think of metaphysics as encompassing religion (although he does think that there are confused ways of construing religion – scientistic or superstitious ways of construing religion[82]). In the *Investigations* Wittgenstein (very briefly) suggests that we should recognize 'theology as grammar' (§373). What this means is that assertions made by theologians, such as 'God exists', are not to be understood as factual claims about a being but as grammatical remarks which tell us how to use theological terms in religious discourse. What 'God exists' tells us is that it is incorrect to use the term 'God' if we are wondering about the existence of a being or ascribing some probability to the existence of a being. 'God exists' is not like 'a planet exists beyond the dwarf planet Pluto' (an empirical claim we might produce evidence for). However, what this also means is that if the theologian thinks of themselves as asserting a true, factual claim, in saying that 'God exists' then they are slipping into metaphysics – confusing factual and conceptual claims.[83] Wittgenstein did not think of religion as being mistaken, nonsensical, or unjustified and so did not think of it as a piece of metaphysics to be overcome or knocked down (although that does not rule out the possibility that theologians might get into metaphysical muddles).

Wittgenstein's position stands in fairly stark contrast with Marx's understanding of religion. Marx saw religion as being 'illusory', as being something

---

[81] K. Marx, *Critique of Hegel's 'Philosophy of Right'*, Cambridge: Cambridge University Press, p. 132.

[82] E.g. in 'Lectures on Religious Belief', Wittgenstein says that 'Father O'Hara is one of those people who make it [religion] a question of science […] I would definitely call O'Hara unreasonable. I would say, if this is religious belief then it's all superstition' (L. Wittgenstein, 'Lectures on Religious Belief', in Cyril Barrett (ed.), *Lectures & Conversations*, Berkeley: University of California Press, 1966, p. 59).

[83] There is a lot of debate even among those who otherwise agree with much of what Wittgenstein has to say on other issues about this way of understanding religion. Kai Neilsen, for example, argues that for the sake of consistency Wittgenstein should claim that religion is incoherent and that it is a 'house of cards' which should fall along with the rest of metaphysics because religion is inescapably metaphysical (see K. Nielsen, 'Wittgenstein and Wittgensteinians on Religion', in Robert L. Arrington and Mark Addis (eds), *Wittgenstein and the Philosophy of Religion*, London: Routledge, 2001).

which had to be overcome in the interest of getting at the truth about the world. Religion, on Marx's view, was used by the ruling class to pacify the populace and prevent them rising up against them. Working people might cling to the promise of happiness in the afterlife rather than fighting to establish a happy situation for themselves in the here and now. They might absorb themselves in religious practice rather than in political organization. It was a part of ruling-class ideology, 'the opium of the people'.[84] Working people under capitalism live in 'a condition which requires illusions'[85] but if they were to succeed in rising up against capitalism and establishing a socialist society then the need for the illusions of religion would disappear and religion would disappear eventually too.[86]

However, despite the clear differences between Marx and Wittgenstein elements of the two positions could be brought together in helping us to understand religion and its role in our lives. Understanding theology as grammar does not rule out it being used to manipulate working people and Wittgensteinian approaches to unmasking nonsense could be used as a tool by Marxists in picking apart the pronouncements of religious figures and theologians.

6.5.7 *Transforming Everyday Life*

Finally I want to consider Eagleton's claim that action to transform our practical or everyday life is the way to abolish metaphysics. Given that Wittgenstein did not think that all philosophical problems were rooted in language and that some of them were rooted in forms of life or cultural factors it is fair to say that Wittgenstein thought that some philosophical problems could be gotten rid of by transforming our practical life as Eagleton suggests. The passage from Wittgenstein's *Remarks on the Foundations of Mathematics* cited above ('the sickness of a time is cured by an alteration in the mode of life of human beings') is evidence that this was Wittgenstein's attitude.[87] However, since it is always

---

[84] Marx *Critique of Hegel's 'Philosophy of Right'*, p. 131.
[85] Ibid.
[86] This is a slightly crude and one-sided account of Marx's understanding of religion. While it is true that Marx viewed religion as illusory and as something used to keep working people from rising up against their oppressors he also saw it as the 'heart of a heartless world' (*Critique of Hegel's 'Philosophy of Right'*, p. 131). Marxists in more recent years (including Terry Eagleton) have also recognized that religion can have emancipatory potential (liberation theology, etc.).
[87] There is also this from Rush Rhees's notes:

Wittgenstein's frequent mentions of the way anti Semitism had disappeared in Russia by a change in the form of society. I think he believed that the central place of manual

possible that concepts like 'knowledge', 'being', and 'I' will be misused in such a way that they are 'idling' metaphysical or philosophical problems can never be shown the door for good. Eagleton may well be right in thinking that dramatic changes in economic and political life would make certain metaphysical views (or 'wrong turnings') less tempting but he has not demonstrated that Marxist philosophy offers a superior way of abolishing metaphysics and it is at best unclear that this could ever be done. Perhaps a better way of thinking about metaphysics would be to think of Marxist and Wittgensteinian philosophies as complementary. Both offer distinctive ways of thinking about and dealing with metaphysical problems that are not obviously in conflict always and everywhere. Their accounts of religion can also be used in conjunction with each other in helping us to understand different aspects of religion. Some philosophical problems (as well as problematic ideology) might pass away as circumstances are transformed and some might be dissolved by putting up signposts to warn against tempting wrong turnings. Marxists must not be racing motorists!

---

labour and the vanishing of the prestige that money gives with us, was one main factor in this. I remember that when I told him there was considerable or growing anti-semitism among the blacks in New York and some other cities, he was astonished and did not really believe it; it was just the sort of thing that was unnatural and couldn't happen. (in 'Wittgenstein's Philosophical Conversations with Rush Rhees', p. 59)

Part 3

APPLYING WITTGENSTEIN'S WORK TO PROBLEMS IN SOCIAL PHILOSOPHY

Chapter 7
WITTGENSTEIN AND FREEDOM OF THE WILL

7.1 Introduction

It might seem that Wittgenstein's philosophical remarks could be useful in getting to grips with traditional problems in epistemology and metaphysics but that they have little bearing on social and political philosophy. However, that would be to draw a conclusion too quickly. Philosophers from the tradition that Wittgenstein distanced himself from concerned themselves with social and political issues going at least as far back as Socrates and Plato. In the *Republic*, for example, Plato presents a philosophy of mind and epistemology that parallels and complements his political philosophy. Traditional philosophers such as Plato saw their political philosophy as something intertwined with their reflections upon knowledge, mind, and reality and there are still plenty of social philosophers today who see their social-philosophical concerns as being entwined with their philosophy of mind and epistemology. So, one way in which Wittgenstein's remarks might have a bearing on political philosophy is that his remarks might undermine political philosophies that are entwined with confused thoughts about language, metaphysics, and epistemology.

Having discussed the nature of philosophy and political ideologies in previous chapters, the focus of this chapter will be on the issue of freedom of the will. This is a traditional philosophical problem (or set of problems) and also one that appears to have implications for social and political philosophy. Conceptions of freedom, and of decision-making, are implicated in discussions of democracy, of legal responsibility, and of morality. If determinism is correct then it would seem to have very profound implications for our understandings of these issues. The role of Wittgensteinian philosophy in discussing these issues, I suggest, is to help us to get clear about the relevant concepts and ultimately to give us the understanding that will make the problems dissolve – to make latent nonsense patent nonsense and to show that the formulation of the problems involves some conceptual confusion.

As hinted at above, there is not one single problem of freedom of the will. Various problems have arisen in the history of philosophy: some relating freedom to goodness and evil, some concerning the role of God in the universe and its compatibility with human freedom, and others concerning causation or mental causation. Philosophers have asked questions like 'Can I freely choose to do evil?', 'If God knows what will happen in the future then how can it be that my actions were freely decided upon by myself?', 'If every action has a cause and causes necessitate their effects then how can my actions be free?', 'How can mental faculties (the will) or mental acts (volitions) bring about movements in a body?', and 'Does my action being free imply that I could have done otherwise?' I cannot possibly hope to give a thorough survey of these problems, let alone solve or dissolve them within this chapter and so the scope of the chapter will be more restricted.

In a recent paper, 'Folk Psychology and Freedom of the Will', Martin Kusch has suggested that it might be fruitful to approach problems surrounding freedom of the will by connecting those problems to debates about folk psychology. Debates about folk psychology would benefit from expanding their focus out from belief, desire, and action into questions about intentions and volitions and philosophers of action would benefit from reflecting on debates about folk psychology.[1] I agree with Kusch that approaching problems concerning freedom of the will in the light of debates about folk psychology could be fruitful and here I will focus on the work of Patricia S. Churchland – a philosopher who discusses both folk psychology and issues surrounding freedom of the will.

Churchland thinks of our ordinary explanations of behaviour in terms of ordinary psychological expressions as being part of a theoretical framework. The framework includes our ordinary psychological concepts (e.g. belief, desire, pain, memory, intention, hunger) and also offers up causal laws (e.g. a person denied food for a great length of time will feel hungry) and warrants predictions. Given that our ordinary psychological concepts and ordinary explanations of action are part of a theory we might ask how that theory has fared and whether other theories might fare better. Churchland does not think that folk psychology has been a successful theory.[2] According to Patricia S. Churchland, and her husband Paul Churchland, folk psychology has failed to explain various things, such as why we get depressed or fall in love,[3] and it

---

[1] M. Kusch, 'Folk Psychology and Freedom of the Will', in D. Hutto and M. Ratcliffe (eds), *Folk Psychology Reassessed*, Dordrecht: Springer, 2007, pp. 175–88.

[2] E.g. in 'The Impact of Neuroscience in Philosophy' she says that 'folk psychology embodies much misdirection' and suggests that we should turn to neuroscience to understand human morality and decision-making (in *Neuron*, vol. 60, 6 November 2008, p. 409).

[3] In 'The Impact of Neuroscience on Philosophy' Patricia S. Churchland says that 'though introspection [the preferred method of folk psychologists] is useful the brain is not rigged to directly know much about itself, such as why we are depressed or in love or that factors such as serotonin levels influence our decisions' (p. 409).

has failed to make progress.[4] It also faces the problem that it cannot be reduced to successful theories in neurobiology, physics, and chemistry.[5] Given its crudity and the fact that it cannot be reduced to more successful, advanced, and advancing theoretical frameworks, folk psychology should be eliminated and replaced with a neuroscientific psychology, according to the Churchlands.[6]

Thinking again about the problems of freedom of the will mentioned above it is clear that they involve the kind of concepts that the Churchlands think are involved in our folk psychological framework. There are questions about *knowledge* of the future, there are questions about *decisions* being made by human beings, and questions about human beings *intending* to do things and *willing* that things should be the case are implicated. Questions about rationality are also clearly closely involved in discussion of human beings making choices or decisions (freely). So, concepts such as *belief, desire, thought,* and *reason* are tied up with questions about freedom of the will. According to the Churchlands these concepts from 'folk psychology' are vacuous and so the formulation of traditional philosophical problems about freedom of the will involves vacuous concepts, on their view.

In a recent article Patricia Churchland and Christopher Suhler have turned to the notion of *control*. In order to understand the notion of control and the implications of self-control within situations where human beings might be held morally or legally responsible Churchland and Suhler think that we should not rely on our ordinary understanding of the notion but should instead formulate a neurobiological model of control.[7] This fits with Churchland's earlier contention that ordinary psychological notions should be eliminated and replaced with sharper notions more suited to advanced scientific theories.

In this chapter I intend to discuss Churchland and Suhler's article and then present some Wittgensteinian criticisms of the arguments they make in it. My purpose is to demonstrate the usefulness of a Wittgensteinian approach to social and political philosophy. I also hope that I make plausible that problems

---

[4] The question of progress in psychology is briefly addressed in the first chapter of this book (Section 1.5) – as is reductionism (Section 1.2).

[5] P. M. Churchland, 'Folk Psychology', in S. Guttenplan (ed.), *A Companion to the Philosophy of Mind*, Oxford: Blackwell.

[6] Patricia Churchland says that 'once folk psychology is held at arm's length and evaluated for theoretical strength in the way that any theory is evaluated, the more folkishly inept, soft and narrow it seems to be', in *Neurophilosophy: Toward a Unified Science of the Mind/Brain*, Cambridge, MA: MIT Press, 1986, p. 395.

[7] P. S. Churchland and C. L. Suhler, 'Control: Conscious and Otherwise', *Trends in Cognitive Science*, vol. 13, no. 8, 2009, pp. 341–47.

of freedom of the will are conceptual problems, although, as mentioned earlier, it would be impossible to discuss all of the problems in a brief chapter.

7.2 Churchland and Suhler on Control

In their article 'Control: Conscious and Otherwise' Churchland and Suhler try to give a clear (re)definition of 'control' in response to concerns raised by what is known as the 'Frail Control hypothesis'. In recent years philosophers and social psychologists have drawn attention to the fact that environmental factors can have a large influence on the way that people behave and the choices they make in ways that they are unaware of. For example, according to Isen and Levin, 'passersby who had just found a dime were twenty-two times more likely to help a woman who had dropped some papers than passersby who did not find a dime'[8] and another similar study has found that when people are in orderly surroundings they are much less likely to litter than when they are in disorderly conditions.[9] The philosopher John Doris has drawn on a range of studies like these to argue that actions can be excused much more frequently than previously assumed because these studies show that choices are strongly affected by circumstances in ways people are unaware of and if that is so then the people in question have an excuse for their action.[10]

In opposition to Doris, Churchland and Suhler argue that if we take into account data from neurobiology and evolutionary theory, as well as behavioural and clinical data, we can arrive at an account of control where people can be held responsible for their actions despite having been influenced by circumstances unknowingly. One of their conclusions is that 'consciousness is not a necessary condition for control' and they think that empirical data supports that conclusion. Moreover, they think that it is a virtue of their account that 'it is agnostic as to whether the underlying processes [supporting control] are conscious or nonconscious'.[11]

The kind of data that Churchland and Suhler deem to be relevant to their conclusion is data from neuroscience such as studies which have shown

---

[8] A. M. Isen and P. F. Levin, 'Effect of Feeling Good on Helping: Cookies and Kindness', *Journal of Personality and Social Psychology*, 21, 1972, pp. 384–88, cited in J. M. Doris and D. Murphy, 'From My Lai to Abu Ghraib: The Moral psychology of Atrocity', *Midwest Studies in Philosophy*, vol. 31, 2007, p. 34.

[9] K. Keizer, S. Lindenberg, and L. Steg, 'The Spreading of Disorder', *Science*, vol. 322, pp. 1681–85.

[10] See Churchland and Suhler, 'Control', p. 342; and J. M. Doris, 'Persons, Situations, and Virtue Ethics', *Nous*, vol. 32, pp. 504–30.

[11] Churchland and Suhler, 'Control', pp. 341–42.

that low serotonin levels are associated with impulsive and violent behaviour and evidence that the dopamine system plays a role in the development of normal social and cognitive abilities, including the development of social skills.[12] Social skills, in turn, are implicated in human beings exercising control. Human beings have to be able to suppress desires (to fight, cheat, etc.) in order to function well in society. Individuals who are able to restrain themselves appropriately, who are able to control impulses and desires, as well as things like when to urinate and defecate, are better able to get on in the world and can be held responsible for breaking social norms or laws. One of Churchland and Suhler's examples is the case of the man who wets his pants through fear when he is about to be executed.[13] The story Churchland and Suhler tell is that man wets his pants because his brain reacts to stress with a rise in corticotrophin releasing factor (CRF), glucocorticoids, epinephrine, and norepinephrine, which disrupts the normal levels of neurochemicals in his brain.[14] As a result of considering cases like these Churchland and Suhler suggest that the meaning of 'control' might be sharpened. Their model of control has two components:

> The first component is anatomical, specifying that the brain regions and pathways implicated in control are intact and that behaviour is regulated by these mechanisms in a way consistent with prototypical cases of good control [...] The second component is physiological, and includes the molecular mechanisms whereby control is regulated [...] functionality requires that the levels of various neurochemicals – neurotransmitters, hormones, enzymes and so on – are maintained normally [...] [T]he account just sketched does not set the unreasonable standard that every relevant neurochemical must be at its ideal level or even within its normal range. Instead, the physiological requirement for being in control is defined in terms of a hyper-region in an n-dimensional 'control space'.[15]

---

[12] Churchland and Suhler, 'Control', p. 343. Churchland and Suhler cite A. Diamond, 'The Early Development of Executive Functions', in E. Bialystok and F. Craik (eds), *Lifespan, Cognition: Mechanisms of Change–*, Oxford: Oxford University Press, 2006, pp. 70–95, in support of their claim about dopamine and they cite P. F. Ferrari et al., 'Serotonin and Aggressive Behavior in Rodents and Nonhuman Primates: Predispositions and Plasticity', *European Journal of Pharmacology*, 526, pp. 259–73, in support of their claim about serotonin.
[13] Churchland and Suhler, 'Control', p. 344.
[14] Ibid., p. 344.
[15] Ibid., pp. 343–44.

This model of control is then deployed in opposition to another model of control – the neo-Kantian one. According to the neo-Kantian picture we reason before we make free decisions and we can be held responsible only for decisions we have made freely. Moreover, that reasoning must be transparent to us; otherwise, it would be a mere cause, 'a reason must be conscious to be a reason at all. Control […] is […] limited to those cases where most or all evidence, reasons, weighting of reasons and so forth that contribute to a choice are consciously accessible.'[16] According to Churchland and Suhler, however, the role of conscious awareness of reasons in considering whether an action is controlled is not something that can be determined a priori (through 'stipulation, intuition, or semantics') because deciding whether an action is controlled, relative to neurobiological criteria, is a matter of scientific discovery.[17]

Churchland and Suhler then give some further examples in an effort to show that their model of control is more plausible than the neo-Kantian one. They argue that the development of skills is often implicated in controlled action and that the development of skills also leads to conscious activity playing less of a role in relevant actions. For example, the development of social skills means that acting nicely, politely, or appropriately becomes second nature and people who have those social skills do not need to consciously work out what to do in many situations. Adults do not have to reason in order not to break wind in polite company and they do not have to consciously figure out that they should shake hands with someone when they meet them.[18] Commenting on the way in which social skills become habitual Churchland and Suhler say that 'habit and routine serve to spare the brain the energetic costs of close attention'[19] and they also suggest that the skills underlying habitual actions provide us with an alternative to the neo-Kantian model, with skills taking the place of reasons: 'Cognitive, motor, and social skills […] are often invoked in later explanations of actions and are certainly robust enough in their guidance of action to be considered genuine reasons […] the idea that reasons and control can be (and often are) nonconscious […] is consistent with the data.'[20] So, as mentioned above, Churchland and Suhler feel justified in concluding that consciousness is not necessary for control. Their new model of control allows us to get around the problems presented by the frail control hypothesis and gives us a sharper definition of control for future studies of the phenomenon, on their view.

---

[16] Ibid., p. 345.
[17] Ibid.
[18] Ibid.
[19] Ibid.
[20] Ibid.

7.3 Problems with Churchland and Suhler's Argument

7.3.1 *Consciousness*

One problem with Churchland and Suhler's argument is that they do not clearly distinguish between forms of consciousness and nor are they clear about the various things that we might be conscious *of* in the kinds of cases they discuss. Churchland and Suhler discuss many cases but their focus is on the kinds of cases mentioned above, of people being more generous after finding a coin or of people being more likely to litter in messy conditions, which are seemingly relevant to the frail control hypothesis. In the case of someone littering in a messy area it is clear that the person is conscious in at least one sense. The person doing the littering is not asleep, not dead drunk, not knocked out, not in a coma. They are conscious in that they are *awake*, what Maxwell Bennett and Peter Hacker call 'intransitive consciousness'.[21] When Churchland and Suhler say that 'consciousness is not a necessary condition for control', presumably they do not have intransitive consciousness in mind. It is clear that in the case of someone finding a coin and then being generous and the case of someone littering in a 'disorderly' area that the people in question are awake. It may be that we can sometimes hold people responsible for things that they do in their sleep but this does not seem to be what Churchland and Suhler have in mind.[22]

Given that Churchland and Suhler are not concerned with intransitive consciousness it seems they must be concerned with one or another form of transitive consciousness – being conscious *of* something or other. In the kinds of cases used to advance the frail control hypothesis what the people are supposedly not conscious *of* is the influence that their circumstances have on their behaviour. But what Churchland and Suhler do not discuss is the various other things that the participants may well have been conscious of and that would be relevant to determining whether the person could be held responsible for their actions. Take the littering case, for example, where more people dropped

---

[21] M. Bennett, M. and P. M. S. Hacker, *Philosophical Foundations of Neuroscience*, Oxford: Blackwell, 2003, p. 244.

[22] Note: It is not totally obvious that Churchland and Suhler are not talking about intransitive consciousness. In her recent book, *Touching a Nerve: Our Brains, Our Selves* (London: W. W. Norton, 2013), Churchland comments on whether consciousness is necessary for speech. She concludes that it is necessary for speech because 'you cannot have a conversation while in deep sleep or in a coma' (p. 198). A few pages later she notes that Jaak Panksepp claims that 'being conscious enables the acquisition of language, not the other way around' and says that 'if you are not conscious, in any of the various ways that a person can be nonconscious (for example, in deep sleep) you are not going to learn much of anything' (p. 204). Here she clearly has *intransitive* consciousness in mind.

litter (a flyer that had been attached to their bicycle) in a 'disorderly' condition (where there was graffiti beside the bicycle rack and a sign prohibiting graffiti) than in an orderly one (with no graffiti).[23] In that case at least two things seem clearly relevant: whether the person was conscious that they were littering in dropping the flyer (presumably they were) and whether the person was conscious that they should not litter (again, presumably they were). In that case it seems we would hold the person responsible for littering. We would say they knew what they were doing, knew that it was wrong, and had no good reason to break the prohibition on littering. It may be that circumstances serve to mitigate responsibility but cases like the littering case do not do anything to demonstrate that our ordinary ways of holding people responsible for actions are in need of revision – that people were not in control of their littering behaviour. That people were influenced by being in an area where anti-graffiti norms were broken does not demonstrate that they were not in control of their actions in dropping litter and nor does it imply that they ceased to be conscious of norms prohibiting littering.

Churchland and Suhler might object that although they do not discuss the various other things that people might be conscious *of* in the littering situation they do at least make it clear that it is transitive consciousness that they have in mind. In making their case they make it clear that they are responding to a neo-Kantian perspective where control (and also presumably responsibility) 'is […] limited to those cases where most or all evidence, reasons, weighting of reasons and so forth that contribute to a choice are consciously accessible'.[24] However, they discuss the Kantian perspective under the heading of 'the role of nonconscious processes'[25] and say that they are agnostic about whether the processes underlying control are conscious or nonconscious.[26] So, there is unclarity surrounding what they mean by 'consciousness' in discussing the Kantian view. It is, at the very best, unclear how it could be that processes could be awake (i.e. be intransitively conscious) or conscious of things (transitively conscious). As Wittgenstein points out, 'only of a living human being and what resembles (behaves like) a living human being can one say: it has sensations; it sees; is blind; hears; is deaf; is conscious or unconscious'.[27] The processes underlying control do not resemble or behave like human beings

---

[23] Keizer, Lindenberg, and Steg, 'The Spreading of Disorder', pp. 1682–83.
[24] Churchland and Suhler, 'Control', p. 345. The Kantian view clearly concerns consciousness *of* various things and so it is concerned with transitive consciousness.
[25] Ibid.
[26] Ibid., pp. 341–42.
[27] L. Wittgenstein, *Philosophical Investigations*, 4th edition, trans. G. E. M. Anscombe, P. M. S. Hacker, and Joachim Schulte, revised by P. M. S. Hacker and Joachim Schulte, Oxford: Wiley-Blackwell, 2009, §281.

in the relevant respects. They do not open their eyes and look at things (they do not have eyes), they do not (and cannot) do things like sit up in bed, or say things, and so we cannot make sense of the claim that they might be conscious. Contrary to what Churchland and Suhler say, it is not a virtue of their account that they are agnostic about whether processes underlying control are conscious, it is a sign of confusion.

However, in their critical discussion of the neo-Kantian perspective, Churchland and Suhler do not always talk about the processes underlying control. They at least sometimes talk about human individuals, their skills and habits, as well as what they – human beings – are conscious or not conscious *of*. They talk about the role of the development of social skills, of social skills becoming second nature, in the controlled behaviour of human beings. They do so in order to make the point that controlled behaviour (that people might be held responsible for) is not always preceded by (conscious) deliberation. For example, they say that 'adults do not have to consciously remind themselves not to break wind in polite company or to shake hands upon meeting someone'.[28] Churchland and Suhler are surely correct about this. We do not always deliberate and are not always aware of deliberating before doing something controlled for which we might be held responsible. However, what Churchland and Suhler have not taken into account is the distinction between *dispositional* and *occurrent* transitive consciousness. Max Bennett and Peter Hacker describe the ways in which we speak about people being conscious *of* various things and make the distinction between dispositional and occurrent transitive consciousness in their book *Philosophical Foundations of Neuroscience*:

> When we say of a person that he is conscious of his ignorance or expertise, or conscious of his superior or inferior social status, we are typically speaking of a *disposition* or *tendency* he has to be conscious [...] of these things [...] *Occurrent* consciousness by contrast, is a matter of currently being conscious of something or conscious that something is thus-and-so.[29]

Given that we recognize this distinction it may be that in the cases Churchland and Suhler describe the people concerned are not *occurrently* conscious of their reason for not breaking wind in polite company but that nonetheless they are *dispositionally* conscious of it. We might say that they are aware or conscious of what they should do in such situations even if they are not conscious of any deliberation (and do not deliberate) about whether they should or should

---

[28] Churchland and Suhler, 'Control', p. 345.
[29] Bennett and Hacker, *Philosophical Foundations of Neuroscience*, p. 248.

not break wind. Similarly, someone might well not deliberate about whether to shake somebody's hand before doing it upon meeting them but we might nonetheless say that they were conscious (*dispositionally*) of what they should do upon meeting someone. What this means is that although Churchland and Suhler have come up with cases that seem to clash with the neo-Kantian picture,[30] they have not demonstrated that 'consciousness is not a necessary condition for control' if we allow that intransitive consciousness and dispositional transitive consciousness count as consciousness.

That is not to say that Churchland and Suhler are wrong, of course. It could be that they only mean 'occurrent transitive consciousness' by 'consciousness' or that they mean something else altogether by 'consciousness'. Given that Churchland is an eliminativist, presumably she thinks that our ordinary concept of consciousness is to be eliminated and replaced by a concept from neuroscience. But the fact remains that it is not clear at all what Churchland and Suhler mean by 'consciousness' and so it is, at best, unclear whether they are correct. As we have already seen they think that 'conscious' and 'nonconscious' might be applied to processes and it is at best unclear what sentences like 'such-and-such a (brain) process is conscious' could mean.[31] To further complicate matters Churchland, in her recent book *Touching a Nerve: Our Brains, Our Selves*, uses 'consciousness' in a neo-Cartesian sense. Descartes extended the concept of 'consciousness' to encompass 'thoughts' of various kinds, including sensation, perceptual experience, cogitation, and volition. Similarly, many modern philosophers, when they speak of 'consciousness', are talking about a range of different 'experiences' and so philosophers discuss things like 'what it is like to see red' under the banner of 'consciousness'. When Churchland discusses philosophical claims that consciousness is fundamentally mysterious she seems to have something like this use of 'consciousness' in mind, since she presents the problem as being 'how the brain gives rise to thoughts and feelings'[32] (not as being about the relation between brain states/processes/events and being *awake* or *conscious of* things or *conscious that* something is the case). Similarly,

---

[30] It is not clear that their cases do actually work as counterexamples to the neo-Kantian account. The neo-Kantians, according to Churchland and Suhler, say that reasons must be 'consciously accessible' in order for an action to count as one that is under someone's control (p. 345). This seems confused to me but it does not obviously mean that the reasons must have been contemplated or that deliberation/working out must have taken place prior to the action.

[31] Elsewhere, Churchland suggests that 'the results of sensory processing' might 'become conscious' (*Touching a Nerve*, p. 204) but as with the case of processes we can respond with Wittgenstein's reminder that only of a living human being or what resembles one can we say that it is conscious.

[32] Churchland, *Touching a Nerve*, p. 56.

when Churchland is discussing whether animals might be conscious she first cites evidence that other mammals experience 'emotions, hunger, pain, frustration, and hot and cold, for starters' in support of the claim that they can be conscious. Whether they wake up, look around themselves, and are clearly aware of things in their environment are not mentioned in the list, although Churchland does go on to suggest that studying animal brains when they are awake, asleep, or in a coma might settle the issue.[33] This is getting things the wrong way around. We could only have knowledge of the brain states, events, or processes necessary for consciousness if we first knew what consciousness was. Tests on human beings or animals to determine what their brain is doing while they are conscious or unconscious are performed on them using our ordinary behavioural *criteria* for consciousness, for being asleep, for being in a coma, and so on. We know when animals are conscious by looking at *them* and seeing if they are moving around or if they have their eyes open and are responding to things in their environment, not by looking at their brains (although looking at images of their brains from a distance might count as *evidence* that they are conscious, asleep, or in a coma, given what we know about how brains are when creatures are conscious or unconscious). As indicated above, it is human beings and creatures that resemble them in relevant respects that we say are conscious, not their brains. We do not need to look at the brains of creatures to determine whether they can be conscious; we should look at the creatures themselves (and it is clear that many creatures are conscious a lot of the time).

But even in cases where Churchland and Suhler use the word 'conscious' in connection with human beings they use it in a peculiar way. So, for example, they say that 'when social niceties become "second nature", one does not have to *consciously* work out what to do'.[34] Here it is unclear what the role of the word 'consciously' is. Do they just mean that when social niceties become second nature one does not have to work out what to do? Similarly, they say that 'adults do not have to *consciously* remind themselves not to break wind in polite company'[35] but what could this mean except that adults do not have to remind themselves not to break wind in polite company?

These objections are not decisive objections against Churchland and Suhler's conclusion. In fact, these examples do seem to be quite good examples of people doing things that are under their control, that they might be held responsible for, where they were not occurrently conscious of any reason for doing so. Churchland and Suhler are right that people do not always have to

---

[33] Ibid., p. 204.
[34] Churchland and Suhler, 'Control', p. 345 (my italics).
[35] Ibid., p. 345 (my italics).

work out what they are doing before acting in order for what they are doing to count as an action that they might be held responsible for (and where they might be said to be in control of what they are doing). They are right that adults do not have to remind themselves not to break wind when they are in polite company. People do sometimes act spontaneously. They sometimes act without deliberating. But we nonetheless sometimes, rightly, hold them responsible for the things that they do spontaneously, where they do not deliberate. It is worth noting here too that acting spontaneously does not mean acting without reason. It may be that someone acts spontaneously and gives you their reason for doing so after the event. As Peter Hacker notes, 'To gives one's reasons for V-ing is not the same as reporting on one's reasoning.'[36] No reasoning needs to have taken place in order for you to be said to have a reason for acting or for you to be able to give a reason after the event.

7.3.2 *Reasons, Control, and Responsibility*

However, to say that Churchland and Suhler's conclusion is, roughly speaking, correct is not to say that the way they got to the conclusion was not muddled or mistaken in some ways. We have already seen that Churchland and Suhler's use of the term 'conscious' is confused and confusing. There are further (conceptual) confusions in what they have to say about the notion of control and the implications of what they say for the frail control hypothesis. The trouble in this case comes from the fact that they use 'control' in its ordinary sense(s) when they are discussing various cases relevant to the frail control hypothesis but switch to their 'neurobiological account of control' when making their arguments. When arguing against the neo-Kantian requirement that people's reasons must be transparent to them in order for them to be said to be in control of their actions Churchland and Suhler talk about the automization of skills involved in driving, reading, gardening, and getting along with people. In the case of driving we understand control in terms of having influence or sway over a car, directing it where we want it to go. We typically determine whether somebody is in control of their car by looking at the car and seeing if it is steadily on course (not skidding around or swerving when the driver does not want it to). Our criteria are not neurobiological. We do not look at a person's brain to decide whether they are in control of a car. And if a person's brain satisfies the neurobiological criteria offered by Churchland and Suhler but the car skids off the road and crashes we take the fact that the person lost direction of the car to be decisive in deciding whether they were in control rather than the condition of their brain. Of

---

[36] P. M. S. Hacker, *Human Nature: The Categorial Framework*, Oxford: Blackwell, 2007, p. 221.

course, a person might deliberately crash their car and so they might be said to be in control of the car despite having crashed but in that case our criteria for deciding whether the person was in control are still behavioural. If the person said that they were going to crash the car in a certain way and then did that then we would say that they were in control when they crashed the car. That is not to deny that there is any connection between the state of a person's brain and their control over things like cars. We know very well that the effect of alcohol on brain chemistry makes people lose control but again, we do not decide whether they are in control by looking at their brains but by looking at what they are doing. We could only learn of the effects of brain chemistry on control by already having independent criteria for deciding when somebody is in control or not. So, the concept of 'control' involved in the case of driving the car in not the same concept as the one devised by Churchland and Suhler. Moreover, it may well be that there is conceptual diversity among the cases. It is not obvious that the concept of control involved in the car case, where a person has control over an inanimate object, is the same as in the kind of cases Churchland and Suhler mention where people are controlling themselves in social situations. We might distinguish cases of control over inanimate objects, like cars, from cases where what is in question is *self-control*, that is, things like the ability to not show one's feelings and to refrain from doing things that your feelings make you want to do. Another concept that Churchland and Suhler mention is executive control, the ability to carry out complex goal-directed behaviour. Churchland and Suhler equivocate between these various uses of 'control' and their own neurobiological concept.

Churchland and Suhler present their neurobiological concept, where 'neurobiological criteria [...] define the boundaries of control' as being a sharpening of the ordinary concept. However, the ordinary concept is not logically or conceptually related to brain states at all. We have recognized when people are in control of themselves or of objects for millennia, long before the empirical discoveries noted by Churchland and Suhler were made. People have held back from expressing their emotions, have held others responsible for their actions, and engaged in goal-directed behaviour throughout human history. As noted above, we could only make empirical discoveries about the contingent relationships between people's brains and their controlled and goal-directed behaviour if we already had a concept of control in place. So, Churchland and Suhler's concept is not a refinement of the ordinary concept at all. Any conclusions they draw about control using that concept will not in fact be about control but about control*. But if they were going to challenge the frail control hypothesis and the neo-Kantian picture they would need to make their argument using our ordinary notion of control and related action concepts. It is those concepts that are related to the concept of responsibility and that are relevant to whether we should hold people responsible or not.

I earlier mentioned Wittgenstein's grammatical observation that 'only of a living human being and what resembles (behaves like) a living human being can one say: it has sensations; it sees; is blind; hears; is deaf; is conscious or unconscious'. Max Bennett and Peter Hacker use the term 'the *mereological fallacy*' to label arguments which break this grammatical rule. Mereology is the study of relationships between wholes and parts of things. They use the term 'mereological fallacy' because while it makes sense to attribute psychological attributes to a human being or to something that resembles one (a whole creature), there is no such thing as a part of a human being (such as their brain or their neurons) having psychological attributes. As Bennett and Hacker note, psychological attributes 'have no intelligible application to the brain'.[37] One of the major conceptual errors made in Churchland and Suhler's paper is to commit this error. For example, they argue that the 'Zeigarnik effect' implies that 'nonconscious processes continue to keep the goal high in priority until resumption of the goal-related action'[38] but while humans can prioritize the goals they want to pursue it makes no sense to say that their nonconscious processes do. Similarly, they say that 'habit and routine serve to spare the brain the energetic costs of close attention',[39] but while we know what it is for a human being to pay close attention to something we have no idea what it would be for a brain to pay close attention to something. I'm sure that Churchland and Suhler would object to being associated with Cartesianism but central to their argument is a kind of neo-Cartesianism. They have replaced mind-body dualism with brain-body dualism. They want to do away with our ordinary psychological concepts in explaining what we do and replace them with neurophysiological ones. However, in making their arguments they equivocate between the ordinary concepts and neurophysiological ones because although they profess to wanting to be rid of our ordinary psychological concepts they cannot make arguments about control, decisions, and responsibility without them.[40] They argue that the role 'awareness of specific factors must have for an action to be considered controlled, relative to neurobiological criteria, is not a matter of stipulation, intuition or semantics, but scientific discovery' but

---

[37] Bennett and Hacker, *Philosophical Foundations of Neuroscience*, pp. 68–74.
[38] Churchland and Suhler 'Control', p. 343.
[39] Ibid., p. 345.
[40] I think there are other conceptual confusions present in Churchland and Suhler's paper. They conflate habits and reasons for no good reason (p. 345). However, there is not space here to discuss that. Bennett and Hacker's book, mentioned earlier, has a good set of arguments against the eliminativist project (pp. 366–77, *Philosophical Foundations of Neuroscience*).

this is confused. To engage with their opponents they must use the ordinary concept of 'control' and in that case it *is* a matter of semantics whether it is possible to be in control and be held responsible without reasoning (transparently). If we are thinking about what is possible with regard to control (as opposed to control* (Churchland and Suhler's neurophysiological notion)) then empirical evidence about brains is irrelevant to our considerations but mapping the grammar of our ordinary concepts of 'control', 'responsibility', 'reasoning', and 'deliberation' is not. This is where Wittgenstein's grammatical observations are helpful in untangling conceptual muddles.

7.4 Conclusion

We have seen in this chapter that philosophical accounts of the conditions under which we hold people responsible at least sometimes involve conceptual confusions. Accounts of the conditions under which people can be held responsible for their actions have clear implications for political philosophy and Wittgenstein's work can help us to get clear about the use of the relevant expressions. In particular, attention to Wittgenstein's remark that 'only of a living human being and what resembles (behaves like) a living human being can one say: it has sensations; it sees; is blind; hears; is deaf; is conscious or unconscious'[41] could be very useful in untangling confusions present in the work of philosophers, political theorists, and neuroscientists.

---

[41] Wittgenstein, *Philosophical Investigations*, §281.

Chapter 8

WITTGENSTEIN AND JUSTICE

8.1 Introduction

This chapter divides into two main parts. The first part will examine Wittgenstein's relevance to problems concerning justice insofar as his philosophy involves getting clear about concepts. Wittgenstein's philosophical remarks could help us to get to grips with philosophical problems about justice by helping us to get clear about the concept of justice and thereby aiding our understanding. The second part of the chapter moves beyond concerns with getting clear about the concept of justice and asks whether Wittgensteinians have reason to criticize particular conceptions or theories of justice that are currently in circulation and whether Wittgensteinians should favour particular conceptions or theories of justice, before finally discussing some ways in which tools from Wittgenstein's later work might help us to understand and overcome injustices.

8.2 Getting Clear about the Concept of Justice

It is possible that the texts of past philosophers might help us to resolve conceptual problems about justice. However, there are various problems with this. One problem is that some past philosophers wrote in languages other than our own and the translations that we have of their work might obscure the fact that they employed different concepts to us. For example, Hanna Pitkin points out that the ancient Greeks used the word *dike* and had no equivalent to our word 'justice'. *Dike* 'came to mean "justice" and to measure the rightness of human action' but it 'originally meant simply "the way": a descriptive account of how things in fact were, or were done'.[1]

It was *dike* or *dikaiosyne* that Plato wrote about in *The Republic*. The words are usually translated as 'justice' in English translations of Plato's work but according to the translator Ernest Barker that is not a very good translation. The Greek word *dike*, according to Barker, 'includes the ethical notions (or

---

[1] H. F. Pitkin, *Wittgenstein and Justice*, Berkeley: University of California Press, 1972, p. 273.

some of the ethical notions) which belong to our word "righteousness" [2] and Pitkin thinks that if we get a better sense of what the Greek expression means then some of Plato's claims become more plausible. For example, whereas it strikes us as odd to say that justice is the 'master virtue', encompassing all other virtues, we can at least see where someone like Plato is coming from if they say that righteousness is the 'master virtue', containing all others.[3]

So careful attention to the use of the word 'justice' in translations of Plato's works might lead to confusion if we think of his term as being equivalent to the way we use 'justice' now, in English. However, that is not to say that studying Plato's work is of no use at all in shedding light on our concept. If we are aware that Plato used the word *dike* and we are clear about what it means then studying Plato's work might shed light on our own term, 'justice', by way of contrast or by highlighting differences. This was one of Wittgenstein's techniques in helping us to gain clarity about the meaning of expressions. When Maurice Drury asked Wittgenstein what he thought of Hegel Wittgenstein said that 'Hegel seems to me to be always wanting to say that things which look different are really the same. Whereas my interest is in showing that things which look the same are really different. I was thinking of using as a motto for my book a quotation from *King Lear*: "I'll teach you differences."'[4]

Wittgenstein's remarks concerning Plato's discussion of concepts that are only distantly related to justice might also help to shed light on the concept of justice. In the *Blue Book* Wittgenstein said that philosopher's attempts to get clear about the use of certain expressions had been held back, 'shackled', by 'the idea that in order to get clear about the meaning of a general term one had to find the common element in all its applications'.[5] The particular case that Wittgenstein uses as an illustration here is Socrates's discussion with Theaetetus concerning the concept of knowledge in Plato's *Theaetetus*.[6] Wittgenstein notices that when Socrates discusses the question 'what is knowledge?' he commits the error of thinking that answering it would involve finding the common element involved in all cases of knowledge. Socrates, Wittgenstein says, 'does not even regard it as a *preliminary* answer to enumerate

---

[2] Aristotle, *Politics*, trans. Sir Ernest Barker, New York: Oxford University Press, 1958, p. 362 (cited on p. 306 of Pitkin's *Wittgenstein and Justice*).

[3] Pitkin, *Wittgenstein and Justice*, pp. 306–7.

[4] M. O'C. Drury, 'Conversations with Wittgenstein', in Rush Rhees (ed.), *Recollections of Wittgenstein*, Oxford: Oxford University Press, 1984, p. 157.

[5] L. Wittgenstein, *The Blue and Brown Books*, New York: Harper & Row, 1965 [1958], pp. 19–20.

[6] Plato, *Theaetetus*, in *Plato: Complete Works*, John M. Cooper (ed.), Indianapolis, IN: Hackett, 1997, PP. 146c–47c.

cases of knowledge' and yet, Wittgenstein says, this would be satisfactory in the case of a term like 'arithmetic'.[7] To understand what arithmetic is it would be useful to investigate a finite cardinal arithmetic, even if this doesn't tell us about every use of the term 'arithmetic', and to then go on to look at other cases. In the *Philosophical Investigations* Wittgenstein makes a similar case about the use of the term 'game'. There is no single defining common feature of all games, just 'a complicated network of similarities overlapping and criss-crossing'.[8] The lesson from all of this in terms of coming to get a clear idea of what 'justice' means is that we should be careful not to assume that there must be some single defining feature in common to all cases of justice. It seems unlikely that we would be able to find a common feature given that we talk about just men, just acts, just outcomes, just states of affairs, distributive justice, procedural justice, social justice, civil justice, and so on. Indeed, David Wiggins notes that Aristotle distinguished at least four kinds of justice; 'justice of allocations, [...] justice of rectifications, [...] commercial justice, [...] equity' – to which neo-Aristotelians could add 'justice of penalties, [...] economic justice, [...] fiscal justice, administrative justice'[9] and Wiggins claims that 'there is no serious question of deducing any one of Aristotle's kinds from any of the others or of deducing all four from a more fundamental idea'.[10]

Returning to Wittgenstein's discussion of games, Wittgenstein also talked about games in relation to language when he was trying to clarify what 'language' is. One of the most well-known pieces of terminology to come out of Wittgenstein's later work is the term 'language game'. In rejecting his own earlier emphasis on assertoric uses of language in the *Tractatus* and his early claim that assertoric sentences depict states of affairs Wittgenstein pointed to the many different uses of language when he discussed it in his later work. So, in the *Philosophical Investigations* he asks us to

> consider the variety of language-games in the following examples and in others:
> Giving orders, and acting on them –
> Describing an object by its appearance, or by its measurements –
> Constructing an object from a description (a drawing) –

---

[7] Wittgenstein, *The Blue and Brown Books*, p. 20.
[8] L. Wittgenstein, *Philosophical Investigations*, revised 4th edition by P. M. S. Hacker and Joachim Schulte, trans. G. E. M. Anscombe, P. M. S. Hacker, and Joachim Schulte, Oxford: Wiley-Blackwell, 2009, §66.
[9] D. Wiggins, 'Neo-Aristotelean Reflections on Justice', *Mind*, vol. 113, no. 451, July 2004, p. 479.
[10] Ibid.

Reporting an event –
Speculating about the event –
Forming and testing a hypothesis –
Presenting the results of an experiment in tables and diagrams –
Making up a story; and reading one –
Acting in a play –
Singing rounds –
Guessing riddles –
Cracking a joke, telling one –
[…] Requesting, thanking, cursing, greeting, praying.

One of the points in using the term 'game' here is to emphasize that we do a variety of different things with language. Language games are diverse in a similar way to which games are diverse. There is no single common feature to all language games just as there is no single common feature to all games. What Wittgenstein also wanted to emphasize was the fact that language is spoken in the course of a variety of different kinds of activities that we engage in as we live our lives: 'the *speaking* of language is part of an activity, or of a form of life.'[11]

Thinking in this way about the various different things we *do* with language and about the various regions of discourse and how they are embedded in our lives draws us away from the temptation to assimilate uses of language and to think in simple terms about words as naming objects and sentences as describing states of affairs. 'Justice' is a noun but that does not mean that we should think about it as a name for an object. Taking on board Wittgenstein's observations about the variety of language games should leave us open to the possibility that we might do various different things with the word 'justice' (it is used in a variety of different language games) and that sentences including the expression might have different logical characteristics to sentences including other kinds of expressions, used in other language games. This is what Hanna Pitkin argues in *Wittgenstein and Justice*. There she contrasts the use of 'justice' with the use of 'delicious' and of 'green'. She points out that we would have different responses to other cultures when it comes to their examples of such things (an example of something that is *just*, an example of something that is *delicious*, an example of something that is *green*). A person from another culture might provide a different example of something delicious (e.g. rotten whale blubber) than someone from our own culture would provide (e.g. chocolate ice cream). Indeed, people within a single culture provide many different examples of what is delicious and they disagree about whether those things

---

[11] Wittgenstein, *Philosophical Investigations*, §23.

are delicious but we nonetheless do not think that the people in question are necessarily using the word incorrectly. If they enjoy what they are eating, have more, recommend it to other people, and we have no reason to think they are being insincere then we recognize that the person eating, say, whale blubber, really does think that it is delicious. It is possible that they are using the concept 'delicious' just as we do. However, if someone provides a colour sample different from our colour samples for green things, for example, a colour sample that we would call 'blue', then we would say immediately that they were not using our concept 'green'. There are then clear logical differences between our colour language and our language concerning matters of taste. Our use of the term 'justice' is in some ways similar to our use of the word 'delicious'. It is possible that we could accept an example unlike any that we had seen before as an example of justice – an example from another culture or from our own. However, we would not be as lax in the case of justice as we would about examples of things that are delicious.[12] As Pitkin says, 'Not merely *any* standards will qualify as standards of justice; not merely any example will be an example of justice. If a speaker considers a certain situation just, he must in principle be prepared to show us *how* it is just, what is just about it.'[13] Justice is the kind of concept that 'involves standards and the possibility of judgement and justification (as the etymology would suggest)'.[14]

As Pitkin suggests, learning about the etymology of a word might help us to get clearer about its meaning. However, we should perhaps be a bit wary of Pitkin's claims that 'a word's former meanings are the root sources of its present ones' and that 'the older meaning is in a way still present in the newer one',[15] since this ties the meaning of a word too closely to its etymology. Wittgenstein remarked that 'for a large class of cases of the employment of the word "meaning" – though not for *all* – this word can be explained in this way: the meaning of a word is its use in the language'.[16] Although etymology can help us to get clearer about the meaning of a word by helping us to recognize its ties with other words (or just earlier meanings of the same word) that might shed

---

[12] Peg O'Connor makes the point that we should be very careful to distinguish matters of taste from moral matters and criticizes C. L. Stevenson for failing to clearly distinguish the two in her (Wittgenstein-inspired) book *Morality and Our Complicated Form of Life* (University Park: Pennsylvania State University Press, 2008). There she says that 'differences in morality cut deeper or go beyond differences in taste, and we are inclined to say that we can have better or worse answers or resolutions to these conflicts, Something more is at stake in moral disagreements than just taste' (p. 146).

[13] Pitkin, *Wittgenstein and Justice*, p. 182.

[14] Ibid., p. 183.

[15] Ibid., p. 10.

[16] Wittgenstein, *Philosophical Investigations*, §43.

light on the meaning of the word in question it is obviously not the case that a word just means what its etymological root means (and, of course, Pitkin does not claim *this*). Etymology does not give us meaning whereas explanations of the meaning of the word, often in terms of the word's use in the language, do give us the meaning of a word. An illustration of how far apart a word can come from etymology is the case of surnames. English people (and people in many other countries) often have surnames that come from words for occupations. People in England have names like Sarah *Baker*, Jonathan *Weaver*, or Polly *Gardener*. However, their surnames are not used as words for occupations when referring to people using their surnames. 'Baker' does not mean 'a person whose trade is making bread and cakes' when it is used as a surname. Indeed, it is not clear that it means anything at all when used as a surname.[17]

However, in the case of the word 'justice' I think it is useful to look at the root of the word and words with common roots. If we examine the etymology of 'justice' we see that it is closely related to words like 'law', 'right', 'judge', and 'judgement' and it is clear that even today justice has something to do with legal systems, judges passing judgements, and with questions about what is right, or what the right thing to do is. What a Wittgensteinian might well also do is to look at words that are closely related in meaning (whether related etymologically or not). In the case of 'just' they might compare words such as 'fair', 'equitable', 'honest', 'right', 'impartial', 'getting what is due', and 'desert/deserved'. If we are having difficulty with grasping the meaning of the word 'justice' then what we might need is a *surveyable representation* – an overview of the use of the word and its relation to other words – which might help us to see the meaning clearly by seeing how its use differs from other words. As Wittgenstein said, 'A main source of our failure to understand is that we don't have *an overview* of the use of our words. – Our grammar is deficient in surveyability. A surveyable representation produces precisely that kind of understanding which consists in "seeing connections". Hence the importance of finding and inventing *intermediate links*.'

So, in summary, Wittgenstein might be of help in philosophical discussions about justice by helping us to achieve clarity about our concepts. We can do that in various ways: by being sensitive to the fact that philosophers in the past may have used words differently to the way we do now, by being aware that we should not look for a single common element in all instances of justice, by being sensitive to the fact that 'justice' has a role in different language games,

---

[17] Compare §3.323 of Wittgenstein's *Tractatus*: 'In the proposition, "Green is green" – where the first word is the proper name of a person and the last an adjective – these words do not merely have different meanings: they are different symbols' (L. Wittgenstein, *Tractatus Logico-Philosophicus*, London: Routledge, 1974, p. 16).

by examining the etymology of the word, and by producing an overview of the word 'justice' in relation to words like 'fairness', 'impartiality', 'judge', 'judgement', and so on. I do not take this list to be exhaustive and following these recommendations may not result in the understanding that we need. There might be other things we can do but these are at least some of the things we can do suggested by Wittgenstein's work.[18]

8.3 Does Wittgenstein's Philosophical Work Suggest That We Should Favour Particular Conceptions of Justice?

We might think that given that Wittgenstein's work is primarily concerned with concepts, moreover that it is a descriptive activity – describing grammar, rather than presenting explanations or theories – that Wittgenstein would not have anything to say to us about which conceptions or theories of justice we should accept. However, we have already seen in the first section that Wittgenstein demonstrated that we should not expect words to refer to things with a single feature in common and we have also seen that we have reason to doubt that instances of justice have a single feature in common. This gives us some reason to be suspicious of Plato's theory of justice. Indeed, if we think that the problems with Plato's 'theory' are really conceptual or grammatical then we have reason to think that it is not really a *theory* at all. Where Plato's work is a search for definitions it seems that his concerns are conceptual rather than theoretical (it does not concern empirical matters or hypotheses). It is not a *theory* that 'justice' means what it does and if we follow Wittgenstein then we would think that what is needed is a description of the relevant region of grammar, a surveyable representation, rather than a theory of any sort, in order to gain understanding of the relevant concepts.[19]

---

[18] For a very rich account of the concept of justice, inspired by Wittgenstein, see Peg O'Connor's *Morality and Our Complicated Form of Life*, particularly the last chapter (pp. 137–68).

[19] See *Philosophical Investigations*, §109, 'We may not advance any kind of theory. There must not be anything hypothetical in our considerations. All *explanation* must disappear, and description alone must take its place', and §128, 'If someone were to advance *theses* in philosophy, it would never be possible to debate them, because everyone would agree to them.' Note: We might also object to philosophical theories being called theories on grounds other than thinking of them as just being concerned with concepts or grammar. Wittgenstein was opposed to scientism in philosophy and thought that we should be sensitive to differences between different language games. If we think of theories as being just like scientific theories, or as, say, being particularly concerned with causation, then it seems mistaken to call accounts of justice theories. 'Justice' is an expression that is not at home in scientific language games and an expression that

But ruling out Plato's take on justice still leaves us with quite a lot of different kinds of theories or conceptions of justice to choose among. Can Wittgenstein be of more help in deciding upon an account of justice from among the current accounts (or in formulating a new one)? One approach to narrowing down the field is to look at what Wittgensteinians in the past few decades have had to say about justice. Wittgenstein himself had very little to say about justice in particular, although he did make remarks about both political and ethical matters that might help to point us in the right direction. However, various Wittgensteinian philosophers *have* had something to say about justice – inspired by their interpretations of Wittgenstein's work.

In his paper 'Wittgenstein vs. Rawls' Rupert Read observes that liberal political philosophy is currently dominant in political philosophy and that many Wittgensteinians and philosophers inspired by Wittgenstein's work have followed the trend.[20] Read notes that Richard Rorty, Stanley Cavell, and Burt Dreben have all praised Rawlsian liberalism. Wittgensteinians such as Alice Crary and James Conant who have deep disagreements with Rorty nonetheless make clear that they agree with him in their liberalism.[21] In Chapter 4 I argued that although Rorty was influenced by Wittgenstein, Rorty's liberal conclusions do not follow from Wittgenstein's philosophical remarks.[22] I also suggested that Richard Eldridge's Cavellian arguments in favour of a liberal Wittgenstein were mistaken, and criticized Alice Crary's claim that lessons learned from her interpretation of Wittgenstein are 'reflected in forms of social life that embody the ideals of liberal democracy'.[23] So, given that I have

---

is clearly tied up with reasons and justification rather than with causal relationships between physical objects.

[20] Read was certainly not the first to use Wittgenstein in criticizing Rawls. For example, back in 1990, Peter Winch developed a Wittgensteinian critique of the social contract tradition using insights from Hume's critique of that tradition. Winch draws out confusions from traditional philosophy about the role of practical reason in political theorizing in his 'Certainty and Authority', *Royal Institute of Philosophy Supplement*, vol. 28, pp. 223–37, 1990. Winch argues, 'The "veil of ignorance" that characterizes this "position" [the 'original position' as described by Rawls] runs foul of Wittgenstein's point that what is "reasonable" cannot be characterized independently of the *content* of certain pivotal "judgements"' (p. 235).

[21] R. Read, 'Wittgenstein vs. Rawls', in V. Munz, K. Puhl, and J. Wang (eds), *Proceedings of the Kirchberg Wittgenstein Symposium 2009: Language and World*, Frankfurt: Ontos, 2010, p. 93.

[22] Chapter 4 was developed from my paper 'Was Wittgenstein a Liberal Philosopher?', *Teorema*, vol. 36, no. 1, 2017, pp. 71–74.

[23] See R. Eldridge, *Leading a Human Life: Wittgenstein, Intentionality, and Romanticism*, Chicago: University of Chicago Press, 1997; R. Eldridge, 'Wittgenstein and the Conversation of Justice', in Cressida Heyes (ed.), *The Grammar of Politics*, Ithaca, NY: Cornell University Press, 2003; A. Crary, 'Wittgenstein's Philosophy in Relation to

looked at arguments from Rorty and Cavellians like Eldridge in favour of a Wittgensteinian liberalism (Rorty) or Wittgenstein being a liberal (Eldridge) and argued that they are mistaken, I will focus on Rawlsian liberalism in this chapter. Would Wittgenstein have been a Rawlsian? Do Wittgenstein's philosophical remarks provide any support for Rawlsian liberal account of justice?

8.3.1 *Did Rawls Put the Question Marks Deep Enough?*

One possible way of arguing against Rawls is to take the Wittgensteinian approach of questioning what are presented as foundational assumptions or first principles. Wittgenstein said that 'one keeps forgetting to go down to the foundations. One doesn't put the question marks *deep* enough down.'[24] Both Rupert Read and Amartya Sen take this approach, although their arguments are different.[25]

In a series of papers Read has argued against Rawls's conception of justice and against liberal conceptions of justice more generally.[26] Read argues that Rawls has not put question marks deep enough down in that Rawls assumes the primacy of justice. Rawls famously claimed that 'a theory however elegant and economical must be rejected or revised if it is untrue; likewise laws and institutions no matter how efficient and well-arranged must be reformed or abolished if they are unjust'.[27] Read thinks that this statement from Rawls is 'the trick that biased the pitch before we even noticed the game had begun'[28] and he cites §308 from Wittgenstein's *Philosophical Investigations* where Wittgenstein talks about how philosophical problems arise because 'the first step [...] escapes notice [...] But that's just what commits us to a particular way of looking at the matter [...] (the decisive moment in the conjuring trick has been made, and it was the very one that seemed to us quite innocent)'. In that context Wittgenstein was talking about behaviourism but the

---

Political Thought', in A. Crary and R. Read, *The New Wittgenstein*, London: Routledge, 2000, p. 141; and Vinten, 'Was Wittgenstein a Liberal Philosopher?', pp. 67–71, 74–75.

[24] L. Wittgenstein, *Culture and Value*, revised edition, ed. G. H. von Wright, Oxford: Blackwell, 1998, p. 71e.

[25] Similarly, Peg O'Connor argues that moral realism and moral antirealism both fail because they share common, mistaken, assumptions (pp. 43–60, *Morality and Our Complicated Form of Life*).

[26] See, e.g. Read, 'Wittgenstein vs. Rawls'; R. Read, 'Why the Ecological Crisis Spells the End of Liberalism: The "Difference Principle" Is Ecologically Unsustainable, Exploitative of Persons, or Empty', *Capitalism Nature Socialism*, vol. 22, 2011; and R. Makoff and R. Read, 'Beyond Just Justice – Creating Space for a Future-Care Ethic', *Philosophical Investigations*, vol. 40, no. 3, 2017.

[27] J. Rawls, *A Theory of Justice*, Oxford: Oxford University Press, 1971, p. 3.

[28] Read, 'Wittgenstein vs. Rawls', p. 99.

same thing could be said of Rawls's argument. Rawls assumes that justice is the first virtue without seriously considering alternatives. However, given that there are serious problems with taking justice to be primary in the way that Rawls does alternatives should be considered.

What are the problems with the Rawlsian account of justice just referred to above? Many of the problems arise from the fact that Rawls gives a contractarian account where representatives of free and equal citizens reason with one another and agree upon principles. Justice is connected to making judgements and so the parties involved in agreeing upon principles must be rational creatures capable of making judgements. However, this excludes various people and also excludes other creatures. As Rupert Read notes in his paper 'Wittgenstein vs. Rawls', 'assuming justice to be the first virtue of social institutions creates real difficulties in taking seriously the claims of those with whom we cannot have a conversation [...] animals, the very ill, the very young, the very disabled, and the unborn'.[29] One thing to notice about these problems is that although they have been introduced here in the context of Wittgensteinian concerns about making unwarranted assumptions these criticisms have been made by non-Wittgensteinian philosophers in the past and there is nothing particularly Wittgensteinian about them. For example, Martha Nussbaum has written extensively about problems with Rawlsian contractarianism excluding animals and the severely disabled, as well as about problems with extending Rawlsian contractualism beyond national borders (and into the future).[30]

Read takes his criticisms of Rawls in a more Wittgensteinian direction by focusing particularly on the unborn, on future generations. In this case the problem with Rawls's contractualism is not merely that future generations are not a part of any (fantasized) discussion but that they *cannot* be. As Read points out, in the case of future people, 'there could not possibly be a contract (in part because our decisions will partly decide which future people there *are*!)'.[31] The absurdity of the notion of a contract with future peoples parallels the absurdity of the idea of a private language, according to Read: 'The "contract" of Rawls and his predecessors is a contract with nobody, a contract "private" to its purveyors. There is no real contract, and *there could not possibly be* a contract with future people.'[32] The focus in contractarianism on discussion and decision-making between contemporaries means that it treats future generations as a

---

[29] Ibid., p. 100.
[30] See, e.g. Nussbaum's *Frontiers of Justice: Disability, Nationality, Species Membership*, Cambridge, MA: Harvard University Press, 2006.
[31] Read, 'Wittgenstein vs. Rawls', p. 101.
[32] Ibid., p. 102.

special case which we consider after everything else is straightened out. But given that we live in a world where issues like climate change are enormously important – issues which clearly involve future generations – it seems as though contractarians are wrong to treat future generations as a secondary case.[33]

But Read does not just discuss future generations in undermining Rawlsian claims about the primacy of justice. In a paper that he wrote with Ruth Makoff they show very clearly how the parent/child relationship reveals limitations of talk of justice. A few obvious points about the relationship between parent and child show that contractarian models do not fit it at all. First of all, when it comes to very small children it makes no sense to think about negotiating, discussing the distribution of goods, or forging contracts. Very young children cannot speak and when they do start to speak we cannot consider them fully rational for some time. There is a clear power imbalance between parent and child, with the parent holding a great deal of power in the relationship and the child having very little. Cool, self-interested discussion about fairness is not suitable for the task of thinking about how parents should act towards children. Read and Makoff point out that Rawlsian contractarianism leaves us in a position where the powerful dictate to the powerless. Somebody who is self-interested and motivated only by cool fairness would not be likely to be fair 'when one controls the very conditions of existence of the other'.[34] What is needed is a warmer motivation than the kind of cool fairness we find in the contractarian tradition. If we *care* about children and about generations yet to come then we might really be fair. But what this means is that justice or fairness is not primary. We are just or fair *because* we care. Justice-first contractarianism, as found in Rawls's work, does not supply us with the conceptual tools for thinking about relationships between parents and children or for thinking about the relationships between ourselves and future generations. A more plausible candidate for a primary virtue is love or care.

Read provides good reasons for questioning Rawls's assumption of the primacy of justice. Amartya Sen makes similar arguments against Rawls. He provides reasons for thinking that the Rawlsian assumption about the priority of identifying a fully just society is mistaken. Rawls makes this assumption in taking the main question to be answered to be 'What is a just society?' Sen, on the other hand, argues that the identification of a fully just society (the Rawlsian 'transcendental' approach to justice) is neither necessary nor sufficient for making comparisons between societies and ranking them as more or less just (the comparative approach to justice). Moreover, we constantly face

---

[33] Ibid.; and also Makoff and Read, 'Beyond Just Justice'.
[34] Makoff and Read, 'Beyond Just Justice', p. 248.

questions about how to advance the cause of justice in our everyday lives and these kinds of comparative questions are urgent.

A Rawlsian might well agree that it is urgent to discuss and act upon cases of injustice to make things more just but suggest that clarity in answering the question 'what is a just society?' is necessary to make judgements about what would make a society more just or that it might be a way of helping us to get clear about comparative judgements. However, Sen questions whether we need a clear picture of the most just society in order to make the kind of comparative judgements that we do. We happily say that a country where slavery has been abolished thereby became more just than it was with slavery. Sen illustrates his position with analogies from aesthetics. He points out that in judging paintings we do not need to identify the best painting in order to argue the case that one painting is better than another: 'In arguing for a Picasso over a Dali we do not need to get steamed up about identifying the perfect picture [...] which would beat the Picassos and the Dalis and all other paintings in the world'[35] and nor does identifying the best picture (if such a thing were possible) tell us how to make comparative judgements about other pictures: 'The fact that a person regards the Mona Lisa as the best picture in the world does not reveal how she would rank a Gauguin against a Van Gogh.'[36] Sen recognizes that this is not a proof that comparing societies in terms of justice works in the same way that comparative judgements about art does. One problem is that we might not be able to form any idea of what a perfect picture is. However, Sen points out that even when making comparative judgements in other regions of discourse where there is clearly a 'top' example – such as judgements about the heights of mountains – we do not need the top case in order to make a judgement about two others. We do not need to understand that Everest is highest or know the height of Everest in order to compare the heights of Kanchenjunga and Mont Blanc.[37] This, again, is not proof that identifying the perfectly just society is not necessary to make comparative judgements about justice but it does at least undermine the claim that it can safely be assumed to be the case. Rawls needs some kind of a justification for taking the principal question to be 'what is a just society?' but he lacks a justification for that.

Wittgensteinians (and others) have good reason to think that Rawls has not put the question marks down deep enough. His whole enterprise rests on shaky assumptions. However, Rupert Read also provides further reasons

---

[35] A. Sen, 'What Do We Want from a Theory of Justice?', *Journal of Philosophy*, vol. 103, no. 5, 2006, p. 222.
[36] Ibid., p. 221.
[37] Ibid., p. 222.

for Wittgensteinians to be wary of Rawls which I will briefly mention here. Rawls introduces what he is doing as a *theory* and Wittgenstein did not think that philosophy, at least as he understood it, was theoretical.[38] Rawls's work has a scientistic flavour, whereas Wittgenstein was opposed to scientism. Wittgenstein describes the kind of confusion philosophers fall into has pictures holding them captive[39] and Read thinks that Rawls is held captive by a set of pictures 'of people as at base individuals, juridical objects; of social institutions as (like) law; of political philosophy as (like) science'.[40]

8.3.2 *José Medina's Portrayal of Wittgenstein as a Rebel and Epistemic Justice*

Wittgenstein's philosophical remarks do not seem to support any kind of liberal political philosophy. Rupert Read has made a good case that, at the very least, Wittgenstein's philosophical remarks are in tension with Rawlsian philosophy and I have already argued in the fourth chapter of this book that Wittgenstein's remarks do not support the 'liberal ironism' of Rorty and nor do they support certain varieties of liberalism inspired by Stanley Cavell. However, there is a more left-wing strand of thought which looks to Cavell for inspiration in the philosophical work of Chantal Mouffe and José Medina. They argue for a form of pluralistic democracy where dissident voices can be heard and given the credibility they deserve.[41] The focus here will be on Medina's work in particular but Medina argues in favour of the roughly the kind of radical and plural democracy which Mouffe favours (despite also having some differences with both Cavell and Mouffe).[42] Medina's work has often focused on cases of epistemic injustice. He argues, for example, that there is injustice in situations

---

[38] See, e.g., *Philosophical Investigations*, §109, where Wittgenstein says that 'we may not advance any kind of theory. There must not be anything hypothetical in our considerations. All explanation must disappear, and description alone must take its place.' Wittgenstein also had this to say in the *Blue Book*: 'Philosophers constantly see the method of science before their eyes, and are irresistibly tempted to ask and answer questions in the way science does. This tendency is the real source of metaphysics, and leads the philosopher into complete darkness' (Wittgenstein, *The Blue and Brown Books*, p. 18).

[39] *PI*, §115: 'A picture held us captive. And we couldn't get outside it, for it lay in our language, and language seemed only to repeat it to us inexorably.'

[40] Read, 'Wittgenstein vs. Rawls', p. 102.

[41] See, e.g. C. Mouffe, *The Democratic Paradox*, New York: Verso, 2000; and J. Medina, *The Epistemology of Resistance*, Oxford: Oxford University Press, 2013.

[42] See pp. 19–24 of J. Medina 'Wittgenstein as a Rebel: Dissidence and Contestation in Discursive Practices', *International Journal of Philosophical Studies*, vol. 18, no. 1, pp. 19–24, where Medina discusses his agreements and disagreements with Mouffe and Cavell.

where people do not have equal access to knowledge practices, where people cannot participate in knowledge practices as equals, where people's testimony is not given the weight it deserves, where people are unfairly denied the resources needed to understand themselves, and in cases where people are not treated with sensitivity because their oppression is ignored or not understood. He suggests that we should build a society where people take on their responsibilities to understand the communities around them, where there is space for people to disagree about norms and rules and to be taken seriously when they make challenges, and where we tackle the kind of bigotry that is intertwined with epistemic injustices. However, he does not propose an ideal. He argues that we should be sensitive to changing circumstances, that we should always be open to changing our norms, and he describes his position as a kind of 'meliorism' – committed to making things better without having a picture of some society being the best.[43] This sounds much closer to someone like Sen, with his comparative approach to justice than to Rawlsian transcendentalism.

In 'Wittgenstein as a Rebel: Dissidence and Contestation in Discursive Practices' Medina argues that Wittgenstein's remarks about meaning and rules have implications for political philosophy. He tries to make a case that Wittgenstein's *Philosophical Investigations* stresses contestation and rebellion as having a crucial role in our normative practices. Although it seems that Wittgenstein emphasizes agreement and appears to give philosophy a conservative role,[44] it is important for Wittgenstein's account of language and philosophy that rules can be broken, that they can change, and that we can rebel against them. According to Medina, in Wittgenstein's discussion of rules, agreement, and disagreement, 'the dialectical relation goes both ways [...] there is a relationship of mutual dependence and support between agreement and disagreement; and, therefore, agreement too depends on and presupposes disagreement, contestation and the possibility of rebellion'.[45]

Medina notes that even while Wittgenstein stresses the importance of agreement in practices he always highlights that there is room for disagreement. For example, in §241 of the *Investigations* Wittgenstein challenges the view (or confused picture) that human agreement decides what is true or false. He observes that 'what is true or false is what human beings *say*; and it is in their *language* that human beings agree. This is agreement not in opinions, but rather in forms of life.' Agreement in language, agreement about what makes sense ('agreement in definitions' (*PI* §242)), is essential for us to make our opinions understood. In order for us to put forward a claim as true we

---

[43] See Medina, *Epistemology of Resistance*, pp. 11–12.
[44] E.g. *PI*, §124: 'Philosophy [...] leaves everything as it is.'
[45] Medina, 'Wittgenstein as a Rebel', p. 3.

must make sense. Our disagreements over matters of opinion rest upon agreement over linguistic norms. Medina also notes that there is also a kind of balance between agreement and disagreement in the situation where someone is trying to understand a completely unknown language. There it would be difficult to understand the people, especially given the variation ('disagreement') in the ways that they behave. In that situation Wittgenstein says that 'shared human behaviour is the system of reference by means of which we interpret an unknown language'.[46] 'Agreement' in ways of behaving – ways of behaving that we have in common, such as smiling when happy, frowning or crying when sad, looking to where a finger is pointing (rather than at the pointing finger), and so on – helps us to make sense of the great variation in human behaviour. In both of these remarks from Wittgenstein's *Philosophical Investigations* we can see that certain kinds of agreement and certain kinds of disagreement are interrelated.

However, it is not only the case that agreements of one sort and disagreements of another are interrelated. The central point that Medina wants to make about agreement and disagreement, as I understand it, is that where we can make sense of saying that there is agreement we must also be able to make sense of saying that there is disagreement. This is presumably what he means when he says that the relation of dependence between agreement and disagreement is mutual. We might agree in language but we might also disagree in language. Disagreement does not only arise between our opinions and in our behaviour, it can also crop up in disputes over meanings and rules. Disagreement, contestation, or rebellion could possibly arise wherever agreement, acceptance, or compliance is found.

A possible problem with this view is that if agreement is a condition of language then it seems to follow that we could not imagine disagreement. If that condition was not met then we would not have a language in which to disagree. However, as Peter Hacker has argued, this reasoning is erroneous. In his commentary on the *Philosophical Investigations* Hacker points out that the reasoning in this case is similar to the fallacy committed by Wittgenstein in the *Tractatus Logico-Philosophicus* when he argued that objects must be sempiternal because it must be possible to describe a state of affairs in which everything destructible is destroyed. Wittgenstein's mistake here, Hacker argues, is that 'it does not follow, from the possibility of such a description, that it must be possible *in that state of affairs* to describe how things are'. Similarly, in a state of affairs where agreement in language has completely broken down there could not be disagreement – disagreement and agreement fall together. But it does

---

[46] Wittgenstein, *Philosophical Investigations*, §206. Medina cites both §241 and §206 on p. 6 of his 'Wittgenstein as a Rebel'.

not follow that in the present, where we do have agreement in language, we cannot imagine disagreement. Hacker explains that

> given that we agree, for example, in our colour-judgements, we can describe such changes in us as would lead to a radical disagreement in our applications (LPE 306[47]). But, of course, beyond a certain point we could not say: 'They disagree in their use of colour-words', for these words would no longer be colour words [...] Only the shell of colour concepts remains, for confusion has supervened. (PPF §§346, 348[48])[49]

This disposes of the problem raised at the beginning of this paragraph and the passages cited by Hacker show clearly that Wittgenstein held the position Medina ascribes to him. Wittgenstein clearly thought that disagreement over linguistic norms was possible and also thought that a host of other kinds of disagreement was possible.

In addition to stressing the ubiquity of the possibility of disagreement, Medina highlights and agrees with Wittgenstein's account of language as a *historical* and *mutable* phenomenon. In §23 of the *Investigations* Wittgenstein emphasizes the diversity in what we call 'words', 'signs', and 'sentences' and remarks that not only is there great diversity but the kind of diversity we have in language changes over time: 'This diversity is not something fixed, given once for all; but new types of language, new language-games, as we may say, come into existence, and others become obsolete and get forgotten.' Medina characterizes these changes in language in terms of agreement and disagreement: 'new agreement [emerges] out of disagreements' and 'established agreement [submerges] into new disagreements'.[50] The fact that language has a history and that it changes over time (sometimes in unpredictable ways) is also emphasized in Wittgenstein's comparison of language to a city developing over time.[51]

Medina thinks that Wittgenstein's remarks that are known as the 'private language argument' add to his case for Wittgenstein being a rebel. The private language argument makes clear that when there is normativity around

---

[47] 'LPE' is the abbreviation that Hacker uses for 'Wittgenstein's Notes for Lectures on "Private Experience" and "Sense Data"', which can be found in *Ludwig Wittgenstein: Philosophical Occasions 1912–1951* (ed. J. Klagge and A. Nordmann, Indianapolis, IN: Hackett, 1993).

[48] 'PPF' is Hacker's abbreviation for *Philosophy of Psychology: A Fragment* which was published in the 4th edition of Wittgenstein's *Philosophical Investigations*.

[49] G. P. Baker and P. M. S. Hacker, *Wittgenstein: Rules, Grammar and Necessity*, 2nd edition, extensively revised by P. M. S. Hacker, Oxford: Wiley-Blackwell, 2009, p. 229.

[50] Medina, 'Wittgenstein as a Rebel', p. 6.

[51] Wittgenstein, *Philosophical Investigations*, §18.

there is also contestability. The private linguist faces the problem that they cannot give their use of a sensation word a private grounding (through, e.g. a private ostensive definition). They cannot demonstrate that they are using the sensation word correctly because there is no criterion of correctness if what they are relying on is just a kind of inner pointing or inner focusing. As Wittgenstein says, 'Whatever is going to seem correct to me is correct. And that only means that here we can't talk about "correct."'[52] We know that someone is in pain through their public behaviour – their cries of pain, their winces, and the things that they say. Our sensation words are part of a public language with public criteria. But this does not mean that the correct use of words is just down to the public – decided on by the community. As Medina notes, there is something similar to be said about the public/community case as in the case of the private linguist. What is right or correct is not whatever *seems* right or correct to either the private linguist *or* the community. We must be able to distinguish what is right/correct from what seems right/correct at the community level as well as at the individual level and we can make sense of collective mistakes too.[53] Meaning is a normative notion and that means that we have *standards* by which we 'measure' the correctness of uses of language which we might fall short of.

8.3.3 *An Assessment of Medina's Account of Rules, Language, and Justice*

8.3.3.1 *What Does Medina Get Right?*

Medina's account of Wittgenstein's philosophical remarks about rules and language emphasizes mutability, history, contestability, disruption, and transformation. Medina wants to challenge the view that our practices might be completely uniform or homogeneous. There is much that is correct in his account. It is clear from the passages Medina cites that Wittgenstein saw language as something mutable and as something that did in fact change. Language changes not only through new terms being introduced and old ones becoming obsolete but also through rules being broken or changed. A word might take on a new meaning as the rules for its use are altered. Whole new practices with their own rules might come into existence and others may disappear. Wittgenstein also clearly thought that rules could be challenged or broken in a variety of ways. In his account of rule-following Wittgenstein discusses a variety of ways in which someone might go wrong in writing the

---

[52] Ibid., §258.
[53] See pp. 9–10 of Medina's 'Wittgenstein as a Rebel'. Medina cites various passages from the *Philosophical Investigations* in support of his argument – §§258, 265, 279, 311.

series of natural numbers as they learn the series. They might produce a *random series*, and communication might break down, they might make a *mistake*, or they might make a *systematic mistake* (misunderstand).[54] Moreover, it is not only the case that people might go wrong or misunderstand when learning about mathematics, they might also *challenge* the rules of mathematics when they have learned the rules. They might propose changes to the way in which mathematics is done.[55] And, of course, it is not only in mathematics that we have rules. We play games according to rules,[56] our civic and political life is governed by norms and rules. We can break rules, challenge rules, bend or stretch rules, disobey rules, violate rules, rules have exceptions, and some rules we say are just rules of thumb. Medina recognizes that there is great diversity in rules in terms of the homogeneity and heterogeneity they admit,[57] and he also thinks that there are big differences in our normative practices in terms of contestability: 'not all practices admit of the same degree of contestability', he says.[58]

So, Medina's account of Wittgenstein is very plausible. There are details of it that are controversial but I will not get into those controversies here. For the sake of argument let us assume that Medina's account of Wittgenstein is at least broadly speaking correct. He is right about Wittgenstein seeing language as being rule-governed, and he is right about it being mutable and having a history. Medina correctly argues that Wittgenstein recognized a variety of rules and a variety of ways in which we might go wrong about them, break them, or contest them. The focus of this chapter is justice and the principal problems with Medina's argument are not with the account of Wittgenstein that he presents but with the political conclusions he draws from it.

8.3.3.2 *What Do Medina and Mouffe Get Wrong?*

The passage in Medina's paper that I want to challenge comes towards the end of 'Wittgenstein as a Rebel'. The first stage of Medina's argument is relatively uncontroversial. From his account of Wittgenstein's philosophy of language and rules he concludes that 'the lesson to be learned from Wittgenstein's discussions is that we should reject any appeal to a final and

---

[54] Wittgenstein, *Philosophical Investigations*, §143.
[55] Wittgenstein mentions changes in mathematics in §23 of the *Philosophical Investigations*.
[56] Wittgenstein mentions chess (§17, §31, §33, §49, §66, §108, §136, §151, §197, §199, §200, §205, §316, §337, §365, §563, §567), ring-a-ring-a-roses (§66), noughts and crosses (§66), tennis (§66, §68), football ('Philosophy of Psychology: A Fragment', xiii), and volleyball (PPF, xiii).
[57] Medina, 'Wittgenstein as a Rebel', p. 23.
[58] Ibid., p. 17.

homogeneous consensus that fixes the normativity of our practices'.[59] It is clear that Wittgenstein did not think that standards of correctness, standards concerning what is right, or behavioural norms were either fixed once and for all or homogeneous, and nor did he think that a consensus determined what is correct, incorrect, right, or wrong. Wittgenstein talked about various ways in which norms might change, bedrock might shift, and rules might be challenged or broken.

However, Medina goes on to claim that the Wittgensteinian view he has outlined has political implications. He agrees with Mouffe in thinking that Wittgenstein's remarks would make democratic thinkers more open to the kind of pluralist society she envisions. This would be a society that avoids striving for consensus and instead allows expression of a variety of conflicting viewpoints. Mouffe thinks that attempts to bring about a democratic consensus are misguided and that 'this is something that Wittgenstein, with his insistence on the need to respect differences, brings to the fore in a very powerful way'.[60]

Despite claiming that she does not want to 'extract a political theory from Wittgenstein, [or] to attempt elaborating one on the basis of his writings'[61] Mouffe nonetheless thinks that Wittgenstein's remarks point to 'a *new way of theorizing* about the political'[62] and she thinks that Wittgenstein's remarks should incline us to be sympathetic to her vision of a radical and plural democracy. She cites two remarks from *On Certainty* that she thinks support her vision. (i) The first is Wittgenstein's remark that 'Giving grounds [...] justifying the evidence, comes to an end; – but the end is not certain propositions striking us immediately as true, i.e. it is not a kind of *seeing* on our part; it is our *acting*, which lies at the bottom of the language game'.[63] This, she says, 'allows us to grasp the conditions of emergence of a democratic consensus'.[64] As she interprets Wittgenstein, 'agreement is established not on significations but on forms of life', and this, she says, distinguishes Wittgenstein's philosophy from Habermas's.[65] Mouffe argues that the significance of this is that it reveals the limits of every consensus. (ii) This is where she again cites Wittgenstein's remarks in *On Certainty*. Wittgenstein remarked, 'Where two principles really do meet which cannot be reconciled with one another, then each man declares the other a fool and a heretic.[66]. I said I would "combat" the other man, – but

---

[59] Ibid., p. 23.
[60] Mouffe, *The Democratic Paradox*, p. 77, cited in Medina, 'Wittgenstein as a Rebel', p. 24.
[61] Mouffe, *The Democratic Paradox*, p. 60.
[62] Ibid., p. 61.
[63] Wittgenstein, *On Certainty*, §204.
[64] Mouffe, *The Democratic Paradox*, p. 70.
[65] Ibid.
[66] Wittgenstein, *On Certainty*, §611.

wouldn't I give him *reasons*? Certainly; but how far do they go? At the end of reasons comes *persuasion*.'[67]

Mouffe finds what she thinks are further remarks in favour of her conception of democracy in Wittgenstein's *Philosophical Investigations*. Wittgenstein famously noted that there is not a single feature that is common to all and only games. 'Game' cannot be defined in terms of necessary and sufficient conditions. Instead what we find is 'a complicated network of similarities overlapping and criss-crossing: similarities in the large and in the small'.[68] Mouffe thinks that Wittgenstein's take on games suggests that 'we should acknowledge and valorise the diversity of ways in which the "democratic game" can be played, instead of trying to reduce this diversity to a uniform model of citizenship'.[69]

There are various problems with Mouffe's arguments and, by extension, with Medina's. Mouffe claims that Wittgenstein insists 'on the need to respect differences' but she does not provide a reference to Wittgenstein's work to clarify what she means by this. In the *Philosophical Investigations* Wittgenstein implores us to 'call to mind the differences between the language games ['I describe my state of mind'/'I describe my room']';[70] he notes that there are differences of degree in the response that one might give to the question 'were you really angry?'[71] and in what has now been denominated *Philosophy of Psychology – A Fragment* he says that we can 'discern conceptual differences' between the various responses to the question 'does he *hear* the plaint?'[72] According to Maurice Drury Wittgenstein said of Hegel that he 'seems to me to be always wanting to say that things which look different are really the same. Whereas my interest is in showing that things which look the same are really different' and Drury recalls that Wittgenstein had considered using a quotation from King Lear – 'I'll teach you differences' – as a motto for his book.[73] In all of these cases the 'differences' referred to are categorial or conceptual differences and this fits with his conception of philosophy – where the problems are not empirical problems but problems which are 'solved through an insight into the workings of our language'.[74] The differences he discusses are differences between concepts or between language games – *not* the kind of differences Mouffe presumably has in mind – differences between citizens in a

---

[67] Ibid., §612.
[68] Wittgenstein, *Philosophical Investigations*, §66.
[69] Mouffe, *The Democratic Paradox*, p. 73.
[70] Wittgenstein, *Philosophical Investigations*, §290.
[71] Ibid., §677.
[72] PPF §§229–30, p. 220e.
[73] Drury, 'Conversations with Wittgenstein', p. 157.
[74] Wittgenstein, *Philosophical Investigations*, §109.

democracy. Wittgenstein's attention to differences had nothing to do with, say, respecting people from other (different) countries, or respecting people regardless of their sexuality, or respecting people with different political affiliations. 'Democracy' is not a term that appears in the *Philosophical Investigations* at all and the book does not have citizenship or justice among its concerns. Mouffe claims, following Cavell, that holding people responsible for their claims was a central concern of Wittgenstein in the *Philosophical Investigations* but if this is so then it is odd that the word 'responsibility' does not appear in it at all, and nor do words like 'obligation' or 'duty'. Wittgenstein *was* occupied with rules, definitions, and language – and the various ways in which we might go wrong, make mistakes, and violate rules where language was concerned. *Normativity* was undoubtedly a central concern of Wittgenstein's but not in a way that obviously supports Mouffe's arguments. So, it seems that Wittgenstein's remarks in the *Philosophical Investigations* do not support Mouffe's suggestion that Wittgenstein's work suggests that we should respect differences between democratic citizens.

Perhaps what Mouffe had in mind was Wittgenstein's remarks in *On Certainty*. There Wittgenstein talks about the possibility that '2 × 2 = 4' might have a *different* meaning or be nonsensical in Chinese,[75] asks whether knowing that here is a hand is *different* in kind from knowing the existence of the planet Saturn,[76] and elucidates the *differences* between belief and knowledge and between knowledge and certainty. He compares *differences* in the meaning of words to *differences* in the functions of officials,[77] talks about a king being brought to look at the world in a *different* way[78] and about the difference between 'us' and someone who says, 'I don't know if I have ever been on the moon: I don't remember having been there.'[79]

On Certainty seems like a more hopeful place to start if what we are developing is an account of differences between people insofar as they are political animals because some of the cases discussed there clearly concern the kind of differences in belief that we might want to think about in thinking about political discussion. A lesson we can learn from Wittgenstein's remarks in *On Certainty* is that people do not just have disagreements of opinion, where each of the people in the conversation are speaking the same language, have the same kind of evidential standards, and have been raised in the same practices. Sometimes people speaking to each other come from an entirely different

---

[75] Wittgenstein, *On Certainty*, §10.
[76] Ibid., §20.
[77] Ibid., §64.
[78] Ibid., §92.
[79] Ibid., §§332–38.

background, have different concepts, and have learned their language through engaging in different kinds of practices. The fact that differently situated people – kings, officials, people from other countries – come into conflict in a variety of ways in *On Certainty* suggests that it is relevant to political discussions. Once we start thinking about these kinds of questions we might well have to revise our conception of rationality and conceptions of rationality are clearly relevant to constructing political visions.[80]

As mentioned earlier, Mouffe cites passages from *On Certainty* which stress that we might not be able to justify our beliefs to another person and that we might have to resort to other means, such as persuasion in order to change someone's mind. These remarks are indeed important for political philosophy. We should recognize that political disagreements might take different forms and that rebellion might not just involve a straightforward disagreement over a matter of opinion where each side would accept the same things as counting as evidence that might settle the matter. To this extent Mouffe is correct. If we want to gain an understanding of people unlike ourselves then we should recognize that their different practices might be tied up with different moral standards, different evidential standards, and different concepts. However, this does not imply that we should 'valorize' alternative ways of playing 'the democratic game' as Mouffe suggests. Wittgenstein's work does not imply that we should aim at democratic pluralism. His work, as he said, was descriptive and angled at enhancing our understanding, not prescriptive. The understanding that we reach having taken Wittgenstein's insights about language games, rationality, argumentation, certainty, and persuasion on board might incline us towards a particular social arrangement but it is not obvious that it does. Recognizing that people might behave in different ways, have different evidential standards, and have different concepts does not imply that we should encourage people to behave in different ways, to have different evidential standards, and to have different concepts.

8.4 Medina, Rules, and Radical Democracy

Having discussed Mouffe's take on Wittgenstein I will now return to Medina's account of Wittgenstein to make a few remarks. Medina recognizes that rules

---

[80] Peter Winch makes a good case that the social contract tradition, from Hobbes to Rawls, is dogged by problems with conceptions of practical rationality in the tradition. It seems plausible that Wittgenstein's work can be used in critiques of certain political theories – highlighting conceptual confusions in them – but less plausible that it can be used to develop a political theory in competition with the ones it critiques (Winch, 'Certainty and Authority', 1990).

and practices are diverse and that rules in some regions of discourse are more contestable than others. However, I do not think that Medina makes enough of differences between rules. We have a variety of different kinds of rules of language, we play games according to rules, there are rules that people obey in public spaces, private clubs, and in religious orders. One difference to note that is relevant to Medina's account is that it does not make sense to speak of *rebellion* in all of the cases where rules are flouted, ignored, or broken. Medina presumably wants to incline us towards considering Wittgenstein's work as particularly suited to his vision of a radical democracy by speaking of rebellion and of Wittgenstein as a rebel. But thinking about many of the cases where rules are flouted, ignored, broken, or misunderstood, rebellion is not in the air at all. We can easily understand what would be involved in someone rebelling against a prohibition on smoking at school but it is less easy to understand what would be involved in rebelling against 'pink is lighter than red'. We can comprehend what someone is saying when they claim that a rule like 'no women on the golf course' is unfair but it is less obvious what is going on when someone claims that it is unfair that 'a bishop moves diagonally remaining on the same coloured squares' in chess. That is not to say that we cannot conceive of some kind of conflict or of changes to rules in the cases of colour language and of chess. There are, as a matter of fact, different sets of colour concepts in different parts of the world today, and people do disagree over the colour of things sometimes (perhaps due to differences in biology). We could imagine the rules of chess being altered to some extent, although it is unclear how much they could be altered with us still being willing to call the game 'chess'. But what is significant here is that the contestability or changeability amounts to something different in the different cases. 'Rule' is a family resemblance concept and it is unclear whether conclusions that we draw about contestability in one region of discourse will carry over to another.[81] What does seem clear is that wherever we can talk about rules we can talk about some kind of contestability (as well as about change, historical development, and mistakes being made) but that is not to say that a society in which rules are in fact contested is desirable. To decide upon whether it is in fact desirable we

---

[81] Peter Hacker makes some good points about the diversity of rules in discussing the notion of logical syntax and Wittgenstein's *Tractatus Logico-Philosophicus* in his paper 'Was he Trying to Whistle it?' There he points out that

not all rules prohibit something that can be done but should not be done [such as the rule against murder]. And one can follow or fail to follow rules even when they do not prohibit something that can be done – as when one follows the rules for making contracts. Failure to follow such rules does not result in illegal contracts, rather it results in invalid contracts. (P. M. S. Hacker, 'Was He Trying to Whistle it?', in *Wittgenstein: Connections and Controversies*, Oxford: Clarendon Press, 2001, pp. 118–22) would have to spell out exactly what we meant by 'a society in which rules are contested'. Even in the cases most fitting to Medina's argument – rules which can be rebelled against, the fact that rebellion is possible implies nothing about it being something desirable or something that we should do. Wittgenstein's comments about rules do not obviously imply anything about the shape that society should take.

8.5 Using Wittgenstein to Advance the Cause of Justice

Medina and Mouffe's political vision is not supported by Wittgensteinian philosophy but it is not obviously in conflict with it either and the fact that remarks from Wittgenstein's philosophy do not justify Medina and Mouffe's political outlook obviously does not imply that they are wrong to hold the positions that they do. The kind of injustices that Medina highlights are ones that we should strive to understand and correct. Recent work on epistemic justice, racial oppression, and feminism suggests that tools from Wittgenstein's later philosophy can be very helpful in helping us to understand and combat oppression and injustice.

For example, in 'Hinges, Prejudices, and Radical Doubters' Anna Boncompagni makes the case that hinge epistemology and accounts of epistemic injustice can be brought together in mutually instructive ways. She looks at ways in which prejudices can lead to people being silenced. It may be that someone is not listened to because they are not asked for information (the dominant group thinks that members of the discriminated group are unlikely to be reliable or trustworthy) or it may be that they are just regarded as sources of information and not as informants (they are objectified). It could be that people are silenced because they are denied the resources to make sense of their own experiences.[82] Or it could be that people are silenced by not being listened to when they raise doubts or ask questions (because their doubts are seen as being unreasonable in the light of the dominant perspective).[83] It is this last case that is the focus of Boncompagni's paper.

She uses the example of the film *Twelve Angry Men* to illustrate how prejudices about the race and upbringing of a boy on trial can affect what is deemed reasonable or not. Initially the jurors in the trial are largely in agreement that the boy is guilty except for one who raises a doubt about his guilt. That guilt is initially seen as unreasonable, due to the prejudice of the rest of the jury, but comes to

---

[82] A. Boncompagni, 'Hinges, Prejudices, and Radical Doubters', in Nuno Venturinha (ed.), Special Section on Wittgenstein and Applied Epistemology in *Wittgenstein Studien*, vol. 10, no. 1, 2019, p. 167.
[83] Ibid., p. 168.

be seen as a reasonable position. What is deemed reasonable or not is affected by prejudices and Boncompagni notes that prejudices share much in common with what have been called 'hinges' in Wittgenstein's work. Wittgenstein compares propositions which are exempt from doubt to the hinges upon which a door turns. Propositions such as 'the earth has existed for a long time' are held fast by us and our empirical questions and doubts turn on us holding to propositions like that and treating them as exempt from doubt. These propositions are often in the background – rarely formulated and often not learned explicitly but picked up along with the things we learn about the things around us, for example, that dinosaurs lived millions of years ago, that we evolved from creatures that existed millions of years ago, that light from stars we see now takes many years to travel through space, and many truths from physics, chemistry, history, and so on. Similarly, prejudices often hang around in the background and affect the way in which we judge and reason about the people around us without necessarily being formulated. Prejudices might be hinges or they might shape our hinges. They affect what is deemed reasonable or unreasonable.

Understanding the role that prejudices play in our societies can help us to understand oppression and should make us open to those who raise, what initially seem like unreasonable doubts. We should be open not only to the possibility that we might be wrong about matters of fact that can be supported with evidence but also about the beliefs we hold fast to – sensitive to the fact that they can shift. So, it seems clear that tools from Wittgenstein's later work can help us to understand and combat oppression, although it certainly does not go all of the way in formulating ways to tackle oppression. Determining strategies for fighting oppression relies on thinking about the current concrete circumstances and so it goes beyond the kind of Wittgensteinian philosophizing we have been discussing here but Wittgenstein's work can complement the work of people fighting oppression by giving us tools to help us to understand epistemic injustices better.

Another recent article makes a case for combining insights from feminist epistemology with hinge epistemology in such a way that both are enriched. In 'The Case for a Feminist Hinge Epistemology', Natalie Alana Ashton argues that developing a feminist hinge epistemology could help overcome some of the problematic aspects of hinge epistemology as it stands. One of those problems is the narrow focus of much of hinge epistemology. Hinge epistemologists often focus on the problem of radical scepticism but there are all kinds of questions about justification in our everyday lives that would still require attention even if the problem of radical scepticism were overcome.[84]

---

[84] N. A. Ashton, 'The Case for a Feminist Hinge Epistemology', in Nuno Venturinha (ed.), Special Section on Wittgenstein and Applied Epistemology in *Wittgenstein Studien*, vol. 10, no. 1, 2019, p. 4.

This narrow focus may well have a distorting influence on our accounts of justification, knowledge, belief, and certainty. Working on developing a feminist hinge epistemology would help to broaden the range of problems dealt with by hinge epistemologists and so would help to overcome this problem. But the narrow focus of much of contemporary hinge epistemology is not the only problem. Ashton thinks that many hinge epistemologists have failed to take pragmatism sufficiently seriously. Works such as Miriam McCormick's *Believing against the Evidence* and Anna Boncompagni's *Wittgenstein and Pragmatism* have not been given the attention they deserve. A further problem is that hinge epistemologists are too quick to dismiss relativism. In both cases, the openness of feminist epistemology to pragmatic approaches and to forms of relativism could help to enliven debates within hinge epistemology. Regardless of one's stance on these issues it is difficult to deny that they should be taken seriously and not be dismissed too readily.[85]

8.6 Conclusion

So, despite the fact that Wittgenstein's work cannot be easily pigeonholed in terms of ideology, and despite the fact that it does not support a particular political programme, it can be used to help untangle conceptual knots in the work of social scientists and can be used to help us to understand other cultures, the ways in which people are oppressed, and the nature of prejudice, as well as many other things. Wittgenstein's relevance to social philosophy and the social sciences should be reaffirmed and there is great promise for its use in work in social epistemology, moral philosophy, and political philosophy, political theory, and psychology.

---

[85] Ashton and Boncompagni are obviously not the first to think that insights from Wittgenstein might help in enriching work in the social sciences and in combatting oppression but I think that they point to interesting new ways in which such work might be developed. An excellent volume, with authors arguing for combining the insights of Wittgenstein with feminism, is *Feminist Interpretations of Ludwig Wittgenstein*, ed. Naomi Scheman and Peg O'Connor (University Park: Pennsylvania State University Press, 2002).

BIBLIOGRAPHY

Agassi, J. *Ludwig Wittgenstein's Philosophical Investigations: An Attempt at a Critical Rationalist Appraisal*, Synthese Library 401, Cham: Springer, 2018.
Ambrose, A. (ed.). *Wittgenstein's Lectures, Cambridge 1932–35, from the Notes of Alice Ambrose and Margaret Macdonald*, Oxford: Blackwell, 1979.
Anderson, P. 'Components of the National Culture', in R. Blackburn and A. Cockburn (eds), *Student Power: Problems, Diagnosis, Action*, London: Penguin Books, 1969, pp. 214–84.
Anderson, P. *English Questions*, London: Verso, 1992.
Anderson, P. *The Origins of Postmodernity*, London: Verso, 1998.
Aristotle. *Politics*, trans. Sir Ernest Barker, New York: Oxford University Press, 1958.
Armitage, D. 'John Locke, Carolina, and the "Two Treatises of Government"', *Political Theory*, vol. 32, no. 5, 2004, pp. 602–27.
Arrington, R. *Rationalism, Realism and Relativism*, Ithaca, NY: Cornell University Press, 1989.
Arrington, R., and H-J. Glock. (eds). *Wittgenstein's Philosophical Investigations: Text and Context*, London: Routledge, 1991.
Arrington, R. L., and M. Addis. *Wittgenstein and Philosophy of Religion*, London: Routledge, 2001.
Ashton, Natalie Alana. 'Scientific Perspectives, Feminist Standpoints, and Non-Silly Relativism', in M. Massimi and Ana-Maria Crețu (eds), *Human Knowledge in Perspective* (Synthese Library), Cham: Springer, 2020, pp. 71–85.
Ashton, N. A. 'The Case for a Feminist Hinge Epistemology', in Nuno Venturinha (ed.), Special Section on Wittgenstein and Applied Epistemology in *Wittgenstein Studien*, vol. 10, no. 1, 2019, pp. 153–63.
Ayer, A. J. *Language, Truth, and Logic*, New York: Dover, 1952.
Backhouse, R. *The Puzzle of Modern Economics: Science or Ideology?*, Cambridge: Cambridge University Press, 2010.
Badiou, A. *Wittgenstein's Antiphilosophy*, London: Verso, 2011.
Baghramian, M. *Relativism*, Abingdon: Routledge, 2004.
Baghramian, M., and A. Coliva. *Relativism (New Problems in Philosophy)*, London: Routledge, 2019.
Baker, G. '*Philosophical Investigations* Section 122: Neglected Aspects', in R. Arrington and H-J. Glock (eds), *Wittgenstein's Philosophical Investigations: Text and Context*, London: Routledge, 1991, pp. 35–68.
Baker, G. P., and P. M. S. Hacker. *Wittgenstein: Rules, Grammar and Necessity*, 2nd edition, extensively revised by P. M. S. Hacker, Oxford: Wiley-Blackwell, 2009.
Bennett, M. R., and P. M. S. Hacker. *Philosophical Foundations of Neuroscience*, Oxford: Blackwell, 2003.
Berlin, I. 'Two Concepts of Liberty', in *Four Essays on Liberty*, Oxford: Oxford University Press, 1969, pp. 118–72.

Blair-Broeker, C. T., R. M. Ernst, and D. G. Myers. *Thinking about Psychology: The Science of Mind and Behavior*, New York: Worth, 2007.
Blakemore, C. *The Mind Machine*, London: BBC, 1988.
Bloor, D. *Wittgenstein: A Social Theory of Knowledge*, London: Macmillan, 1983.
Boncompagni, A. 'Hinges, Prejudices, and Radical Doubters', in Nuno Venturinha (ed.), Special Section on Wittgenstein and Applied Epistemology in *Wittgenstein Studien*, vol. 10, no. 1, 2019, pp. 165–81.
Brice, R. G. *Exploring Certainty: Wittgenstein and Wide Fields of Thought*, Lanham, MD: Lexington Books, 2014.
Bricmont, J., and A. Sokal. *Intellectual Impostures*, London: Profile, 1998.
Caldwell, B., and L. Montes. 'Friedrich Hayek and His Visits to Chile', *Review of Austrian Economics*, vol. 28, no. 3, 2015, pp. 261–309.
Callinicos, A. *Marxism and Philosophy*, new edition, Oxford: Oxford University Press, 1985.
Cameron, D. 'PM's Speech at Munich Security Conference', 5 February, 2011, https://www.gov.uk/government/speeches/pms-speech-at-munich-security-conference, (accessed 19 December 2014).
Cavell, S. *The Claim of Reason: Wittgenstein, Skepticism, Morality and Tragedy*, Oxford: Clarendon, 1979.
Cavell, S. *Conditions Handsome and Unhandsome: The Constitution of Emersonian Perfectionism*, Chicago: University of Chicago Press, 1990.
Chang, H.-J. *Economics: The User's Guide*, London: Pelican Books, 2014.
Churchland, P. M. 'Folk Psychology (2)', in S. Guttenplan (ed.), *A Companion to the Philosophy of Mind*, Oxford: Blackwell, 1994, pp. 308–16.
Churchland, P. S. *Neurophilosophy: Toward a Unified Science of the Mind/Brain*, Cambridge: MIT Press, 1986.
Churchland, P. S. 'The Impact of Neuroscience in Philosophy', *Neuron*, vol. 60, 6 November 2008, pp. 409–11.
Churchland, P. S. *Touching a Nerve: Our Brains, Our Selves*, London: W. W. Norton, 2013.
Churchland, P. S., and C. L. Suhler. 'Control: Conscious and Otherwise', *Trends in Cognitive Science*, vol. 13, no. 8, 2009, pp. 341–47.
Citron, G., R. Rhees, and L. Wittgenstein. 'Wittgenstein's Philosophical Conversations with Rush Rhees (1939–50): From the Notes of Rush Rhees', *Mind*, vol. 124, no. 493, January 2015, pp. 1–71.
Conant, J. 'Introduction' to Putnam, H. *Realism with a Human Face*, Cambridge: Harvard University Press, 1990, pp. xv–lxxiv.
Courtland, D., G. Gaus, and D. Schmidtz. 'Liberalism', in *Stanford Encyclopedia of Philosophy*, http://plato.stanford.edu/entries/liberalism/ (first published in 1996, revised in 2014).
Crary, A. 'Wittgenstein's Philosophy in Relation to Political Thought', in A. Crary and R. Read (eds), *The New Wittgenstein*, London: Routledge, 2000, pp. 118–45.
Crary, A. 'Wittgenstein's Pragmatic Strain', *Social Research*, vol. 70, no. 2, Summer 2003, pp. 369–91.
Crary, A., and R. Read (eds). *The New Wittgenstein*, London: Routledge, 2000.
Crick, F. *The Astonishing Hypothesis*, London: Touchstone, 1995.
Dancy, J., and C. Sandis (eds). *Philosophy of Action: An Anthology*, Oxford: Wiley-Blackwell, 2015.
Danford, J. W. *Wittgenstein and Political Philosophy: A Reexamination of the Foundations of Social Science*, Chicago: University of Chicago Press, 1978.
Davidson, D. 'Actions, Reasons, and Causes', *Journal of Philosophy*, vol. 60, no. 23, 1963, pp. 685–700.

Davidson, D. 'On the Very Idea of a Conceptual Scheme', *Proceedings and Addresses of the American Philosophical Association*, vol. 47, 1973–74, pp. 5–20.
Davies, H. (interview with Terry Eagleton). 'A Theoretical Blow for Democracy', *Times Higher Education*, 1 June 2001, https://www.timeshighereducation.com/news/a-theoretical-blow-for-democracy/160508.article.
Diamond, A. 'The Early Development of Executive Functions', in E. Bialystok and F. Craik (eds), *Lifespan, Cognition: Mechanisms of Change*, Oxford: Oxford University Press, 2006, pp. 70–95.
Dienes, Z. *Understanding Psychology as a Science: An Introduction to Scientific and Statistical Inference*, Basingstoke: Palgrave-Macmillan, 2008.
Doris, J. M. 'Persons, Situations, and Virtue Ethics', *Noûs*, vol. 32, no. 4, December 1998, pp. 504–30.
Doris, J. M., and D. Murphy. 'From My Lai to Abu Ghraib: The Moral Psychology of Atrocity', *Midwest Studies in Philosophy*, vol. 31, 2007, pp. 25–55.
D'Oro, G., and C. Sandis. *Reasons and Causes: Causalism and Anti-Causalism in the Philosophy of Action*, London: Palgrave Macmillan, 2013.
Douglass, F. 'What to the Slave Is the Fourth of July?' (speech) – available at https://www.thenation.com/article/what-slave-fourth-july-frederick-douglass/ (accessed 26 May 2018).
Drury, M. O'C. 'Conversations with Wittgenstein', in Rush Rhees (ed.), *Recollections of Wittgenstein*, Oxford: Oxford University Press, 1984, pp. 97–171.
Dummett, M. *Truth and Other Enigmas*, London: Duckworth, 1978.
Dupré, J. *The Disorder of Things*, Cambridge, MA: Harvard University Press, 1993.
Dupré, J. 'Social Science: City Centre or Leafy Suburb', *Philosophy of the Social Sciences*, vol. 46, no. 6, May 2016, pp. 548–64.
Dyson, F. Interview on 'Web of Stories' website, http://www.webofstories.com/play/freeman.dyson/47;jsessionid=27BB84B2E9D0A7D1F0C0C403063703B9 (accessed 15 December 2014).
Eagleton, T. *Saints and Scholars*, London: Futura, 1987.
Eagleton, T. 'Wittgenstein's Friends', in *Against the Grain*, London: Verso, 1991, pp. 99–130.
Eagleton, T. *Wittgenstein: The Terry Eagleton Script, The Derek Jarman Film*, London: British Film Institute, 1993.
Eagleton, T. *Ideology: An Introduction (New and Updated Edition)*, London: Verso, 2007 (originally published 1991).
Eagleton, T. *The Meaning of Life*, Oxford: Oxford University Press, 2007.
Eagleton, T. *Materialism*, New Haven, CT: Yale University Press, 2016.
Easton, S. *Humanist Marxism and Wittgensteinian Social Philosophy*, Manchester: Manchester University Press, 1983.
Eldridge, R. *Leading a Human Life: Wittgenstein, Intentionality, and Romanticism*, Chicago: University of Chicago Press, 1997.
Eldridge, R. 'Wittgenstein and the Conversation of Justice', in Cressida Heyes (ed.), *The Grammar of Politics*, Ithaca, NY: Cornell University Press, 2003, pp. 117–28.
Engelmann, P. *Letters from Ludwig Wittgenstein. With a Memoir*, trans. L. Fürtmüller, ed. Brian McGuinness, Oxford: Blackwell, 1967.
Epstein, K. *The Genesis of German Conservatism*, Princeton, NJ: Princeton University Press, 1966.
Ferrari, P. F., P. Palanza, S. Parmigiani, R. M. de Almeida, and K. A. Miczek. 'Serotonin and Aggressive Behaviour in Rodents and Nonhuman Primates: Predispositions and Plasticity', *European Journal of Pharmacology*, vol. 526, no. 1–3, 2005, pp. 259–73.

Flowers, F. A., *Portraits of Wittgenstein*, London: Thoemmes Continuum, 1999.
Fricker, M. *Epistemic Injustice*, Oxford: Clarendon Press, 2007.
Gellner, E. *Reason and Culture*, Oxford: Blackwell, 1992.
Gellner, E. *Language and Solitude*, Cambridge: Cambridge University Press, 1998.
Gellner, E. *Words and Things: An Examination of, and an Attack on, Linguistic Philosophy*, London: Routledge, [1959] 2005.
Glock, H.-J. 'Philosophical Investigations Section 128: "Theses in Philosophy" and Undogmatic Procedure', in R. Arrington and H-J Glock (eds), *Wittgenstein's Philosophical Investigations: Text and Context*, London: Routledge, 1991, pp. 69–88.
Glock, H.-J. *A Wittgenstein Dictionary*, Oxford: Blackwell, 1996.
Glock, H.-J. 'Relativism, Commensurability and Translatability', in J. Preston (ed.), *Wittgenstein and Reason*, Oxford: Blackwell, 2008, pp. 21–46.
Glock, H.-J. *What Is Analytic Philosophy?*, Cambridge: Cambridge University Press, 2008.
Green, T. H. *Lectures on the Principles of Political Obligation and Other Essays*, Paul Harris and John Morrow (eds), Cambridge: Cambridge University Press, [1895] 1986.
Griffiths, A. Phillips (ed.). *Wittgenstein Centenary Essays*, Cambridge: Cambridge University Press, 1991.
Gunnell, J. *Social Inquiry after Wittgenstein & Kuhn*, New York: Columbia University Press, 2014.
Hacker, P. M. S. 'On Davidson's Idea of a Conceptual Scheme', *Philosophical Quarterly*, vol. 46, no. 184, July 1996, pp. 289–307.
Hacker, P. M. S. 'Developmental Hypotheses and Perspicuous Representations: Wittgenstein on Frazer's Golden Bough', in *Wittgenstein: Connections and Controversies*, Oxford: Oxford University Press, 2001, pp. 74–97.
Hacker, P. M. S. 'Gordon Baker's Late Interpretation of Wittgenstein', in G. Kahane, E. Kanterian, and O. Kuusela (eds), *Interpretations of Wittgenstein*, Oxford: Blackwell, 2007, pp. 88–122.
Hacker, P. M. S. *Human Nature: The Categorial Framework*, Oxford: Blackwell, 2007.
Hacker, P. M. S. *Wittgenstein: Comparisons & Context*, Oxford: Oxford University Press, 2013.
Hayek, F. A. *The Constitution of Liberty*, Chicago: University of Chicago Press, 1960.
Hayek, F. A. 'Remembering My Cousin, Ludwig Wittgenstein', *Encounter*, August 1977, pp. 20–22.
Held, V. *Feminist Morality: Transforming Culture, Society, and Politics*, Chicago: University of Chicago Press, 1993.
Heyes, C. (ed.). *The Grammar of Politics*, Ithaca, NY: Cornell University Press, 2003.
Hutchinson, P., R. Read, and W. Sharrock (eds). *There Is No Such Thing as a Social Science: In Defence of Peter Winch*, Aldershot: Ashgate, 2008.
Isen, A. M., and P. F. Levin. 'Effect of Feeling Good on Helping: Cookies and Kindness', *Journal of Personality and Social Psychology*, vol. 21, 1972, pp. 384–88.
Janik, A. 'Nyíri on the Conservatism of Wittgenstein's Later Philosophy', in Allan Janik's *Essays on Wittgenstein and Weininger*, Amsterdam: Rodopi, 1985, pp. 116–35.
Janik, A. 'Wittgenstein, Marx and Sociology', in Allan Janik's *Essays on Wittgenstein and Weininger*, Amsterdam: Rodopi, 1985, pp. 136–57.
Jarman, D. (dir.). *Wittgenstein* [film], Japan/UK: BFI Production/Bandung Productions/Channel Four Films/Uplink, 1993.
Karczmarczyk, P. 'Althusser and Wittgenstein: Ideology and Therapeutical Analysis of Language', *Rethinking Marxism*, vol. 25, no. 4, 2013, pp. 534–48.
Keizer, K., S. Lindenberg, and L. Steg. 'The Spreading of Disorder', *Science*, vol. 322, no. 5908, 2008, pp. 1681–85.

Kenny, A., and B. McGuinness (eds). *Wittgenstein and His Times*, Chicago: University of Chicago Press, 1982.
Kitching, G., and N. Pleasants. *Marx and Wittgenstein: Knowledge, Morality and Politics*, London: Routledge, 2002.
Klein, D. B. 'The Origin of "Liberalism"', *The Atlantic*, 13 February 2014.
Kusch, M. 'Folk Psychology and Freedom of the Will', in D. Hutto and M. Ratcliffe (eds), *Folk Psychology Reassessed*, Dordrecht: Springer, 2007, pp. 175–88.
Kusch, M. 'Epistemic Relativism, Scepticism, Pluralism', *Synthese*, vol. 194, 2017, pp. 4687–703.
Kusch, M. 'Disagreement, Certainties, Relativism', *Topoi*, 2018.
Kusch, M. 'Introduction: A Primer on Relativism', in *Routledge Handbook on Relativism*, London: Routledge, 2019.
Landau, S. 'The Chilean Coup', *Counterpunch*, 11 September 2003, available here: https://www.counterpunch.org/2003/09/11/the-chilean-coup/ (accessed 27 June 2018).
Leavis, F. R. 'Memories of Wittgenstein', in *Recollections of Wittgenstein*, Oxford: Oxford University Press, 1984, pp. 50–67.
Leavis, F. R. 'Luddites? Or, There Is Only One Culture (1966)', in *Two Cultures? The Significance of C. P. Snow* (with Introduction by Stefan Collini), Cambridge: Cambridge University Press, 2013, pp. 89–112.
Leavis, F. R. 'Two Cultures? The Significance of C. P. Snow (1962)', in *Two Cultures? The Significance of C. P. Snow* (with Introduction by Stefan Collini), Cambridge: Cambridge University Press, 2013, pp. 53–76.
Lenin, V. I. 'The Junius Pamphlet', *Collected Works*, vol. 22, pp. 305–19.
Lovibond, S. *Realism and Imagination in Ethics*, Minneapolis: University of Minnesota Press, 1983.
Lugg, A. 'Wittgenstein and Politics: Not Right, Left, or Center', *International Studies in Philosophy*, vol. 36, no. 1, 2004, pp. 61–79.
Mackie, J. *Ethics: Inventing Right and Wrong*, New York: Penguin, 1977.
Makoff, R., and R. Read. 'Beyond Just Justice – Creating Space for a Future-Care Ethic', *Philosophical Investigations*, vol. 40, no. 3, 2017, pp. 223–56.
Malcolm, N. *Ludwig Wittgenstein: A Memoir*, 2nd edition, Oxford: Clarendon Press, 2001.
Manser, A. R. *The End of Philosophy: Marx and Wittgenstein*, Southampton: Camelot Press, 1973.
Marcuse, H. *One Dimensional Man*, New York: Routledge, [1964] 2007.
Marx, K. 'Theses on Feuerbach', in *Selected Works in One Volume*, London: Lawrence and Wishart, 1970, pp. 13–15.
Marx, K. *Critique of Hegel's 'Philosophy of Right'*, Cambridge: Cambridge University Press, 1982.
McCauley, H. C. 'Wittgenstein: Philosophy and Political Thought', *Maynooth Review*, vol. 2, no. 2, 1976, pp. 13–26.
McGinn, C. 'Soul on Fire', *New Republic*, vol. 210, no. 25, 20 June 1994, pp. 34–39.
Medina, J. 'Wittgenstein as a Rebel: Dissidence and Contestation in Discursive Practices', *International Journal of Philosophical Studies*, vol. 18, no. 1, 2010, pp. 1–29.
Medina, J. *The Epistemology of Resistance*, Oxford: Oxford University Press, 2013.
Mill, J. S. *On Liberty*, London: Longman, Roberts & Green, 1869.
Milner, A. (ed.). *Postwar British Critical Thought*, vol. 2, London: Sage, 2004.
Moi, T. *Revolution of the Ordinary: Literary Studies after Wittgenstein, Austin, and Cavell*, Chicago: University of Chicago Press, 2017.
Monk, R. *Ludwig Wittgenstein: The Duty of Genius*, London: Vintage, 1991.

Moran, J. 'Wittgenstein and Russia', *New Left Review*, vol. I/73, 1972, pp. 85–96.
Mouffe, C. *The Democratic Paradox*, New York: Verso, 2000.
Moyal-Sharrock, D. 'Fighting Relativism: Wittgenstein and Kuhn', in C. Kanzian, S. Kletzl, J. Mitterer, and K. Neges (eds), *Realism, Relativism, Constructivism*, Berlin: De Gruyter, 2017.
Nash, G. *The Conservative Intellectual Movement in America Since 1945*, Wilmington, DE: Intercollegiate Studies Institute, 1976.
Neurath, O. 'Physicalism: The Philosophy of the Viennese Circle', in *Philosophical Papers 1913–1946 (Vienna Circle Collection) Vol. 16*, ed. and trans. Robert S. Cohen and Marie Neurath, Dordrecht: D. Reidel, pp. 48–51.
Nussbaum, M. *Frontiers of Justice: Disability, Nationality, Species Membership*, Cambridge, MA: Harvard University Press, 2006.
Nyiri, J. C. 'Wittgenstein's New Traditionalism', *Acta Philosophica Fennica*, vol. 27, 1976, pp. 503–9.
Nyiri, J. C. 'Wittgenstein's Later Work in Relation to Conservatism', in Anthony Kenny and Brian McGuinness (eds), *Wittgenstein and His Times*, Chicago: University of Chicago Press, 1982, pp. 44–68.
Nyiri, J. C. 'Wittgenstein 1929–31: The Turning Back', in Stuart Shanker (ed.), *Ludwig Wittgenstein: Critical Assessments (Vol. 4)*, London: Routledge, 1986, pp. 29–59.
O'Connor, P. *Morality and Our Complicated Form of Life: Feminist Wittgensteinian Metaethics*, University Park: Pennsylvania State University Press, 2008.
Oppenheim, P., and H. Putnam. 'The Unity of Science as a Working Hypothesis', in H. Feigl et al. (eds), *Minnesota Studies in the Philosophy of Science*, vol. 2, Minneapolis: University of Minnesota Press, 1958, pp. 3–36.
Pascal, F. 'Wittgenstein: A Personal Memoir', in Rush Rhees (ed.), *Recollections of Wittgenstein (Revised edition)*, Oxford: Oxford University Press, 1984, pp. 12–49.
Pitkin, H. F. *Wittgenstein and Justice*, Berkeley: University of California Press, 1972.
Plato, *Republic*, in John M. Cooper (ed.), *Plato: Complete Works*, Indianapolis, IN: Hackett, 1997, pp. 971–1223.
Plato, *Theaetetus*, in John M. Cooper (ed.), *Plato: Complete Works*, Indianapolis, IN: Hackett, 1997, pp. 157–234.
Pohlhaus, G., and J. Wright. 'Using Wittgenstein Critically: A Political Approach to Philosophy', *Political Theory*, vol. 30, no. 6, 2002, pp. 800–27.
Preston, A. 'The War against Humanities at Britain's Universities', in *The Guardian*, 29 March 2015, https://www.theguardian.com/education/2015/mar/29/war-against-humanities-at-britains-universities (accessed 27 June 2018).
Preston, J. (ed.). *Wittgenstein and Reason*, Oxford: Blackwell, 2008.
Putnam, H. *Pragmatism*, Oxford: Blackwell, 1995.
Quine, W. V. O. 'Two Dogmas of Empiricism', *Philosophical Review*, vol. 60, no. 1, 1951, pp. 20–43.
Quinton, A. 'Conservatism', in Robert E. Goodin, Philip Pettit, and Thomas W. Pogge (eds), *A Companion to Contemporary Political Philosophy*, 2nd edition,, Oxford: Blackwell, 2009, pp. 285–309.
Rawls, J. *A Theory of Justice*, Oxford: Oxford University Press, 1971.
Rawls, J. *The Law of Peoples*, Cambridge: Harvard, 1999.
Rawls, J. *Political Liberalism*, New York: Columbia University Press, 2005.
Read, R. 'Wittgenstein vs. Rawls', in V. Munz, K. Puhl, and J. Wang (eds), *Proceedings of the Kirchberg Wittgenstein Symposium 2009: Language and World*, Frankfurt: Ontos, 2010, pp. 93–110.

Read, R. 'Why the Ecological Crisis Spells the End of Liberalism: The "Difference Principle" Is Ecologically Unsustainable, Exploitative of Persons, or Empty', *Capitalism Nature Socialism*, vol. 22, 2011, pp. 80–94.
Rhees, R. (ed.). *Recollections of Wittgenstein (Revised Edition)*, Oxford: Oxford University Press, 1984.
Rhees, R. 'Postscript', in *Recollections of Wittgenstein (Revised edition)*, Oxford: Oxford University Press, 1984, pp. 172–209.
Robin, C. *The Reactionary Mind: Conservatism from Edmund Burke to Sarah Palin*, Oxford: Oxford University Press, 2011.
Robinson, C. *Wittgenstein and Political Theory: The View from Somewhere*, Edinburgh: Edinburgh University Press, 2009.
Rooney, P. 'Philosophy, Language, and Wizardry', in Naomi Scheman and Peg O'Connor (eds), *Feminist Interpretations of Ludwig Wittgenstein*, University Park: Pennsylvania State University Press, 2002.
Rorty, R. *Contingency, Irony, and Solidarity*, Cambridge: Cambridge University Press, 1989.
Rorty, R. *Objectivity, Relativism and Truth: Philosophical Papers: Volume 1*, Cambridge: Cambridge University Press, 1991.
Rorty, R. 'The Priority of Democracy to Philosophy', in Douglas Tallack (ed.), *Critical Theory: A Reader*, London: Routledge, 1995, pp. 369–88.
Rorty, R. 'Hilary Putnam and the Relativist Menace', in *Truth and Progress: Philosophical Papers, Volume 3*, Cambridge: Cambridge University Press, 1998, pp. 43–62.
Rorty, R. *Philosophy and Social Hope*, London: Penguin Books, 1999.
Rorty, R. 'Wittgenstein and the Linguistic Turn', in *Philosophy as Cultural Politics, Philosophical Papers: Volume 4*, Cambridge: Cambridge University Press, 2007, pp. 160–75.
Rubinstein, D. *Marx and Wittgenstein: Social Praxis and Social Explanation*, London: Routledge, 1981.
Russell, B. *My Philosophical Development*, London: Allen and Unwin, 1959.
Ryan, A. 'Liberalism', in *A Companion to Contemporary Political Philosophy*, Oxford: Blackwell, 1993, pp. 291–312.
Sandis, C. (ed.). *New Essays on the Explanation of Action*, London: Palgrave Macmillan, 2009.
Sanfélix Vidarte, V. 'Was Wittgenstein a Liberal?', in K. Wojchiechowski and J. Joerden (eds), *Ethical Liberalism in Contemporary Societies*, Frankfurt am Main: Peter Lang, 2009, pp. 117–37.
Scheman, N., and P. O'Connor (eds). *Feminist Interpretations of Ludwig Wittgenstein*, University Park: Pennsylvania State University Press, 2002.
Schroeder, S. *Wittgenstein: The Way Out of the Fly-Bottle*, Cambridge: Polity Press, 2006.
Schulte, J. 'Wittgenstein and Conservatism', in Stuart Shanker (ed.), *Ludwig Wittgenstein: Critical Assessments (Vol. 4)*, London: Routledge, 1986, pp. 60–69.
Sen, A. 'What Do We Want from a Theory of Justice?', *Journal of Philosophy*, vol. 103, no. 5, May 2006, pp. 226–38.
Soifer, E., and B. Szabados. *Hypocrisy: Ethical Investigations*, Toronto: Broadview Press, 2004.
Sparti, D. 'Rules and Social Community: Does Wittgenstein's Philosophy Have Conservative Implications?', in W. Lütterfelds, A. Roser, and R. Raatzsch (eds), *Wittgenstein Jahrbuch 2001/2002*, Frankfurt: Peter Lang, 2003, pp. 139–49.
Tanney, J. *Rules, Reason, and Self-Knowledge*, Cambridge: Harvard University Press, 2013.
Tawney, R. H. *Equality*, New York: Harcourt Brace, 1931.
Thomas, D. L. *Routledge Philosophy Guidebook to Locke on Government*, London: Routledge, 1995.
Thomson, G. 'Wittgenstein: Some Personal Recollections', *Revolutionary World*, vol. XXXVII, no. 9, 1979, pp. 87–88.

Trigg, R. 'Wittgenstein and Social Science', in A. Phillips Griffiths (ed.), *Wittgenstein Centenary Essays*, Cambridge: Cambridge University Press, 1991, pp. 209–22.
Tsilipakos, L. *Clarity and Confusion in Social Theory*, Farnham: Ashgate, 2015.
Uschanov, T. P. 'Ernest Gellner's Criticisms of Wittgenstein and Ordinary Language Philosophy', in Gavin Kitching and Nigel Pleasants (eds), *Marx and Wittgenstein: Knowledge, Morality and Politics*, London: Routledge, 2002, pp. 23–46.
van Riel, R., and R. Van Gulick. 'Scientific Reduction', in Edward N. Zalta (ed.), *The Stanford Encyclopedia of Philosophy*, http://plato.stanford.edu/entries/scientific-reduction/ (accessed 29 August 2016).
Venturinha, N. 'Introduction', in António Marques and Nuno Venturinha (eds), *Wittgenstein on Forms of Life and the Nature of Experience*, Bern: Peter Lang, 2010, pp. 13–19.
Venturinha, N. 'Wittgenstein and the Natural History of Human Beings', in J. P. Gálvez (ed.), *Philosophical Anthropology: Wittgenstein's Perspective*, Frankfurt: Ontos, 2010, pp. 91–110.
Venturinha, N. 'Sraffa's Notes on Wittgenstein's "Blue Book"', *Nordic Wittgenstein Review*, vol. 1, 2012, pp. 181–91.
Venturinha, N. 'Moral Epistemology, Interpersonal Indeterminacy and Enactivism', in J. P. Gálvez (ed.), *Action, Decision-Making and Forms of Life*, Berlin: Walter de Gruyter, 2016, pp. 109–20.
Vinten, R. 'Leave Everything as It Is: A Critique of Marxist Interpretations of Wittgenstein', *Critique*, vol. 41, no. 1, 2013, pp. 9–22.
Vinten, R. 'Was Wittgenstein a Conservative Philosopher?', *Revista Estudos Hum(e)anos*, no. 8, 2014/1, pp. 47–59.
Vinten, R. 'Eagleton's Wittgenstein', *Critique*, vol. 43, no. 2, 2015, pp. 261–76.
Vinten, R. 'Mackie's Error Theory: A Wittgensteinian Critique', *Kínesis*, vol. 7, no. 13, 2015, pp. 30–47.
Vinten, R. 'Review of "Clarity and Confusion in Social Theory" by Leonidas Tsilipakos', *Nordic Wittgenstein Review*, vol. 4, no. 2, 2015, pp. 153–56.
Vinten, R. 'Book Review of Revolution of the Ordinary by Toril Moi', *Nordic Wittgenstein Review*, vol. 6, no. 2, 2017, pp. 99–103.
Vinten, R. 'Was Wittgenstein a Liberal Philosopher?', *Teorema*, vol. 36, no. 1, 2017, pp. 57–82.
von Wright, G. H. (ed.). *A Portrait of Wittgenstein as a Young Man: From the Diary of David Hume Pinsent 1912–1914*, Oxford: Blackwell, 1990.
Warman, M. 'Stephen Hawking Tells Google "Philosophy Is Dead"', in *Telegraph*, 17 May 2011, http://www.telegraph.co.uk/technology/google/8520033/Stephen-Hawking-tells-Google-philosophy-is-dead.html (accessed 24 October 2016).
Weaver, M. (and agencies). 'Angela Merkel: German Multiculturalism Has "Utterly Failed"', *Guardian*, 17 October 2010, http://www.theguardian.com/world/2010/oct/17/angela-merkel-german-multiculturalism-failed (accessed 19 December 2014).
Whiting, D. 'Introduction', in Daniel Whiting (ed.), *The Later Wittgenstein on Language*, Basingstoke: Palgrave Macmillan, 2010, pp. 1–16.
Whiting, D. (ed.). *The Later Wittgenstein on Language*, Basingstoke: Palgrave Macmillan, 2010.
Wiggins, D. 'Neo-Aristotelean Reflections on Justice', *Mind*, vol. 113, no. 451, July 2004, pp. 477–512.
Williams, B. 'Pluralism, Community and Left Wittgensteinianism', in B. Williams (ed.), *In the Beginning Was the Deed: Realism and Moralism in Political Argument*, Princeton NJ: Princeton University Press, 2005, pp. 29–39.

Winch, P. 'Certainty and Authority', *Royal Institute of Philosophy Supplements*, vol. 28, March 1990, pp. 223–37.
Winch, P. *The Idea of a Social Science*, 2nd edition, London: Routledge, 1990.
Wisdom, J. *Philosophy and Psycho-analysis*, Oxford: Basil Blackwell, 1953.
Wittgenstein, L. *Philosophical Investigations*, trans. G. E. M. Anscombe, Oxford: Basil Blackwell, 1953.
Wittgenstein, L. *Tractatus Logico-Philosophicus*, London: Routledge, 1961.
Wittgenstein, L. *The Blue and Brown Books*, New York: Harper & Row, [1958] 1965.
Wittgenstein, L. *Lectures & Conversations on Aesthetics, Psychology and Religious Belief*, in Cyril Barrett (ed.), Berkeley: University of California Press, 1966.
Wittgenstein, L. *Zettel*, ed. G. E. M. Anscombe and G. H. von Wright, trans. G. E. M. Anscombe, Berkeley: University of California Press, 1967.
Wittgenstein, L. *On Certainty*, Oxford: Blackwell, 1969.
Wittgenstein, L. *Philosophical Grammar*, ed. Rush Rhees, trans. Anthony Kenny, Berkeley: University of California Press, 1974.
Wittgenstein, L. *Wittgenstein's Lectures on the Foundations of Mathematics, Cambridge 1939*, ed. Cora Diamond, Hassocks: Harvester, 1976.
Wittgenstein, L. *Wittgenstein's Lectures, Cambridge 1932–1935*, from the notes of A. Ambrose and M. Macdonald, ed. A. Ambrose, Oxford: Blackwell, 1979.
Wittgenstein, L. *Culture and Value*, trans. Peter Winch, Oxford: Blackwell, 1980.
Wittgenstein, L. *Remarks on the Philosophy of Psychology*, vol. 1, ed. G. E. M. Anscombe and G. H. Von Wright, trans. G. E. M. Anscombe, Blackwell: Oxford, 1980.
Wittgenstein, L. *Last Writings on the Philosophy of Psychology*, vol. 1, ed. G. H. Von Wright and H. Nyman, trans. C. G. Luckhardt and M. A. E. Aue, Oxford: Blackwell, 1982.
Wittgenstein, L. *Ludwig Wittgenstein: Philosophical Occasions 1912–1951*, ed. J. Klagge and A. Nordmann, Indianapolis, IN: Hackett, 1993.
Wittgenstein, L. *Culture and Value: Revised Edition*, ed. G. H. von Wright and H. Nyman, revised by Alois Pichler, trans. Peter Winch, Oxford: Blackwell, 1998.
Wittgenstein, L. *Remarks on the Foundations of Mathematics*, 3rd edition, Oxford: Blackwell, [1956] 2001.
Wittgenstein, L. *Big Typescript: TS 213*, trans. C. Grant Luckhardt and Maximilian E. Aue, Chichester: Wiley-Blackwell, 2005.
Wittgenstein, L. *Philosophical Investigations*, revised 4th edition by P. M. S. Hacker and Joachim Schulte, trans. G. E. M. Anscombe, P. M. S. Hacker, and Joachim Schulte, Oxford: Wiley-Blackwell, 2009.
Zeki, S. 'Splendours and Miseries of the Brain', *Philosophical Transactions of the Royal Society B*, vol. 354, 1999, pp. 2053–65.

INDEX

50 Shades of Grey 133

absolutism 49n2
  moral 13
action 25, 26, 130, 162
  and reasons 37
  intelligibility of 36
actions 166
  and habitual behaviour 33
  free 161
  future 161
aesthetics 188
Agassi, J. 70n2
agreement 53, 190
  in behaviour 190
  in forms of life 190
  in language 190, 191
  in practices 190
agreement in definitions 190
alienation 112n122
Althusser, L. 134n6
Ambrose, A. 75
analytic-synthetic distinction 58, 60
anarchism 98, 135
Ancombe, G. E. M. 10
Anderson, P. 7, 69n1, 89n10, 114, 114n3, 114n7, 115n9, 115n9, 116, 117, 118, 120, 122, 123, 124, 125, 127, 130, 137, 138, 149, 150
animals 170, 186
  political 197
Anscombe, G. E. M. 10, 75
anthropology 44, 45, 47, 99
anti-Semitism 140, 156n87
Aristotle
  on justice 178

Arrington, R. 49, 49n2, 56, 56n32, 57, 62, 63, 154n79
Ashton, N. A. 49, 49n2, 55n28, 201, 202n85
Augustine 25, 42, 57, 94, 143, 144, 152, 153n76
authority 5, 13, 17, 19, 78, 84
autonomy 89, 92, 101
Ayer, A. J. 12n41

Backhouse, R. 46
Baghramian, M. 5, 9, 51, 51n10
Baker, G. 49, 57, 63, 104, 105, 106
Bakhtin, M. 141n39
Bakhtin, N. 78, 140, 141n39
Barker, E. 177
Beckett, S. 13
behaviour 33
  and language 190
  and verificationism 38
  controlled 169
  habitual 33
  impact of circumstances on 167
  pain 40
  pre-linguistic 57
  violent 164
behaviourism 57, 185
belief 31, 54, 84, 99, 162, 163
  religious 130n67
Benjamin, W. 141n42
Bennett, M. 30, 31, 42, 124n45, 167, 169, 174, 174n40
Berkeley, G. 30n27
Berlin, I. 116
bewitchment 103n78
biology 32, 42. *See also* natural sciences
  progress in 40

Blair, T. 73, 91n16
Blakemore, C. 30
Bloor, D. 97, 100, 139n29
Boncompagni, A. 200, 201, 202n85
Brice, R. G. 6, 87, 88, 91, 92, 97, 99, 100, 106, 112
Bricmont, J. 51
Broad, C. D. 118n24
Broer, M. 89n10
Bruckner, A. 76, 82
Burke, E. 72

Callinicos, A. 7, 69n1, 114, 114n7, 125, 127, 128, 129, 130, 137, 138, 150
Cameron, D. 82
Capital 133
capitalism 110, 133, 153, 155
catalyst example 37
causation 161
  mental 161
causes 4, 12, 26, 161
Cavell, S. 17, 19, 88n4, 111n118, 184, 189, 196
Cerbone, D. 18
certainty 84
Chang, H.-J. 46
chemistry 46, 162. *See also* natural sciences
  progress in 40
children 187
Churchland, P. M. 40, 43, 162, 163
Churchland, P. S. 8, 162, 163, 164, 166, 167, 167n22, 168, 169, 170, 170n30, 170n31, 171, 172, 173, 174
class 91, 97, 124, 132, 153, 155
climate change 22, 112n122, 186
cognitive science 8
Coliva, A. 51n10
colour 192, 198
commodities 143
common sense 120, 122, 125, 145n55, 150
communism 97
Communist Manifesto 133
communitarianism 95
Conant, J. 106, 110, 184
conceptual schemes 53, 58, 59, 60
  translatability of 58
consciousness 167, 170
  animal 170
  behavioral criteria for 170
  and the brain 170
  and control 164, 166, 169, 174
  dispositional 169
  dispositional transitive 169
  in human beings 171
  intransitive 167, 167n22, 168, 169
  neo-Cartesian account of 170
  occurrent 169, 171
  occurrent transitive 169, 170
  and processes 168
  and speech 167n22
  transitive 167, 168, 169
consensus 194
  democratic 195
conservatism 5, 6, 13, 17, 19, 22, 69–85, 117, 118
  central aspects of 71
  and Conservative parties 70
  cultural 73, 85, 116
  defined 70–73
  and diversity 76, 82, 83
  and liberalism 87n3
  and power 72, 78. *See also* organicism *and* traditionalism
  and sexism 74n14, 75
  and theory 81. *See also* theory
conservativism 100
context 20
contextualism
  felted 12, 13
  strong 20
contradiction 118
control 8, 163, 164, 166, 172
  over bodily functions 164
  of a car 172
  and consciousness 171
  over desires 164
  executive 172
  neo-Kantian model of 165, 166, 168, 169, 170n30, 172, 173
  neurobiological model of 163
  neurophysical account of 164, 165, 166, 172, 173, 174
  ordinary meaning of 172, 173, 174
  processes underlying 168
  and responsibility 171
  self- 172

Copernicus, N. 125
Courtland, S. D. 89
Crary, A. 6, 87, 88, 91, 95, 96, 106, 110, 112, 184
Crick, F. 29, 30
Critchley, S. 113n1
cultural theory 7, 133

Dali, S. 188
Dancy, J. 26n9
Danford, J. W. 9, 17
Darwin, C. 125
Davidson, D. 27, 33, 35, 36, 37, 58, 59, 60, 61, 62, 63, 64, 65, 130
deconstructionism 137
deflationism. *See also* truth
democracy 89, 96, 161
  differences within a 196
  direct. *See also* liberal democracy
  pluralistic 189, 195, 196, 198
  radical 189, 195, 196, 198
depression 162
Descartes, R. 118n24, 130, 131, 170, 174
description 15
desire 162, 163, 164
determinism 161
Dewey, J. 94n39
dialectics 80, 118n24
dialogue 17, 19
dike 177, 178
disagreement 190
  in behaviour 190
  in language 191
  over meanings 191
  over rules 191
disagreements 22
  in opinion 190, 197
  political 198
Dobb, M. 78
dogmatism 102, 103, 104
Doris, J. 164
Dostoevsky, F. 79
Douglass, F. 11
Dreben, B. 184
Drury, M. O'C. 75–76, 118n24, 178, 196
dualism 30, 38
  brain-body 174
  Cartesian 57

Dummett, M. 127, 128, 129
Dupré, J. 9, 26, 28, 31n30, 32, 45, 47n87
Dyson, F. 74, 75

Eagleton, T. 7, 114n6, 136, 137, 138
  on being deluded 136n18
  on ideology 151, 153
  on meaning 142
  on metaphysics 141, 142, 143, 144, 145, 146, 147, 148, 150, 151, 155, 156
  on pain 148, 153n77
  on philosophy 149, 150, 151, 153, 153n78
  on religion 155, 156n86
  on the *Philosophical Investigations* 137
  on Wittgenstein and conservatism 137, 138, 140, 141, 150, 151. *See also* conservatism
Easton, S. 9, 114n6
ecology 32
economics 28, 44, 45, 46, 47
Einstein, A. 58, 61, 125
Eldridge, R. 6, 18, 87, 88, 91, 92, 95, 101, 102, 103, 104, 105, 106, 106n89, 112, 184
eliminativism 162, 163, 170, 174n40
empiricism 117
Engels, F. 80, 133
epistemic injustice 189, 200, 201. *See also* justice
epistemology 12, 120, 130, 137, 144, 152, 153, 161
  feminist 201
Epstein, K. 72, 76
equality 112n122, 153
essences 129, 153
ethics
  Aristotelian 41
  verification and 38
evil 161
explanation 4
  in terms of reasons 4
explanations
  of actions 166
  in anthropology 99
  causal 26, 33–38
  context-placing 37

explanations (cont.)
  Marxist 141
  nonteleological causal 35
  in philosophy 15
  in science 27
  in social sciences 11
  in terms of habituation 35
  in terms of reasons 26, 33–38, 39
  in terms of rules 35

fairness 187
fascism 97, 122, 135
feminism 11, 17, 20, 49n2, 55n28, 200, 202n85
Ferkiss, V. 133n1
Feyerabend, P. 58, 60
Figdor, F. 76
Fleming, W. 89n10
folk psychology 40, 43, 162, 163. *See also* psychology
forms of life 21n96, 52, 53, 55, 57, 94, 96, 100, 180, 190
  and conservatism 139
Frail Control hypothesis 8, 164, 166, 167, 172, 173
Frazer, J. 99
free markets 89, 92, 110
free speech 131
freedom 89, 96
  expressive 92, 101
  negative 89
  positive 89
  of the will 126, 161–75. *See also* will
freedom of the will 8
Frege, G. 83, 125, 129
  on sense and force 127, 129
French revolution 72
Freud, S. 125

Gaita, R. 10
Gakis, D. 114n6
Galileo 125
games
  rules of 193
Gauguin, P. 188
Gaus, G. 89
Gellner, E. 17, 96, 113, 114n3, 139n29
generalizations 116, 118, 120
  in social sciences 44

genetics 32
Glock, H.-J. 3n5, 9, 49, 51, 54, 56, 57, 60, 61, 62, 63, 64, 65, 65n66, 73n13, 113n1, 115n9
goals 38, 39, 174
God 120, 155, 161
Gombrich, E. 116
grammar 3, 4, 15, 17, 31, 40, 42, 47, 53, 54, 57, 60, 63, 83, 103, 104, 110, 126, 150, 153
  arbitrariness of 56, 65n66, 105
  autonomy of 104, 105, 150
  and conceptual relativism 50n6, 56
  describing 183
  and empirical investigations 128
  of meaning 128
  and realism 20
  and religion 155
  and theology 156
  and therapy 64
Gramsci, A. 78, 140
Grillparzer, F. 6, 76, 78, 81, 82, 83
Gunnell, J. 50n3, 64

Habermas, J. 115n9, 195
  on ideology 151, 153
habits 166, 169, 174
Hacker, P. M. S. 16n68, 17n70, 30, 31, 42, 49, 53, 54, 56, 57, 61, 62, 63, 64, 65, 65n66, 99, 104, 105, 106, 106n89, 124n45, 128n62, 133, 149n64, 167, 169, 171, 174, 174n40, 191, 192
  on rules 199n81
Harkin, J. 18n79, 19, 21n96
Harman, G. 12, 20
Harvey, D. 133
Hawking, S. 40, 41, 43
Haydn, J. 76
Hayek, F. 70, 89, 90n15, 91, 92, 97
Hegel, G. W. F. 80, 118, 118n24, 178, 196
Held, V. 11, 12n38
Heraclitus 42
Hertz, H. 125
Heyes, C. 17
hinge epistemology 200, 201
  and prejudice 200
  feminist 201. *See also* feminism
hinge propositions 123

hinge-commitments 50
history 34, 118, 125
Hobbes, T. 5, 19, 89, 90n12, 198n80
Hobhouse, L. T. 91
Horwich, P. 128n62
human geography 45, 47
humanities 11, 16, 28, 45
Hume, D. 130, 184n20
Hutchinson, P. 9, 10, 26, 28, 45, 47n88, 62, 63
hypotheses 15, 39
   compared to grammatical remarks 40

idealism 20, 30n27, 50, 108n105
   linguistic 150
ideology 2, 3, 5, 17, 151
   as a family resemblance concept 136
   and language 124
   and religion 155
   ruling class 117, 122, 125, 130
illusions 153, 154, 154n79, 155
imagination 110, 111n118
immanent theorizing 13. *See also* theory
inequality
   economic 92
   of opportunity 92
inner/outer picture 40
intentions 162, 163
interpretation 3
introspection 162n3
Isen, A. M. 164
Islam 131

Janik, A. 18
justice 5, 8, 9, 22, 177–202
   comparative approach to 187, 188, 189
   compared to colour expressions 180
   conceptions of 183
   contractarian account of 186, 187
   and *dike* 177, 178
   etymology of 181, 182
   and neurobiology 40
   standards of 180
   theories of 183, 188
   trancendental theories of 5
   transcendental approach to 187

Kant, I. 58, 60, 94n39, 106, 130
Kanterian, E. 141n39
Karczmarczyk, P. 134n6
Keynes, J. M. 79, 122
Kitching, G. 134
Klein, D. B. 89n10
knowledge 4, 12, 31, 84, 120, 129, 145, 148, 163
   as ability-like 31
   as an inner state 84
   in mathematics 84
   Plato on 41
   Socrates on 178
Köhler, W. 44
Kuhn, T. 58, 60, 65n66
Kusch, M. 49, 49n2, 51n10, 162

Labor, J. 76
Labour Party (U. K.) 98
language. *See also* theory, of language
   Augustinian picture of 25
   as historical 192, 193, 194
   on holiday 147, 150
   as like a city 192
   as mutable 192, 193, 194
   ordinary 125, 146, 148
   philosophy of 152
   social practice theory of 106
   theory of 127
language games 25, 53, 55, 94, 95n44, 123, 179, 180
   incommensurability of 115n9
language-games 52
Laugier, S. 88n4
Leavis, F. R. 28, 46
Lenau, N. 76
Lenin, V. 76, 79
Levin, P. F. 164
liberal democracy 6, 87, 95, 110
liberal dictatorship 89
liberal ironism 92, 94, 106, 108n101, 189
liberalism 5, 6, 22, 87–112
   as bourgeois ideology 98
   and capitalism 91, 98
   classical 89, 91, 92
   and conservatism 70
   defined 89–91
   and democracy 89, 89n11
   and free speech 131

liberalism (cont.)
  modern 91, 96
  origins of the term 89n10
  perfectionist 101, 106
  Rawlsian 184, 185
  utopian 92, 93, 94
  weak perfectionist 87
Libet, B. 126, 126n56
linguistics 47
lion 55
literarism 28. *See also* scientism
literary studies 47
literary theory 7
literature 28, 34, 47
  and philosophy 106n89
Locke, J. 89, 91, 92
  and democracy 90n14
logic 83
logical constants 83
logical positivism 40, 58, 60, 133
logical positivists 38
Lord Salisbury 72
love 162, 187
Lovibond, S. 95n44, 111n118
Lugg, A. 69n1, 145n55, 146n57, 148n63
Lyotard, J.-F. 115n9

Macdonald, M. 75
Mackie, J. 12, 12n41
magic 99
Makoff, R. 187
Malcolm, N. 98n52
Malinowski, B. 116
Manser, A. R. 134n6
Marcuse, H. 113
Marx, K. 7, 20, 76, 79, 80, 91, 113, 114,
   118, 119, 125, 133, 138, 142, 149,
   151, 153, 153n78, 154
  and liberalism 91
  on Feuerbach 149
  on history. *See also* history
  on ideology 151, 153, 154
  on illusions 154
  on religion 155, 156, 156n86
  compared to Wittgenstein 131, 133, 134
Marxism 7, 76, 78, 79, 80, 98, 113, 114,
   116, 119, 120, 122, 127, 129, 130,
   131, 132, 135, 138, 140, 141

  and analytic philosophy 125
  on ideology 151
  and liberalism 97
  and metaphysics 142, 147, 156
  and money 143
  and non-scientific explanations 136
  and racing motorists 135
  as similar to Wittgensteinian
    philosophy 131
Masterman, M. 75
materialism 30, 38, 40, 114n6, 119,
   136n19, 150
  and reductionism 30, 30n27
mathematics 39
McCauley, H. C. 69n1, 117n20
McCormick, M. 201
McDowell, J. 108n101
meaning 81, 82, 96, 144, 190
  and etymology 181
  and use 57, 83n51, 94, 106, 110, 117,
   127, 128, 128n62, 142, 143, 143n52,
   144, 181
meaninglessness
  and utility 106
  vs. utility 94n37
mechanism 119
Medina, J. 9, 189–94, 196, 198, 200
  on democracy 195
meliorism 189
mereological fallacy 126, 174
Merkel, A. 82
metaethics 12, 38n58
metaphysical 129
metaphysics 16, 21, 22, 104, 106, 110,
   120, 130, 141, 142, 143, 144,
   145, 145n55, 146, 150, 152, 153,
   154n80, 156, 161
  and grammar 153
  and religion 155
methodology 3, 4, 11, 26, 27
  in anthropology 99
  in the humanities 11
  in the natural sciences 38–40
  in philosophy 8, 11, 94
  in science 94, 145
  scientific 28
  in social science 11
  in the social sciences 38–40

INDEX 219

Mill, J. S. 33, 35, 91, 92
    influence on Rorty 93
Miller, J. 126
mind 120, 121, 137, 145, 152
Mind (journal) 120
modes of representation 57
Moi, T. 69n1
money 143, 145
monism 38
Monk, R. 75, 79, 97, 112n121, 118n24, 122, 140
Moore, G. E. 84, 122
moral antirealism 12, 20
moral epistemology 12, 56
moral realism 12, 20
morality 21, 161, 198
    and matters of taste 180, 181n12
    and prudence 106
motives 26, 38, 39
Mouffe, C. 9, 189, 195, 196, 197, 198, 200
Moyal-Sharrock, D. 50n3, 65n66
multiculturalism 82, 92
Murdoch, I. 75
myth of the given 60

Nash, G. 72
natural history 134
natural sciences 2, 3, 4, 11, 26, 27, 35
    methodology in 28
    methods in the 38–40
    and philosophy 40. *See also* philosophy, and science
    progress in 4, 27
    and reductionism 32
    and social sciences 38
    and sociology 35
    supported by social studies 46
nature 13
Neilsen, K. 155n83
neoliberalism 89
Nestroy, J. 76
Neurath, O. 27n14, 38
neurobiology 8, 40, 162, 164
    and control 172
neurophysiology 3
neuroscience 42, 43, 44, 122, 162n2, 164
    and consciousness 170
New Wittgensteinians 17, 19

Newton, I. 58, 61, 125
Nietzsche, F. 7
non-realism 18. *See also* realism
nonsense 106, 110, 148, 150, 156
    latent 161
    patent 161
    and religion 155
normativity 13
Nussbaum, M. 186
Nyiri, J. C. 6, 6n8, 17, 69, 69n1, 72, 72n7, 76, 76n24, 76n25, 77n26, 77n27, 77n28, 77n29, 77n30, 77n31, 78, 78n32, 78n33, 79n42, 81, 82, 83, 83n50, 84, 85, 87n1, 96, 97, 100, 138n26, 139n29

O'Connor, P. 10, 11, 12, 17, 18, 20, 21, 38n58, 55, 181n12, 183n18, 185n25, 202n85
    on relativism 49n2
objectivity 94, 106, 110
objects 191
observation 39
    and morality 12
    in the social sciences 39
observations 15
Oppenheim, P. 30n25
organicism 71, 72, 75

pacifism 98
pain 40, 148, 162, 192
Panksepp, J. 167n22
paradox 43
Pascal, F. 74, 78, 79, 140
patriotism 92
perception 104, 170
persuasion 195, 198
philosophy 1, 2, 4, 116n11
    of action 162
    analytic 113, 113n1, 125, 130
    as conceptual cartography 2
    as contemplative 135
    common sense approaches to 122
    continental 113, 113n1
    as a descriptive enterprise 32
    and other disciplines 94
    elucidatory 116n11, 119
    emancipatory 116n11, 119
    not empirical 118

philosophy (*cont.*)
  and language 146
  Marxist 7
  modern 131
  of mind 161
  ordinary language 125, 142
  political 5, 8, 161, 163, 175
  positions in 63, 64
  progress in 4, 27, 40, 41, 42
  relationship to other disciplines 14, 16
  and science 1n4, 4, 16, 22, 42, 47, 94, 106
  scientific 120
  social 1, 2, 3, 161, 163
  speculative 131
  theories in 64
  theory in 113
  as therapy 64
  traditional 106, 110, 112n122, 116n11, 161, 163
  and understanding 43
  and the will 102, 103
  Wittgenstein's conception of 4, 5, 7, 16
  Wittgenstein's understanding of 1
physicalism 38
physics 32, 46, 58, 61, 162. *See also* natural sciences
  Newton's vs. Einstein's 58
  progress in 40
  and psychology 44
Picasso, P. 133, 188
Pinochet, General A. 89, 91n16
Pinsent, D. 73
Pitkin, H. 8, 9, 17, 177, 180, 181
Plato 41, 137, 146, 161, 183
  on justice 177, 178, 183, 184
  Theaetetus 178
Platonism 57
pluralism 91
Pohlhaus, G. 17, 18, 88n4, 92n27, 108n101, 109n115, 111n118, 112n122
political disagreements 9
political theory 19
  transcendental 14
politics 4, 47
  and theory 5
Popper, K. 116
positivism 27
postmodernism 115n9

post-structuralism 137
practical rationality 19, 19n86
practices 131
pragmatism 87, 94, 106, 201
  and liberalism 106, 110
predictions 162
prejudice 200, 201
private language 186, 192
private property 110
problem of other minds 130n67
progress 4, 27, 28, 38, 40
  in the natural sciences 40
  in science 125, 126
  in the social sciences 40
psychoanalysis 16n68. *See also* Wittgenstein, and therapy
psychology 3, 4, 8, 16, 16n63, 28, 34, 40, 42, 43, 44, 45, 119, 119n28, 126, 133
  causal laws in 162
  cognitive 104
  laws of 39
  materialist 119
  neuroscientific 40, 162
  predictions in 162
  progress in 43
  and science 44
  as a science 46
  social 164
  Witttgenstein on 44
Ptolemy 41
Putnam, H. 30n25, 106, 108n104

Quine, W. V. O. 58, 60
Quinton, A. 70, 71, 72

racing motorists 135, 137, 141, 157
Ramsey, F. 98n51
rationality 52, 69, 163
  and justice 186, 187
  and politics 197
  practical 5, 198n80
Rawls, J. 5, 19, 91, 92, 185, 186, 187, 188, 198n80
Read, R. 9, 10, 18n79, 19, 21n96, 26, 28, 45, 47n88, 62, 63, 88n4, 187
  on justice 187
  on Rawls 184, 185, 186, 187, 188, 189
Reagan, R. 89

realism 20, 106. *See also* moral realism
  perspectival 49n2
  and relativism 50
reasons 4, 26
  awareness of 172
  and causes 33–38, 166
  and skills 166
rebellion 198
redness 153
reductionism 2, 4, 11, 27, 28, 29–32, 38, 45, 119, 162
  in Marxism 119, 119n28
  and materialism 30n27
  and psychology 31
Rees, J. 119n28
referentialism 81, 83
relativism 5, 11, 12, 19, 21, 49–65
  alethic 5, 51–56, 65
  cognitive 5, 49, 51, 52, 56, 65
  conceptual 2, 5, 50, 51, 56, 58, 59, 62, 65, 65n66
  epistemic 50, 51
  about existence 2
  and hinge epistemology 201
  about justification 2
  about knowledge 2
  metaethical 49n2
  moral 13, 50
  non-silly 49n2
  ontological 51, 52, 56, 65
  about rationality 51, 55
  social 51
  subjective 51
  as a theory 62
  about truth 2
religion 2, 99, 155, 156
representationalism 106
responsibility 8, 164
  and consciousness 175
  and control 173
  and deliberation 169, 171
  legal 161, 163, 164
  moral 163, 164
  neo-Kantian account of 168
  and transitive consciousness 167
Rhees, R. 76, 79, 80, 135, 140, 156n87
Robin, C. 9, 72, 75
Robinson, C. 10, 13, 14, 15, 16
Rooney, P. 103n78

Rorty, R. 6, 87, 88, 91, 92, 93, 94, 106, 110, 112, 112n122, 184, 189
  differences with Wittgenstein 106, 110
  on realism 110. *See also* realism
  on science 106
Rubinstein, D. 114n6
rule
  as a family resemblance concept 198
rule-following 33, 69
rules 190, 193
  contestability of 198
  diversity in 193
  diversity of 198
  in mathematics 193
  rebellion against 190
Russell, B. 83, 133, 137
Russian revolution 79, 122, 140, 156n87
Ryan, A. 90n12, 91

Sandis, C. 26n9, 121n34
Sanfélix Vidarte, V. 89n11, 89n6
scepticism 17, 18, 19, 20, 41, 84, 102, 108n101, 120, 122
  and hinge epistemology 201
  in politics 71, 72
  therapeutic 17
Scheman, N. 202n85
Schmidtz, D. 89
Schroeder, S. 153n76
Schubert, F. 76, 82
Schulte, J. 69n1
science 3n5, 16, 26, 27
  concepts in 124
  conceptual confusions in 126
  conceptual innovation in 125
  cultural 27n14
  and knowledge 43
  and philosophy 135
  progress in 30, 42. *See also* progress
  and theory 43
  unity of 119, 119n28
scientism 3, 3n5, 11, 12, 26, 28, 38n58, 46, 50, 120, 145, 183n19, 188
  in Marxism 119
  and religion 155
Sen, A. 185, 187, 188, 189
sensations 170, 192
sexism 73–75

Sharrock, W. 9, 10, 26, 28, 45, 47n88, 62, 63
skills 172
Skinner, Q. 17
slavery 188
Snow, C. P. 28, 46
social contract theories 198n80
social science 1, 4
  methodology in 1
social sciences 1, 2, 3, 4, 5, 11, 25–47
  and explanation 2
  generalisations in 11
  legitimacy of 45
  methods in the 38–40
  as scientific 2
  progress in 27, 40
social skills 164, 166, 169, 172
socialism 5, 6, 70, 97, 98, 151
  Fabian 72, 73
  reformist 72
sociology 28, 34, 35, 44, 45, 47, 116, 119, 119n28, 133, 137
Socrates 161, 178
Soifer, E. 90n14
Sokal, A. 51
solidarity 92, 94
solipsism 20, 108n105
souls 119
speech therapy. *See also* Wittgenstein, and therapy
Spengler, O. 104
Sraffa, P. 78, 122, 140
Stevenson, C. L. 181n12
Straw, J. 91n16
Strawson, P. 58, 60
Sturgeon, N. 12, 20
substance 30, 121
Suhler, C. 8, 163, 164, 166, 167, 167n22, 168, 169, 170, 170n30, 171, 172, 173, 174
superstition 155, 155n82
surveyable representations 42, 103, 182
Szabados, B. 90n14

Tanesini, A. 17
Tanney, J. 37–38
Tarski, A. 59, 60, 61, 62, 63, 64
Taylor, C. 17
Teichmann, R. 10

Temelini, M. 10, 17, 18, 19, 20, 21, 21n96
testimony 189
Thatcher, M. 70, 89
theology 155, 156
theory
  in Davidson 59
  empirical 15
  evolutionary 164
  and language 61
  literary 137
  of language 123, 127, 129. *See also* language
  and meaning 58, 60
  and metatheory 13, 14, 15
  and philosophy 40, 63, 106, 117, 119, 125. *See also* philosophy
  political 13, 137
  and psychology 43
  in psychology 162
  and rules 128
  social 137
  and truth 58
  and Wittgensteinian philosophy 62
therapy 17
theses 103
  in philosophy 106. *See also* theory
Thomson, G. 78, 79, 97, 122, 140
thought 163
time 76, 83, 84n52, 152, 153n76
tolerance 91, 92, 99, 100, 101
toleration 89, 91, 96
  religious 89
Tolstoy, L. 79, 112
trade unions 72, 89, 92, 92n28, 97
traditionalism 71, 72, 78
training 17
Travena, J. 126
Trigg, R. 49, 49n1, 52, 53, 55, 55n28, 65
Trotsky, L. 119, 120
truth 52, 53, 58, 59, 61, 62, 63, 64, 147
  as an aim in philosophy 153n78
  obtainment theory of 54
  Tarski and 59, 60
Tsilipakos, L. 27n15
Tully, J. 17

Uschanov, T. P. 114n3
utility 94, 106

Van Gogh, V. 188
Varoufakis, Y. 133
Venturinha, N. 12n40, 57n36, 79n36, 200n82, 201n84
verificationism 38, 40
Vienna Circle 27, 27n14
virtues 177
vocabularies 106
volition 170
volitions 161, 162

walking 13, 16
war 91, 97, 98, 98n52, 112n122, 122
 and science 98
Weininger, O. 75
welfare states 92
white emigration 116
Whiting, D. 106, 128n62
Wiggins, D. 178
will 102, 103, 161, 163
Williams, B. 88n5
Winch, P. 5, 10, 17, 18n79, 19, 26, 33, 34, 35, 36, 62, 198n80
 and authority 19
 on action 26
 on Rawls 184n20
Wisdom, J. 95n43
Wittgenstein (film) 136
Wittgenstein, L.
 on behaviourism 185
 Big Typescript 16n68, 42n66, 146
 Blue Book 11, 16, 20, 32, 50, 75, 83, 178
 On Certainty 1, 6, 9, 15, 19, 21, 50, 78, 84, 100, 122, 123, 195, 197
 on class 79, 97, 114
 comparative dialogical reading of 17
 and conservatism 69–85
 Culture and Value 29n19
 on differences 195, 196, 197
 on essence 145
 on fascism 140
 and freedom of the will 161–75
 on games 178, 179, 180, 196
 on Marxism 79, 122, 135, 140
 as a materialist 150, 151n69
 Philosophical Grammar 56
 Philosophical Investigations 1, 1n4, 10, 14, 15, 20, 25, 31, 57, 62, 63, 69, 75, 78, 81, 87, 92, 94, 101, 117, 123, 129, 133, 137, 140, 144, 147, 151, 178, 190
 Philosophy of Psychology - A Fragment 16
 on progress 41
 on realism 20
 Remarks on Frazer's *Golden Bough* 99
 on reductionism 32
 on religion 155, 155n82, 155n83, 156
 remarks on politics 69
 Remarks on the Foundations of Mathematics 156
 sexism of 73–75
 and Stalinism 140n37
 therapeutic-sceptical interpretation of 17, 19, 20
 and therapy 13, 14, 16, 16n68, 17
 on tolerance 99
 Tractatus Logico-Philosophicus 1, 1n4, 16, 54, 133, 142
 on war 98, 98n52
 Zettel 50n6, 56, 105
women's suffrage 74, 75, 89
Wood, A. W. 133n1
Wright, J. 17
Wright, J. R. 18, 88n4, 92n27, 108n101, 109n115, 111n118, 112n122

Zeigarnik effect 174
Zeki, S. 40, 43
Zeno 41
Zerilli, L. 18
Žižek, S. 126n56

www.ingramcontent.com/pod-product-compliance
Lightning Source LLC
Chambersburg PA
CBHW020911020526
44114CB00039B/332